IMAGES
of America

CRAWFORDSVILLE

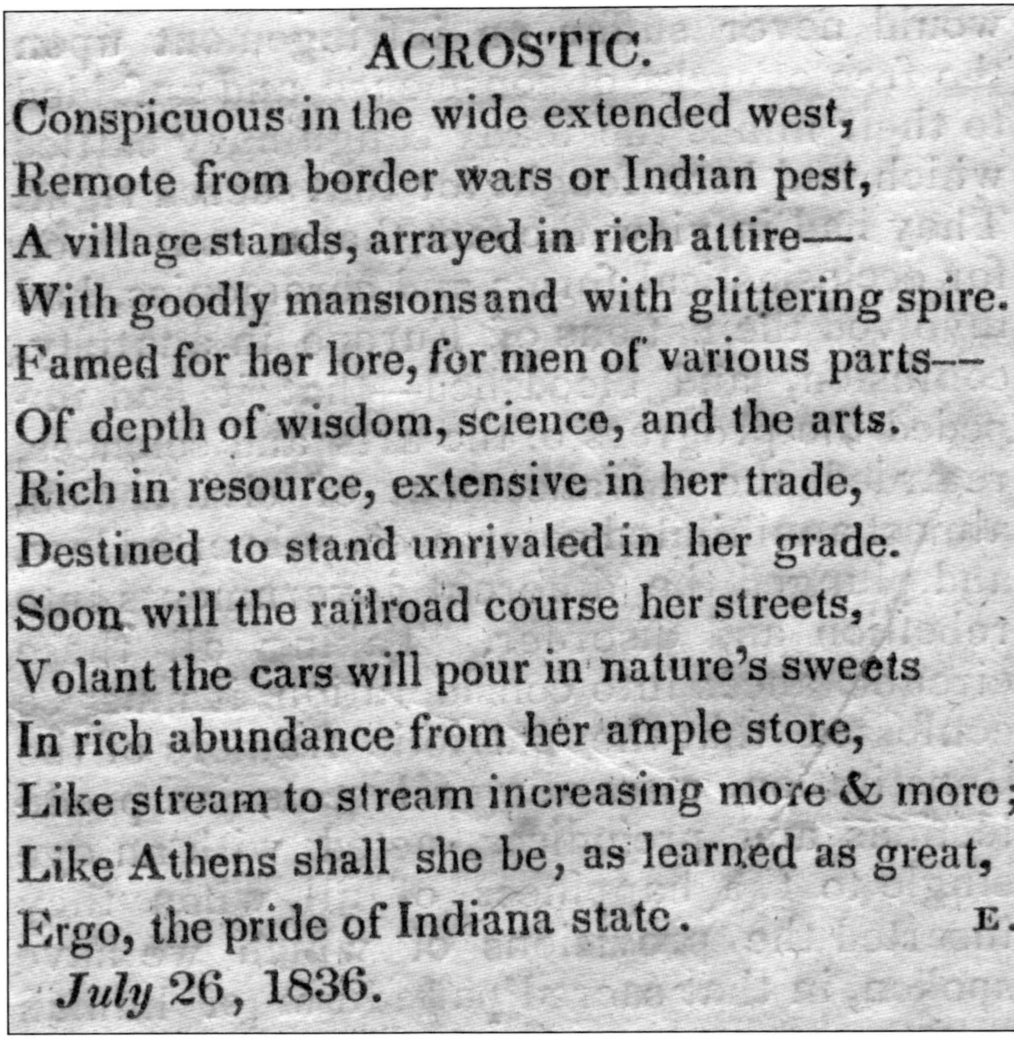

ACROSTIC.

Conspicuous in the wide extended west,
Remote from border wars or Indian pest,
A village stands, arrayed in rich attire—
With goodly mansions and with glittering spire.
Famed for her lore, for men of various parts—
Of depth of wisdom, science, and the arts.
Rich in resource, extensive in her trade,
Destined to stand unrivaled in her grade.
Soon will the railroad course her streets,
Volant the cars will pour in nature's sweets
In rich abundance from her ample store,
Like stream to stream increasing more & more;
Like Athens shall she be, as learned as great,
Ergo, the pride of Indiana state. E.

July 26, 1836.

Crawfordsville was always a town with much potential. In 1836, an anonymous contributor published an acrostic (a composition, usually in verse, in which the first letter of each verse spells out a word) in the *Crawfordsville Record*. In this poem, the writer spelled "Crawfordsville" while attempting to express the strengths of the new community and dreams for what Crawfordsville would one day become. (Crawfordsville District Public Library.)

ON THE COVER: In 1916, Crawfordsville residents volunteered in large numbers to participate in the Montgomery County Pageant commemorating Indiana's centennial. One of the volunteers, Lillian Lollis, shows off her costume for this photograph taken near Dry Branch in what was then called Crawford's Woods (southwest of Wabash College). This quiet spot provided an ideal location for the thousands of spectators attending the festivities. The pageant held in Crawfordsville was reportedly one of the best in the state and much admired by Indiana centennial officials. (Crawfordsville District Public Library.)

IMAGES
of America

CRAWFORDSVILLE

William P. Helling for the
Crawfordsville District Public Library

ARCADIA
PUBLISHING

ISBN 978-0-7385-8354-9

Published by Arcadia Publishing
Charleston, South Carolina

Printed in the United States of America

Library of Congress Control Number: 2010931934

For all general information, please contact Arcadia Publishing:
Telephone 843-853-2070
Fax 843-853-0044
E-mail sales@arcadiapublishing.com
For customer service and orders:
Toll-Free 1-888-313-2665

Visit us on the Internet at www.arcadiapublishing.com

To Jane, who will always know that I am serious (and I'm not kidding either!)

Contents

Acknowledgments 6

Introduction 7

1. Streetscapes 9
2. Schools and Churches 25
3. The Age of the Interurban 41
4. Celebrating the Indiana Centennial 53
5. Crawfordsville at Work 67
6. Crawfordsville at War 79
7. Crawfordsville at Play 89
8. Town and Gown 103
9. People, Famous and Forgotten 111

ACKNOWLEDGMENTS

Every author should one day have the opportunity to work with a competent publishing company that employs professional and responsive staff. I have had that pleasure in my dealings with Arcadia Publishing, including John Pearson, Midwest publisher, and the delightfully supportive Anna Wilson, acquisitions editor. I sincerely thank Karen Bazzani Zach for her keen review of my historical accuracy—any errors found in this book are mine, and mine alone. Karen's book, *Crawfordsville: Athens of Indiana* (Arcadia Publishing), served as my original inspiration to research our community. I am also grateful for the continued support of Crawfordsville District Public Library director Larry Hathaway, who is responsible for managing a diverse staff and putting together a wonderful collection. In addition, I could not have completed this task without the assistance of the reference department staff. Special thanks go to Dellie Craig, whose tireless energy and enthusiasm will never be exceeded. Dellie touched every image I have included in this book, and she was relentless in pursuit of my whims, no matter how trivial. Jodie Steelman Wilson researched and uncovered every fact or figure that I needed about Crawfordsville (very often at a moment's notice) and has contributed in untold ways. Her astute observations on every aspect of this book were always most welcome and made the task very enjoyable. Reference department staff members Adam Rice, Emily Griffin, and Dian Moore were willing to look at anything at any time, and for that I will always be grateful. Most of all, my wife, Jane, supports me in everything that I undertake, and I often undertake some ill-advised ventures (not including this book, of course). I know she will support me through all, and I am fortunate to be able to share my life with her. My children, John, Ryan, and Elizabeth, are a constant source of joy and wonder to me. And my mother and father, so far away in distance but so near to me in my heart, deserve a special mention. If anyone says I work hard, I know it is because I have my father as a model. And if anyone notices my love of learning, I remember all those wonderful days when my mother took me to the library and simply encouraged me to enjoy.

Unless otherwise noted, all photographs and images appear courtesy of the Crawfordsville District Public Library.

INTRODUCTION

In 1813, three years before Indiana was admitted into the Union, ranger officers Ambrose Whitlock, Henry Ristine, and Williamson Dunn scouted a frontier location with farming potential near a small but steady waterway. They knew that they had found an excellent site for a settlement—a spot that would become Crawfordsville. Upon their return 10 years later, Whitlock laid out the town, which he named in honor of Secretary of the Treasury William H. Crawford, who had granted Whitlock the commission of Receiver of Public Lands. The state had created Montgomery County in 1822, and Crawfordsville—situated in the center of the county and being its only town—became the county seat. When land sales opened at the Crawfordsville office in late 1823, the future of the town was assured.

However, this book does not try to tell the story of Crawfordsville; the bibliography that I include provides enough works for any reader interested in knowing more about the history of the Athens of Indiana. Rather, *Crawfordsville* tries to evoke the uniqueness of a small city that has its own story to tell.

In order to portray the important aspects of Crawfordsville, I divided this book into several chapters based on different themes. "Streetscapes" presents views of the town during many stages of its development. Crawfordsville residents will easily recognize some structures that look much the same today as they did many years earlier. The same readers may also regret the loss of some views that no longer exist except in photographs. In "Schools and Churches," I combine two of the elements most often mentioned in early publications that aimed to attract people to this community. For example, in 1911, a civic pamphlet praised, along with other features, the "splendid schools" and the "handsome churches" that served citizens who were "cultured, refined, and enterprising."

"The Age of the Interurban" may surprise some readers who have never ventured beyond their town's limits except by automobile. Few traces remain of the interurban traffic that, at convenient times and affordable rates, catered to the needs of residents leaving and returning to Crawfordsville for three decades.

Crawfordsville residents already know that their community works together to plan and conduct festivities, but in "Celebrating the Indiana Centennial," I show scenes from those few days in 1916 when Crawfordsville outdid itself and just about every other celebration in the state. This town produced a parade and pageant that it will probably never be able to match.

Because this is a community built on heavy toil, it is only fitting that I include a few samples of the people and businesses that have shaped this town. For "Crawfordsville at Work," I chose images that represent the industriousness of its citizens. And because its men and women have unhesitatingly served their country in the time of need, "Crawfordsville at War" includes some of those stories as well as people who should be honored. Our community is more than work and strife, however, and the chapter "Crawfordsville at Play" shows the leisure and sports activities, organized or otherwise, that made up a very important part of the town's daily life. Another essential part of Crawfordsville is Wabash College, which was founded in 1832 when the town was less than a decade old and had less than a thousand citizens. In "Town and Gown," the spirit of cooperation between Crawfordsville and the college is the theme.

Finally, in "People, Famous and Forgotten," I attempt to display men and women who made Crawfordsville what it is, whether they have accomplished extraordinary actions or have simply contributed to their town on a smaller scale. This chapter was the most difficult to compose, simply because there are so many faces that make up the spirit of Crawfordsville.

Some readers may wonder why I left out this or that person, perhaps a famous name that appears frequently in our local brochures and advertisements. Space was limited, of course, but I also wanted to avoid repeating some of the characters that are always described in any history of the area. That is why Gen. Lew Wallace, whose military career and novel *Ben-Hur* are still used to promote Crawfordsville, appears in the same chapter as an unknown tailor and an obscure socialite who were, at least to someone at one time, just as important as the famous general.

With few exceptions, the photographs used in this book are held by the Crawfordsville District Public Library, which is committed to preserving the county's heritage while making it accessible to its residents. These images are in our database (www.cdpl.lib.in.us/lh), which is just one of the numerous resources we provide at the Crawfordsville District Public Library. I am fortunate to be the head of the reference department and its local history resources, and as such I have at my fingertips the archives of our community, which grows constantly through thoughtful patron donations and our own collection development efforts. Because of space limitations, I unfortunately could not include in my index to this book all the deserving people, places, and events. Nevertheless, the small index I provided can serve as a starting point for those who want to find quickly the most deserving or interesting images.

Finally, what qualifies me to write this book? I am not a native of Crawfordsville. When I came to this town as an adult more than 25 years ago from my much larger home city in another state, I expected to stay only a short time. As I occasionally traveled away from Crawfordsville, people would inevitably ask me where I was from. For several years, I would simply state my place of birth; sometimes I would say that I was from Crawfordsville, but I always qualified it by adding "temporarily." Something changed, however, and it is difficult to say when it happened. Certainly this change was not caused by one incident—it must have been a slow accumulation of experiences as I began to discover the people and events that made up the fabric of this community. I thought long ago that I had left a place full of vitality and history for one of those innumerable small towns that dot any map, but I was wrong. After all, this town became my home, and I no longer hesitate to claim it as such. I can't say for sure that I will forever remain in Crawfordsville, but I can promise that it will forever remain in me—and in creating this book I can attempt to give back to Crawfordsville some of what it has shared with a person who thought he was just passing through but has decided to stick around a while.

One

STREETSCAPES

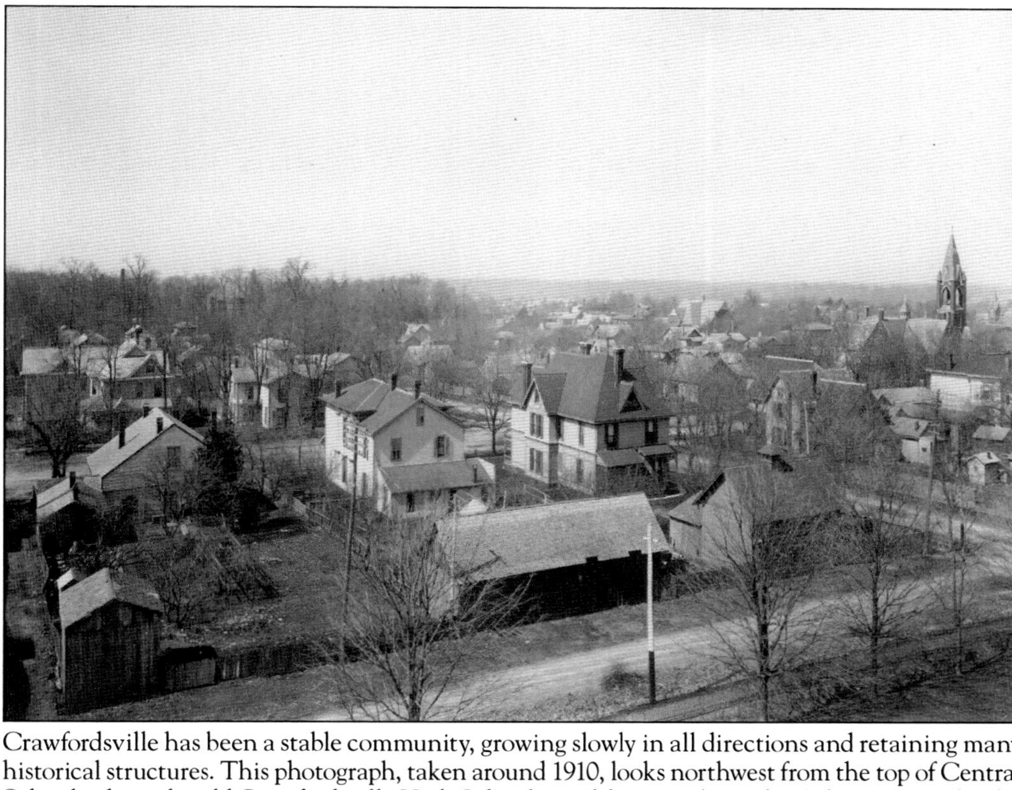

Crawfordsville has been a stable community, growing slowly in all directions and retaining many historical structures. This photograph, taken around 1910, looks northwest from the top of Central School, where the old Crawfordsville High School stood for years (now the Athena Center). The view from this spot would be recognizable to Crawfordsville residents past or present. On the right appears the tall steeple of Center Church, now the Wabash Avenue Presbyterian Church at the corner of Washington Street and Wabash Avenue (it has marked the skyline since 1880). Farther west on Wabash, the distinctive features of the First Christian Church rise above the surrounding houses. The tower of Wabash College's Yandes Hall (now Detchon Center) peaks through the trees to the left.

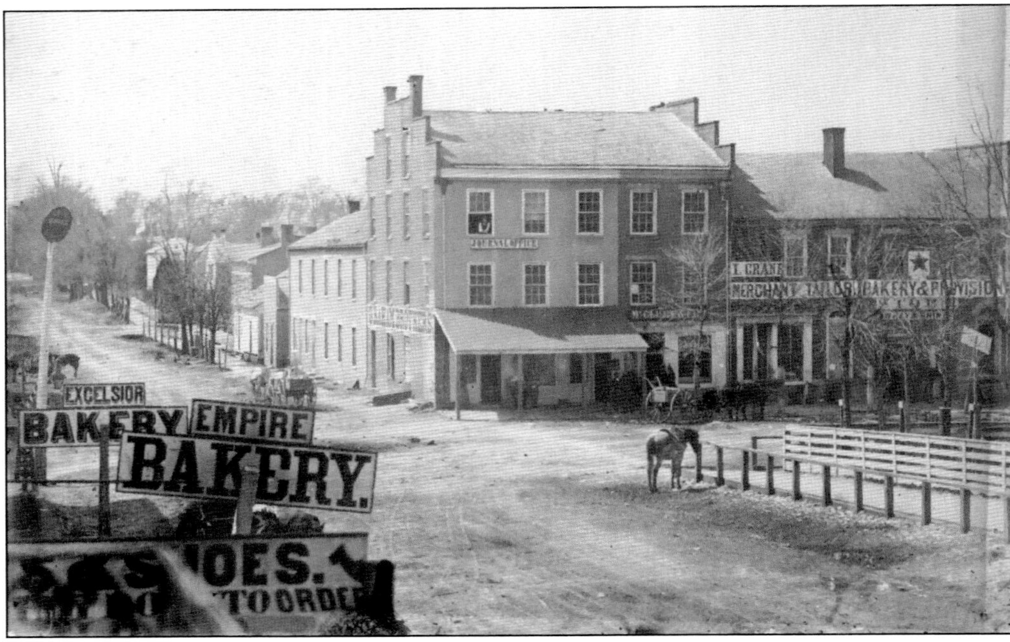

A series of photographs from 1865 reveals that Crawfordsville looked like many other towns of the era—from the dirt streets to the wooden sidewalks. The view above looks west on Main Street where it crosses Washington Street. To the right appears a fence and hitching post that bordered what was then the courthouse (before the present-day courthouse was built in 1876). The *Crawfordsville Journal* office was in the four-story building, which was erected in 1836. Wabash College held classes in this building from 1838 to 1839 after its only structure was destroyed in a fire. The photograph below looks north on Green Street from the corner of Main Street. The township trustee's office is visible in the center of the image. A dry goods store is to the far right in the picture with a sign for groceries, boots, shoes, and clothing.

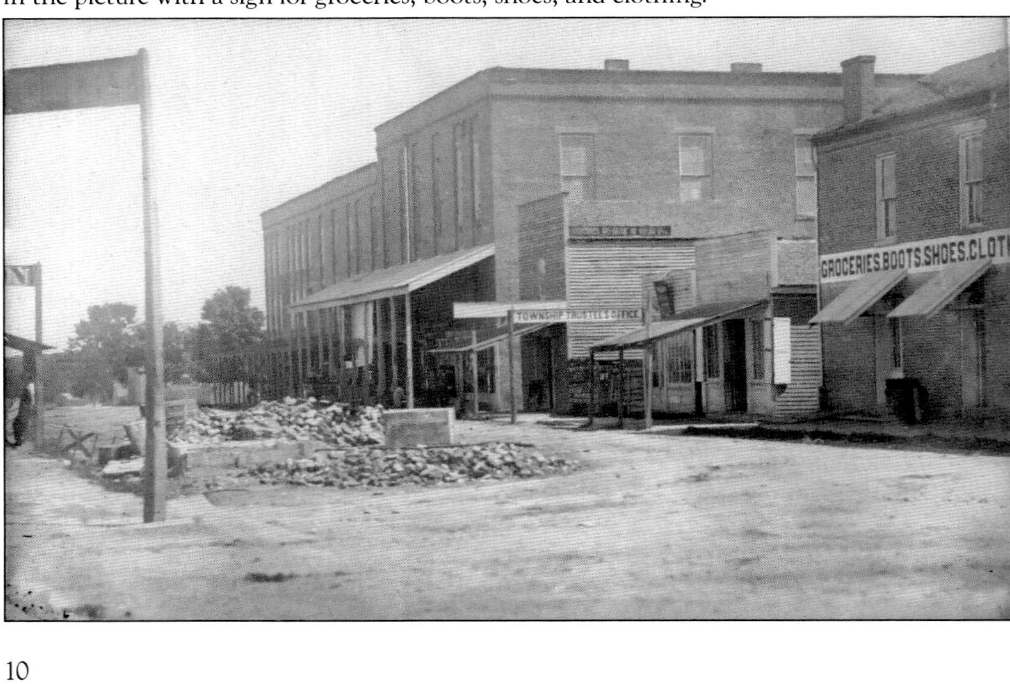

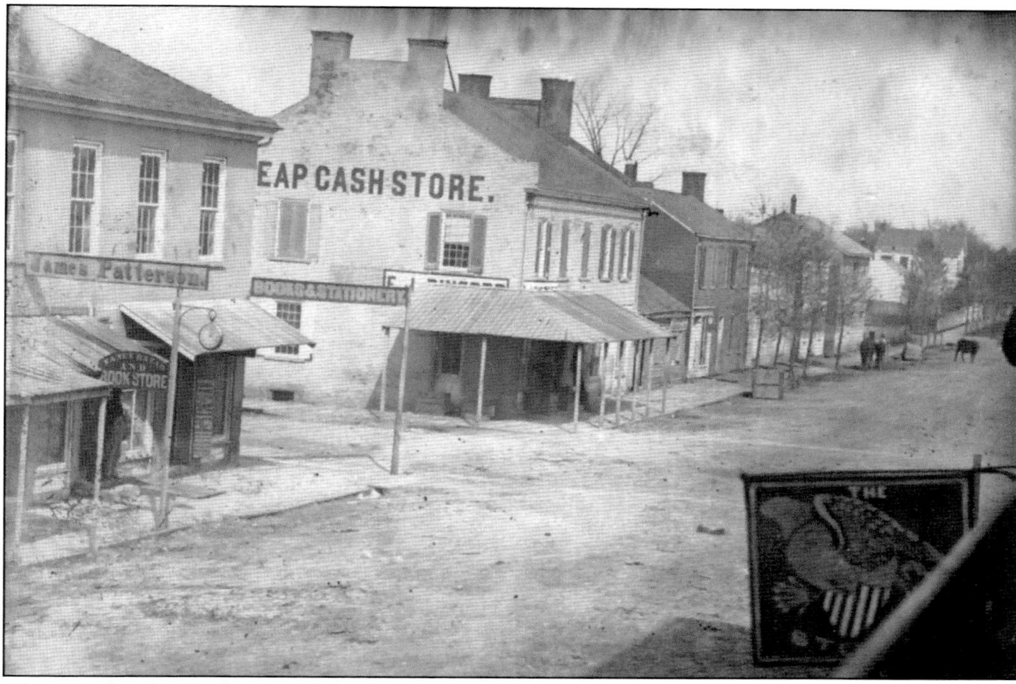

The sign for the Eagle Store, which dealt in dry goods, is in the foreground of this view looking east on Main Street (above). James Patterson, a jeweler and watchmaker, has a store on the left next to Frank M. Heaton's bookstore and stationery shop. The Cheap Cash store stands prominently on the northwest corner of Main and Green Streets. Another glance east (below) but on the south side of Main Street shows Bill Bowers's Banner Store. Bowers was a master at creative advertising, as seen by his poetically inspired advertisement in the *Crawfordsville Weekly Review*: "Then as you are passing around this fall / At the banner please make a call; / For Bill's resolved, as heretofore, / To sell at cost and a little more."

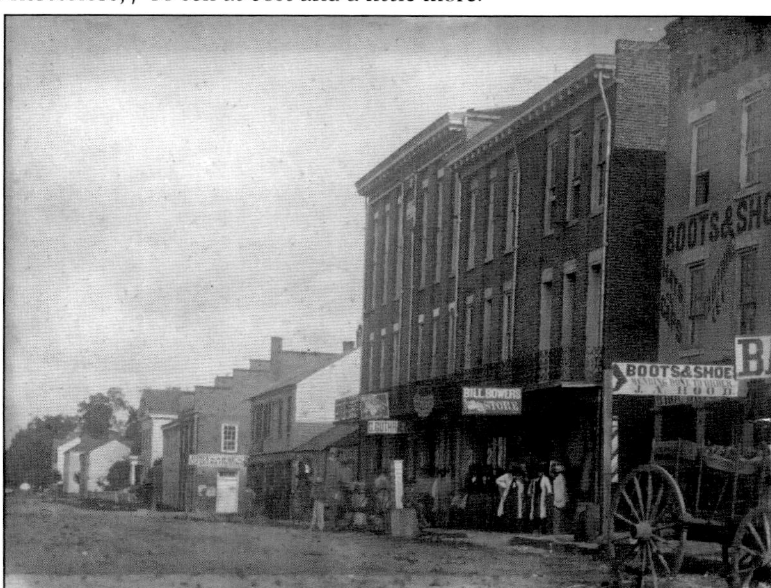

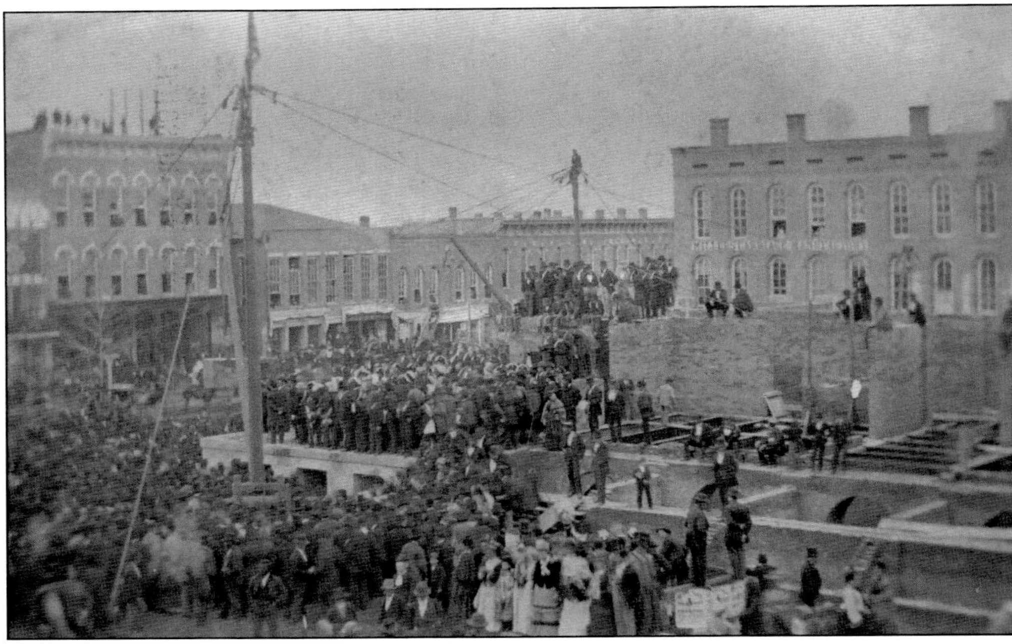

The *Crawfordsville Star* of May 4, 1875, predicted that the laying of the new courthouse cornerstone at Main and Washington Streets would "call together on the streets of our beautiful and growing city such a multitude of happy people as has seldom been called together." A crowd estimated at more than 6,000 people gathered two days later for a parade and ceremony where Lew Wallace was scheduled to speak. Just after the introduction, rain forced the ceremony into a nearby hall, where Wallace was able to finish his delivery.

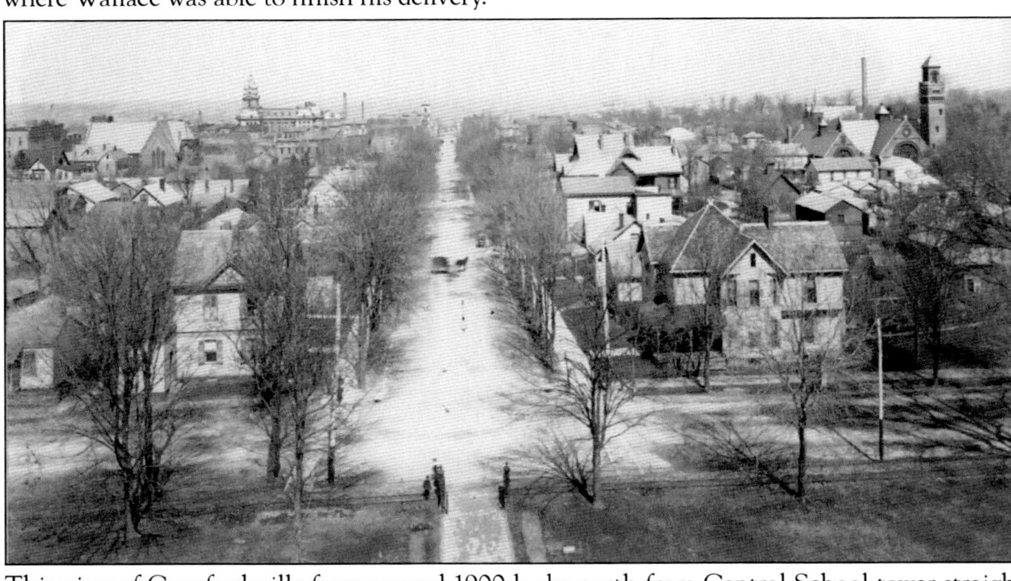

This view of Crawfordsville from around 1900 looks north from Central School tower straight down Green Street where it meets Jefferson Street. The courthouse, with its tower intact, can be seen in the distance to the left (west) of Green Street. The Methodist church and tower on the right were replaced by a new structure in 1976. Toward the end of Green Street, on the left side, appears the tower for the old city hall, which stood there until 1936.

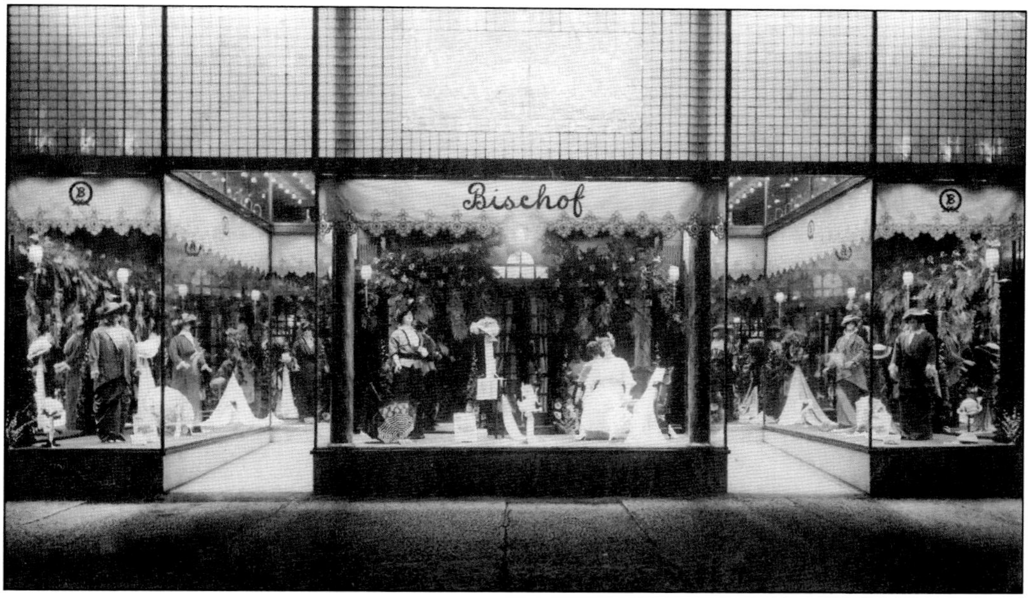

Crawfordsville was a well-lighted city by all early accounts, and a stroll along East Main Street in the early 1900s was a pleasant experience, especially when one reached the corner of Green and Main Streets where Bischof's Big Store stood for decades. Bischof was a cooperative that sold anything from clothes to toys. The latest in women's fashions make up this attractive storefront display.

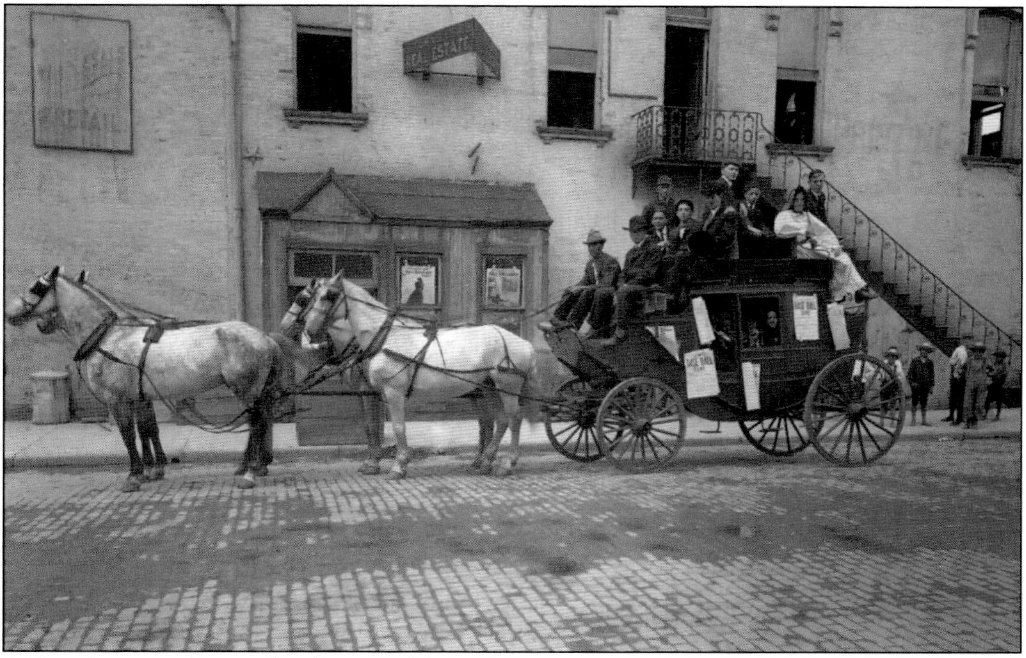

Although interurban and trolley travel became a mainstay in Crawfordsville, at the time of this photograph around 1903, horses still provided a common means of transportation. This stagecoach is stopped in front of 102 West Main Street. Flyers on the coach advertise a "Base Ball Game," which was very popular in town at that time. Some of the building's windows are now bricked up, but this edifice on West Main Street still exists.

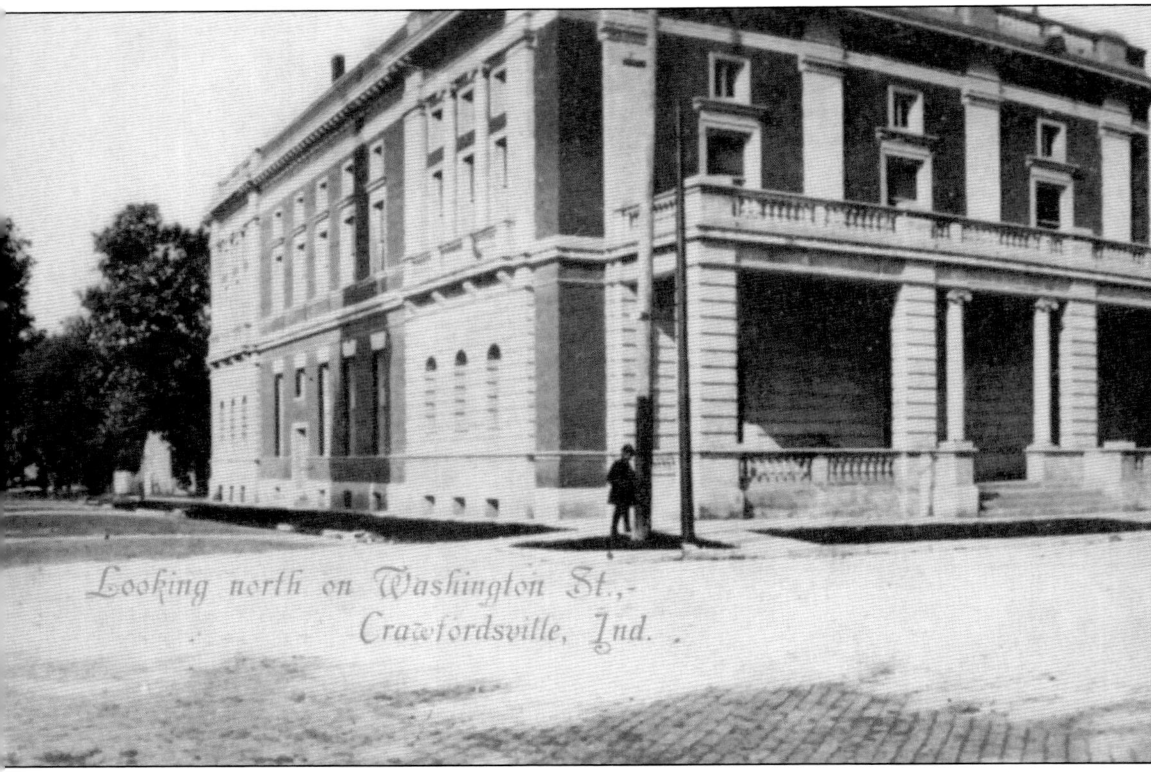

Some 60 years after the Masons began to organize in Crawfordsville, they erected their current lodge, the Masonic Temple, whose cornerstone was laid in 1901. Besides being the lodge, this building was often used by the community for its convenient theater. The view looks north on Washington Street from the corner of Wabash Avenue. This twofold postcard was created shortly

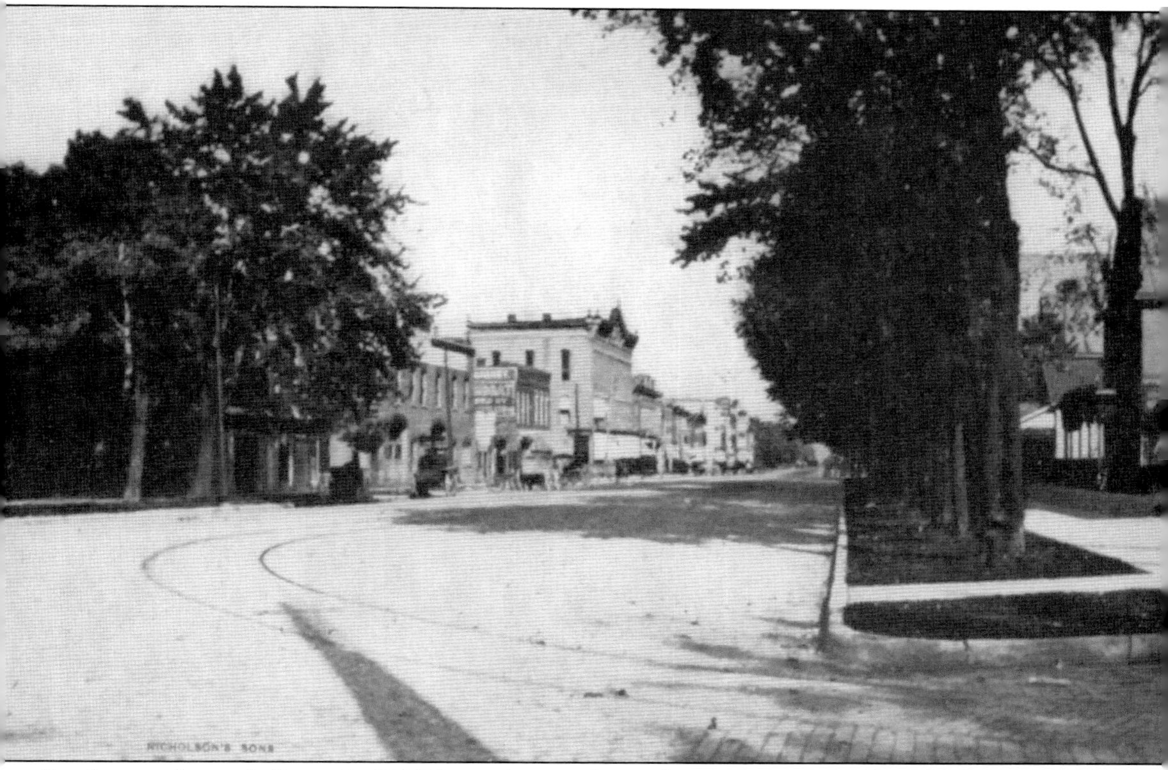

after the temple was dedicated in 1904. Interurban tracks can be seen coming south on Washington Street and turning east on Wabash Avenue. Just to the left but out of sight, on the corner, stands the Carnegie Library, which was dedicated in 1902. The Masonic Temple and the Carnegie Library (now the Carnegie Museum of Montgomery County) still face each other today.

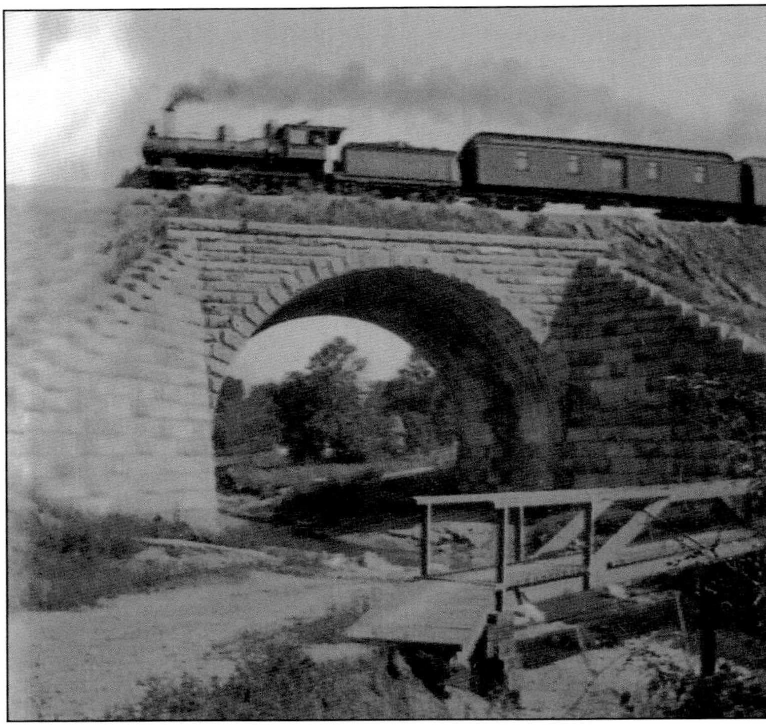

Most Crawfordsville residents will recognize the Big Four Arch. This photograph shows the arch after its completion in 1902, spanning what was then called Perrysville Road (now Big Four Arch Road, which becomes Jennison Street beyond the bridge). The stone block overpass was constructed to replace a wooden trestle that had existed since 1869. Dry Branch still flows under the arch today.

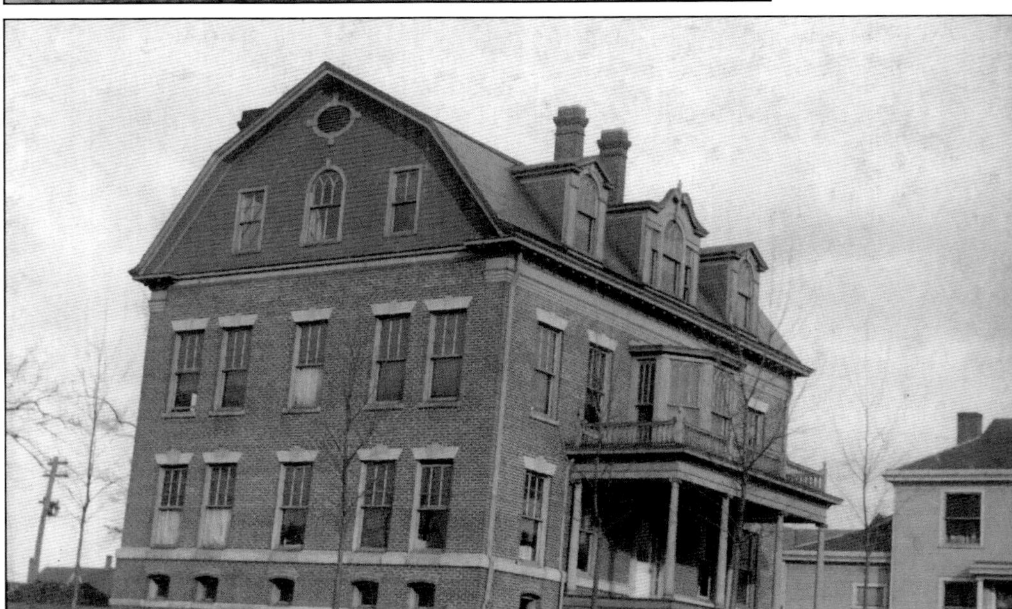

The original Culver Union Hospital was built in 1902 (shortly before this picture was taken) at what is now 308 Binford Street (between Jones and Dubois Avenues). Mrs. Hattie Strikey of Clinton, Iowa, had the honor of being the first person operated on (by Dr. Barcus); the hospital's janitor was the second, for an abscess under his arm. This Culver Union Hospital building was used as a nurses' home after a new hospital was built in 1929.

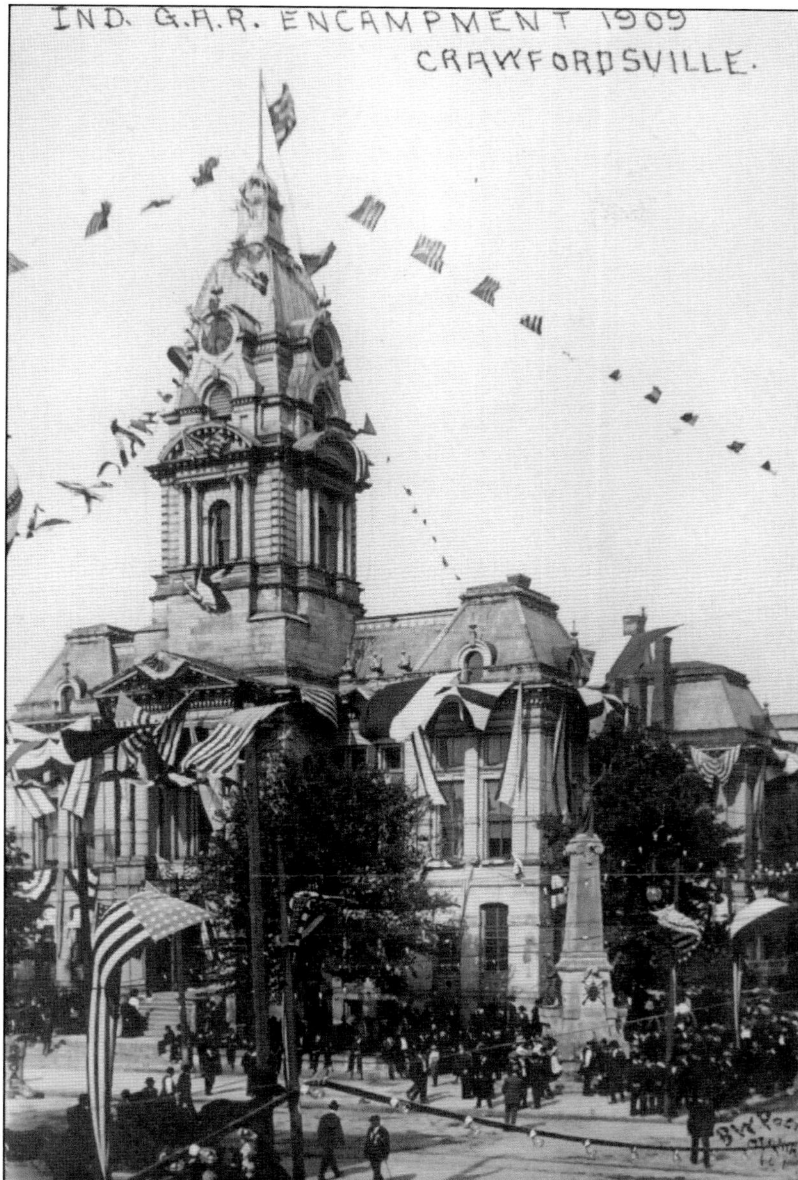

The Indiana Department of the Grand Army of the Republic (a fraternal organization of Union army veterans) was holding a large encampment in May 1909 in Crawfordsville, complete with activities and parades, when this photograph was taken to commemorate the event. This view is of the Montgomery County courthouse (on the northeast corner of Washington and Main Streets), and it is only one example of the effort the city took to welcome what was estimated to be as many as 40,000 potential visitors. American flags and pennants bedecked every major downtown building, and some 7,000 lightbulbs hung on and between structures. Crawfordsville fluttered by day and shone at night. The courthouse still stands on the same busy corner today but without its tower, which was removed in 1940 because of structural problems. The Soldiers and Sailors Monument in the lower right, however, is still a familiar sight for current courthouse visitors. It was erected in 1906 as a memorial to all veterans.

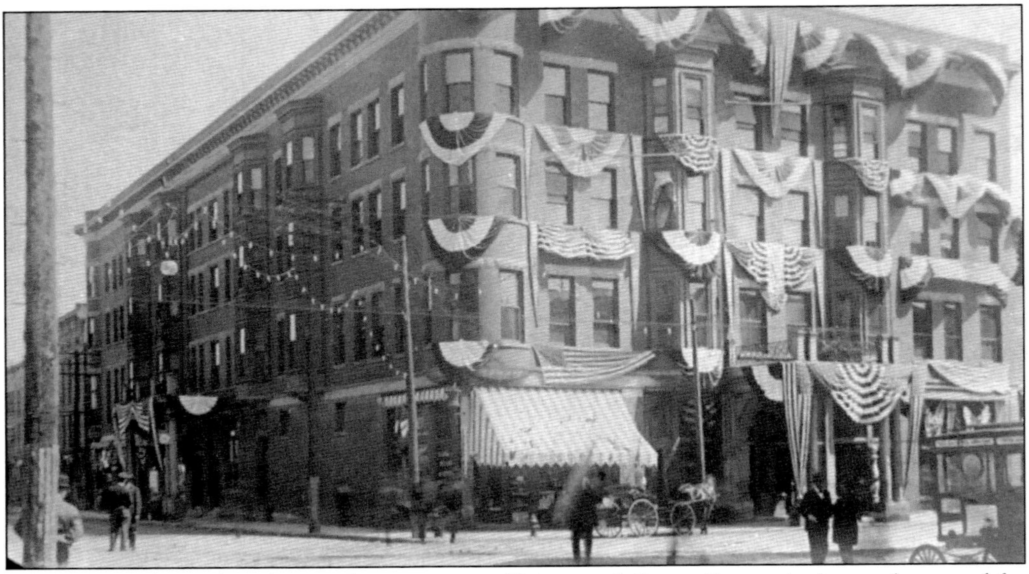

The Crawford Hotel at the northeast corner of Main and Green Streets is shown decorated for the Grand Army of the Republic encampment of 1909. The Crawford Hotel opened in early 1900, with "every modern convenience known in the hotel line," according to the *Crawfordsville Journal*. The hotel enjoyed its own electric plant, as well as an elevator, café, barbershop, drugstore, clothing store, and other various shops. The hotel fell to the wrecking ball in 1975, and a local gathering place, the Canine Plaza, now occupies this spot.

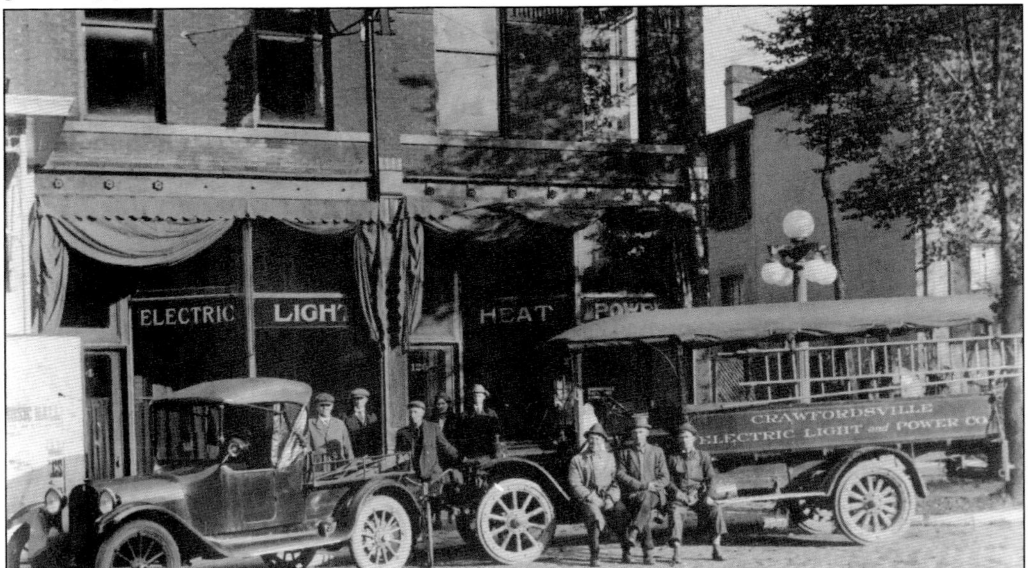

The Crawfordsville Electric Light and Power Company was once located on 124–126 South Green Street, shown here around 1916. Twenty years earlier, in 1890, the Crawfordsville City Council voted to operate its own electric power plant (the first municipality to ever take this step), which was built on the corner of Washington and North Streets. By 1891, the city considered itself the best lighted in Indiana. In 1911, a new power plant was finished north of the city on the banks of Sugar Creek.

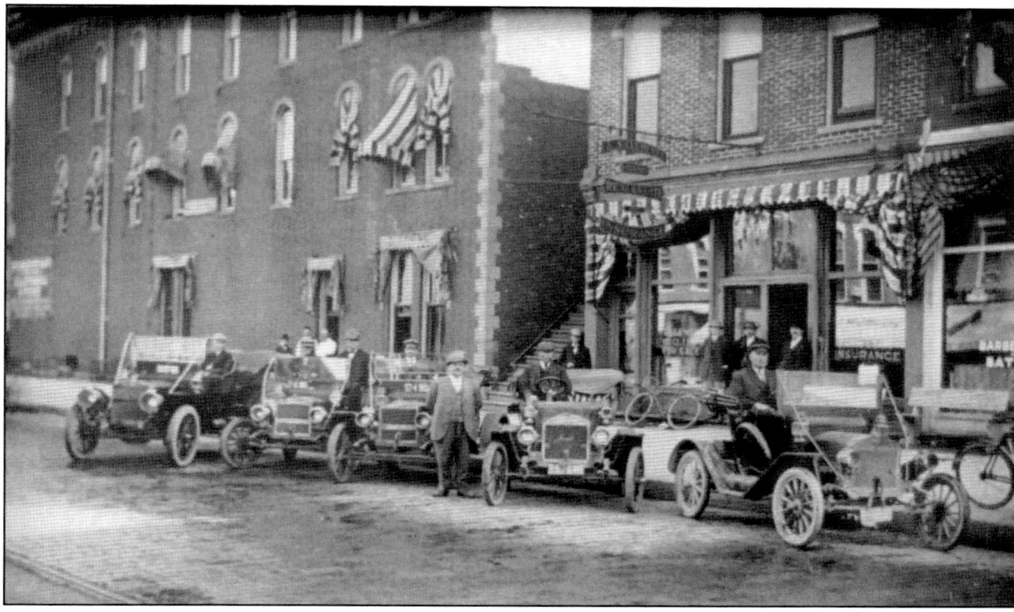

Several cars are being displayed along Washington Street for this *c.* 1908 photograph, where Andrew Clements moved his real estate and insurance office (114 South Washington Street). Sitting in the far left car is Andrew's son John, while Andrew himself stands in the center. All the structures in this view still exist. The building to the left of Clements's office, once a bank and later a jewelry store, has served as a small restaurant and coffee bar for several years.

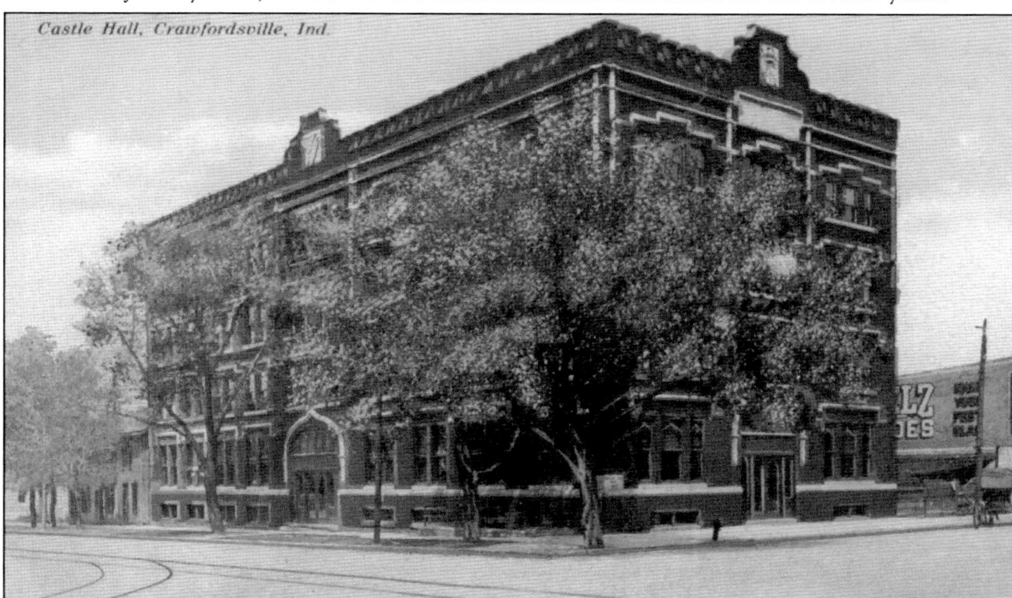

This building (on the corner of Market and Washington Streets) was known for almost a century as Castle Hall because of its crenellated roofline, but it was later known as Commerce Hall. The Indiana Life Insurance Company erected the structure in 1907, but in 1912 the Knights of Pythias purchased it. The hall was an automotive parts store when it was demolished to make way for a pharmacy parking lot in 1999.

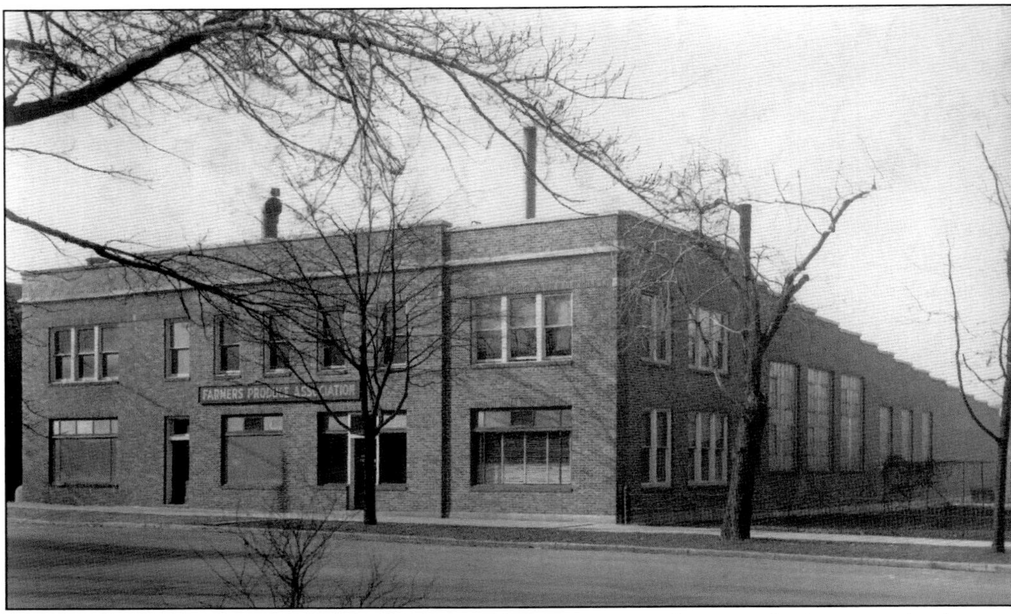

In 1923, the County Farm Bureau championed a cooperative dairy marketing organization and appealed to the farmers to band together and obtain better prices for their production. The Farmers Cooperative Creamery (later the Farmers Produce Association) opened the next year at 211 North Washington Street. By the time the cooperative closed in 1957, it employed some 70 residents. The building still remains, however, just south of the Rotary Jail Museum.

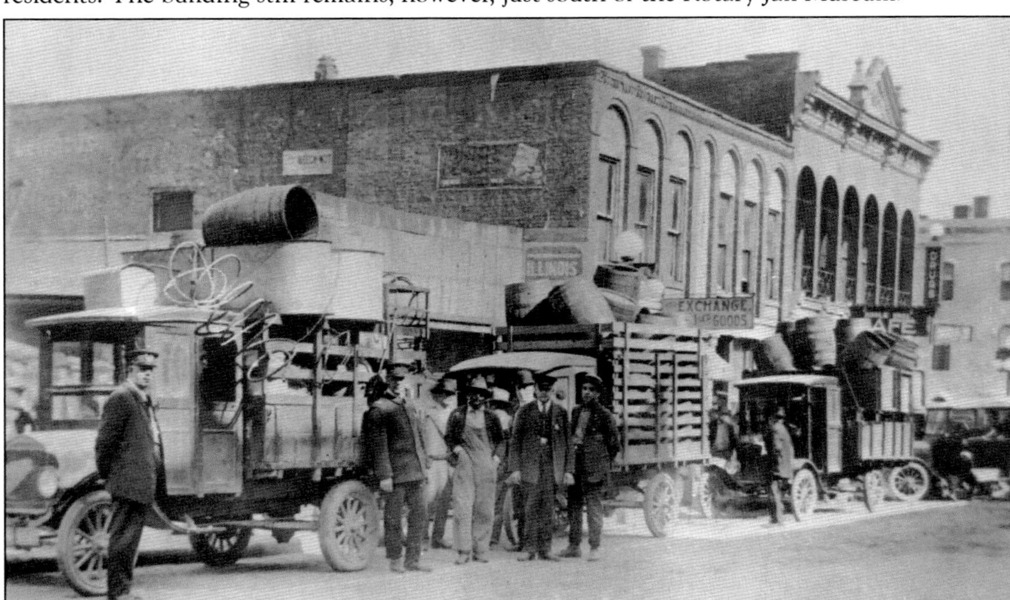

On June 30, 1923, local law agencies raided two county moonshine sites and destroyed some 3,400 gallons of mash. The confiscated copper tubing, barrels, and other paraphernalia are shown here in trucks parked in front of the city building, then located at 117–119 North Green Street. In the background can be seen the Otto Schlemmer Building, with its distinctive six round-headed brick arches. The Schlemmer Building was beautifully restored in 1978 and now houses a law office.

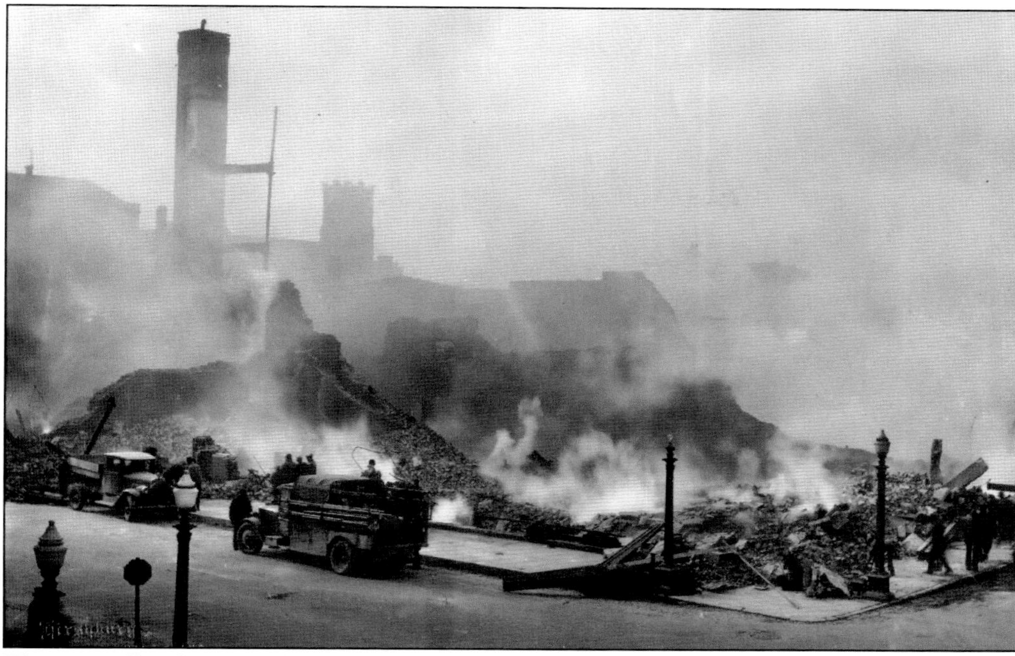

The city suffered a major disaster on January 10, 1933, when a quarter of a city block burned to the ground, destroying more than a dozen stores and businesses and damaging several others (above). Heaps of smoldering bricks and other debris remain piled by the sidewalks on the morning after the blaze. Shown is the intersection of Green and East Main Streets, where Goodman's Department Store (formerly Bischof's Big Store) was housed. Some days after the fire, crowds still congregated at the scene to wonder at the destruction and witness the cleanup effort (below). The *Crawfordsville Journal and Review* observed that the city was "shaken and staggered but not disheartened or discouraged" by what it called the worst disaster of Crawfordsville. This view is looking east on Main Street. Some still-familiar buildings that line Green Street are clearly visible (including the Strand Theater, which no longer exists, on the far right).

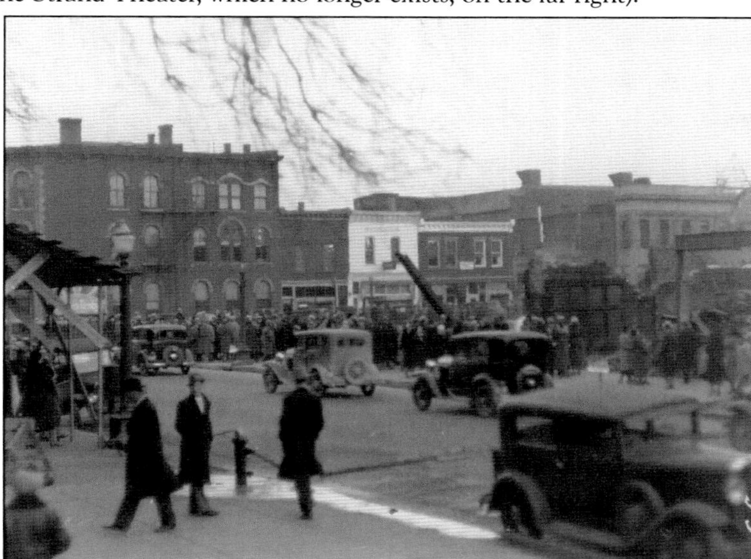

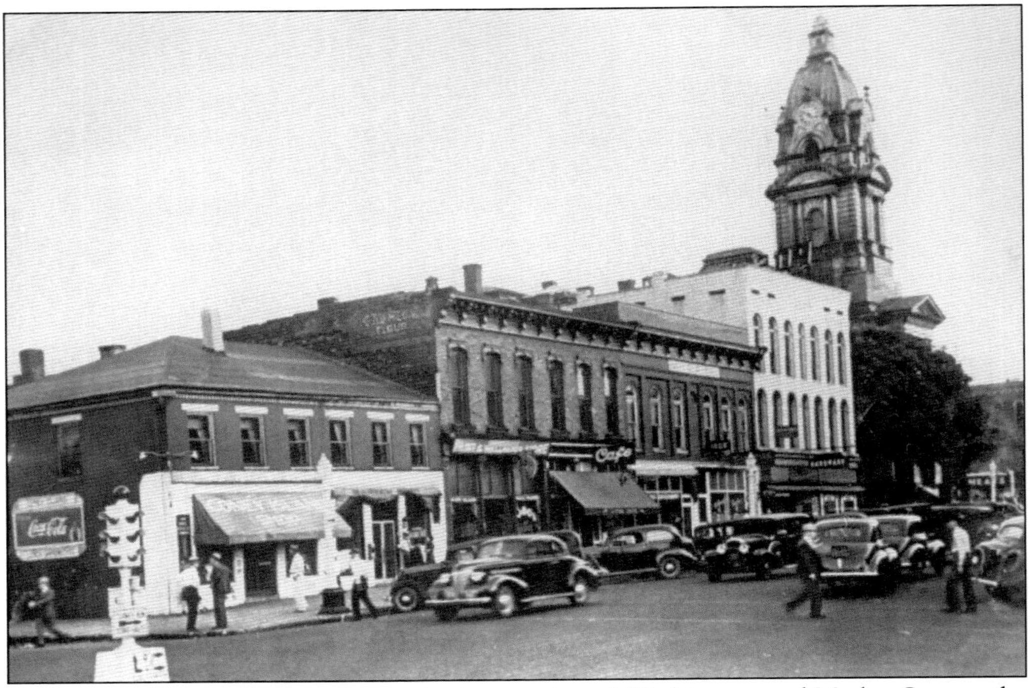

This 1940s photograph was taken at the intersection of Washington and Market Streets; the Montgomery County Courthouse dominates the downtown district. The popular Coney Island Shop on the corner operated until 1956. All the buildings up to the courthouse are now gone, replaced by a city parking lot.

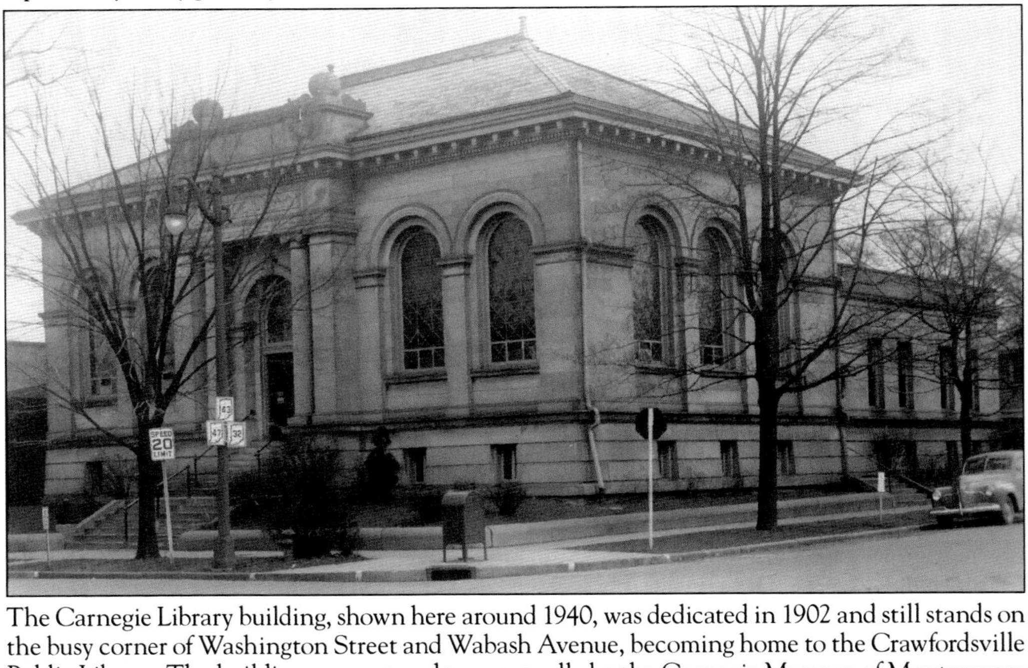

The Carnegie Library building, shown here around 1940, was dedicated in 1902 and still stands on the busy corner of Washington Street and Wabash Avenue, becoming home to the Crawfordsville Public Library. The building was restored to eventually be the Carnegie Museum of Montgomery County after the new library opened in 2005 just across the street.

The block just north of the present-day courthouse on Washington Street was, at one time, a busy commercial district. This picture from the late 1940s shows B. F. Goodrich, Sherwin-Williams Paints, the Western Auto Associate Store, and the Coney Island Shop on the corner. Across the street, on Market Street, is Castle Hall (also known as Commerce Hall). None of these structures remain today, having been replaced by parking lots.

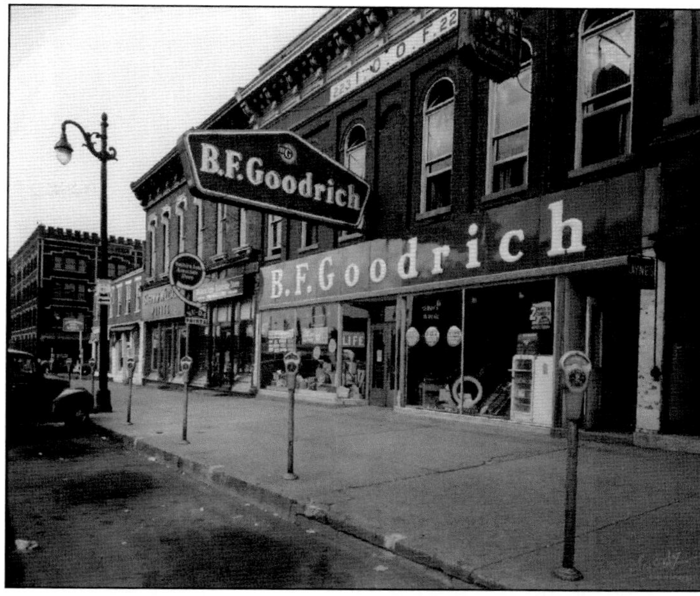

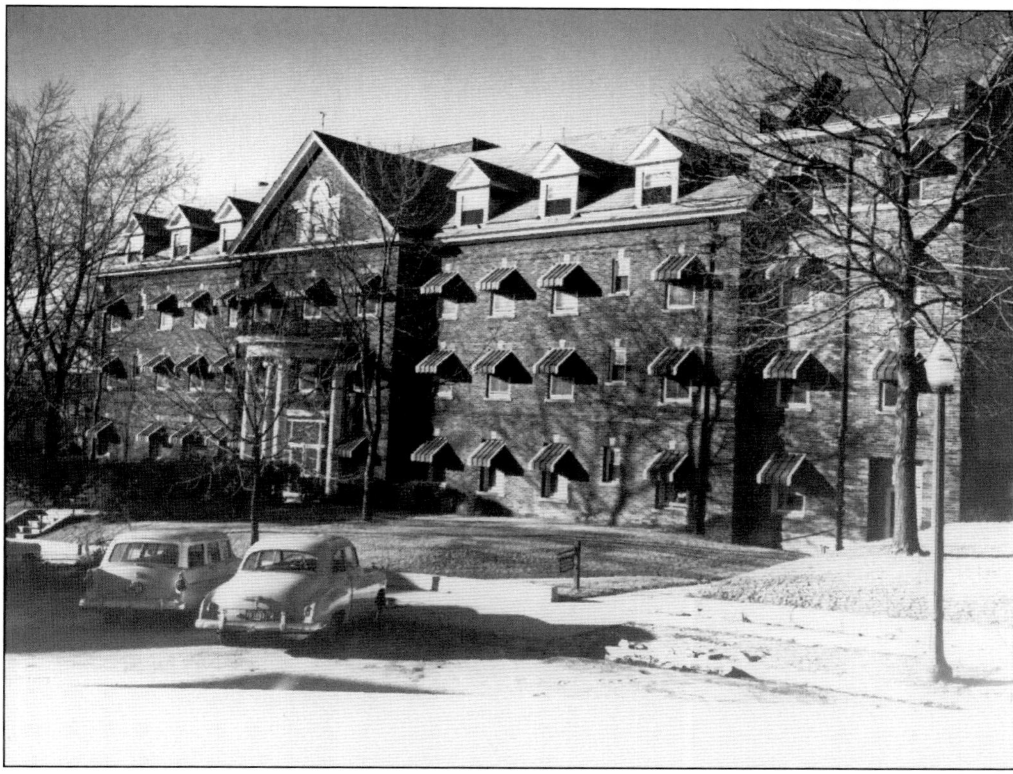

The second Culver Union Hospital opened in 1929, replacing the original structure. At the dedication ceremony, the public (estimated at 4,000 people) was invited to wander through the building. This picture shows the hospital in the 1950s after several modifications and expansions. The building was abandoned in 1984 when the AMI/Culver Hospital (now St. Clare's) was built north of the city.

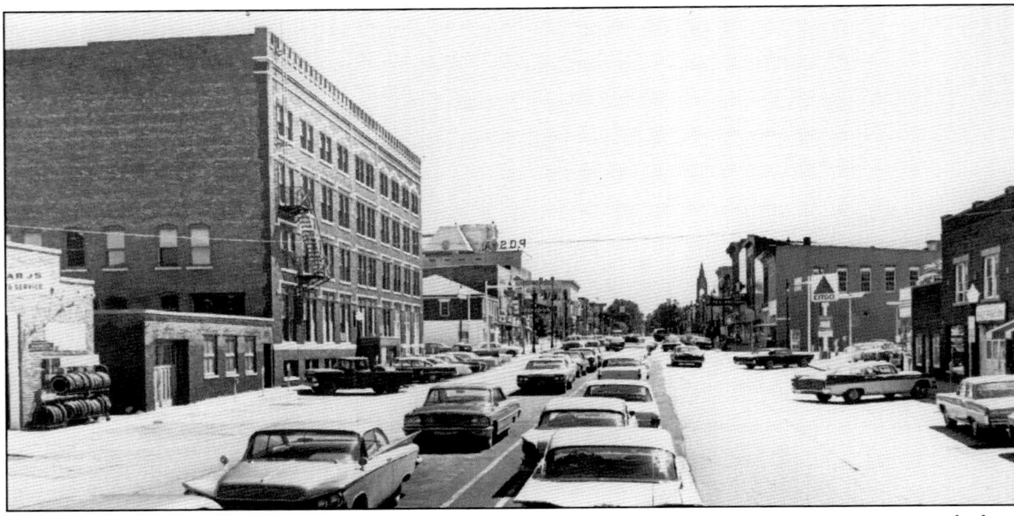

This 1950s view of downtown Crawfordsville looks from North Washington Street south from Spring Street; Castle Hall appears to the left. The end of the downtown district is marked by the steeple of the Wabash Avenue Presbyterian Church. Washington Street is now busy U.S. 231, bisecting Crawfordsville, and cars are no longer permitted to park in the center lanes.

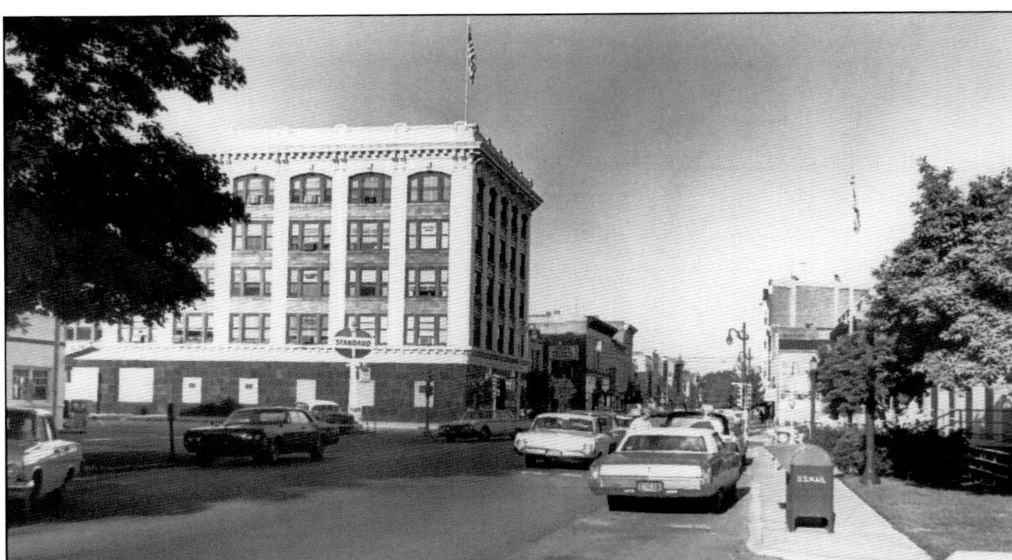

This late-1950s view looks east on Main Street; the Crawfordsville Post Office is visible to the right. Most prominent, of course, is the Ben-Hur Building, which was constructed in 1912. At its dedication, the *Crawfordsville Weekly Journal* proclaimed, "It is doubtful if there is a city of the same size of the Athens of Indiana in the whole country that has such a splendid structure." The Standard gas station no longer remains.

Two

SCHOOLS AND CHURCHES

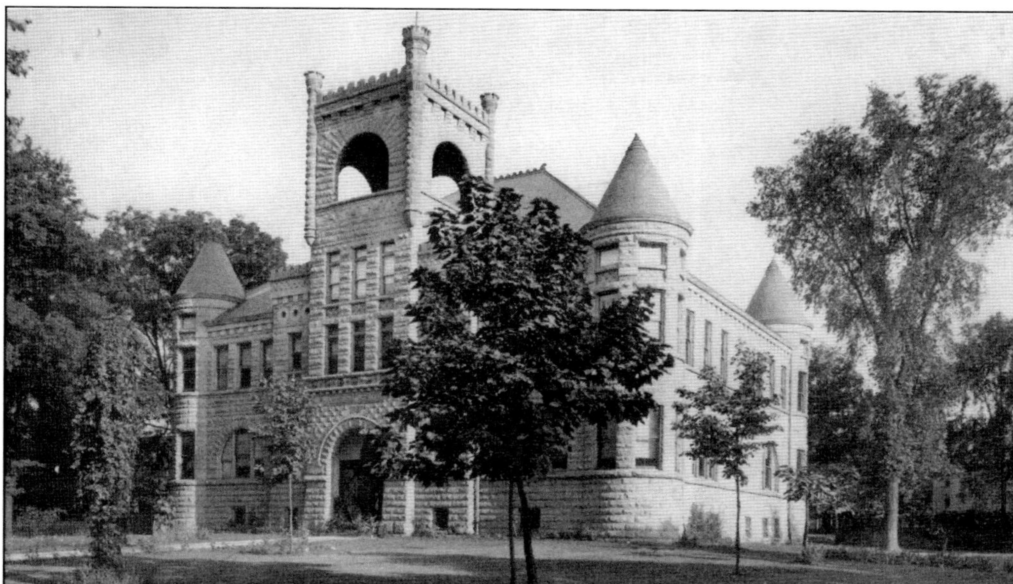

In the late 19th century, Laura Willson's home on East Wabash Avenue was used for a ward school because of overcrowding at the city's Central School. In 1897, the castle-like and imposing Willson School building was constructed on her property with an entrance facing East Wabash Avenue. When the new building was dedicated on February 22, 1898, the *Crawfordsville Journal* called it "one of the handsomest edifices of the kind in Indiana." Dr. Joseph F. Tuttle, president of Wabash College, gave the dedicatory prayer. In 1911, when this photograph was taken, Willson School served 356 students in six grades. In 1964, it was torn down and replaced by a newer building at the same location named the Anna Willson School after a popular teacher and school administrator, the granddaughter of Laura Willson.

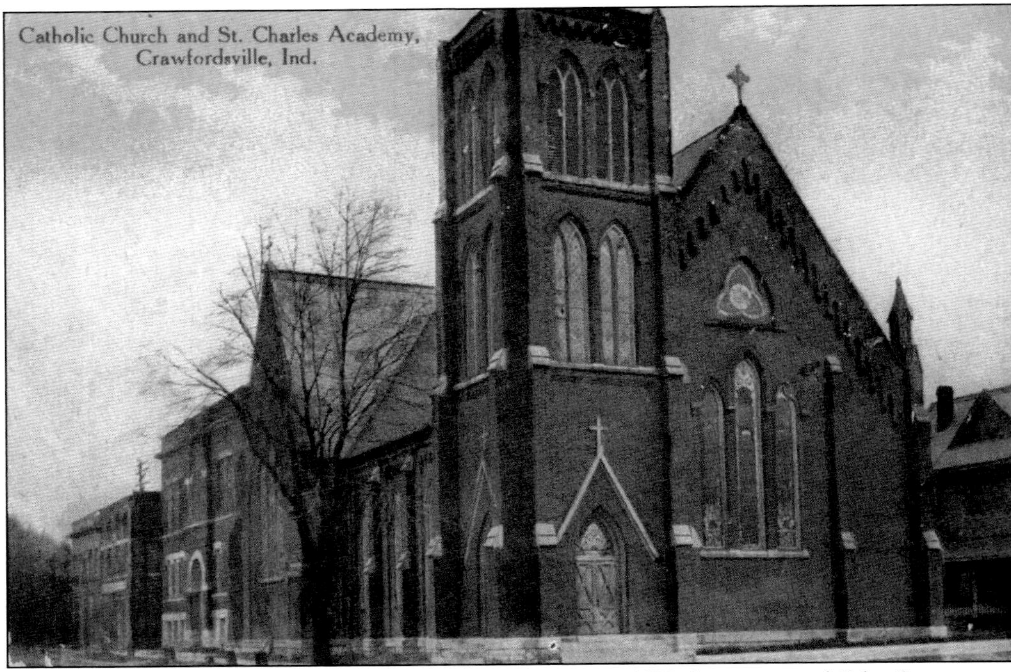

St. Bernard's Catholic Church (above), on the corner of Washington and Pike Streets, was dedicated on September 17, 1876. The *Crawfordsville Star* noted that many well-wishers were expected and warned: "Owing to the immense throng from abroad, no person will be admitted at the morning services unless upon presentation of a ticket." The entire community was proud of the church, which was a more impressive structure after its bell tower was completed in 1881. The church served as a backdrop (below) for this *c.* 1906 photograph of children preparing for their First Holy Communion. A new church and school were built on East Main Street in 1956. The original structure was eventually torn down to make way for a bank.

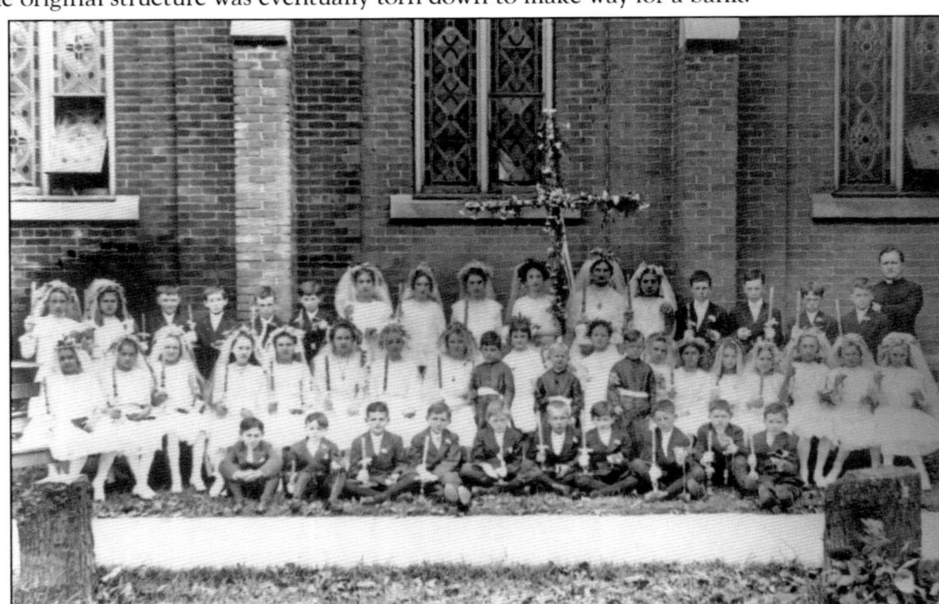

The Crawfordsville Methodist Episcopal Church (right), built in 1855 for $3,200, is shown here on the corner of Wabash Avenue and Water Street. The eastern façade entrance faced Water Street and what is now the restored Lane Place (note the iron fence). The church was the second Methodist Episcopal church on the site and served until its demolition in 1886. The Old First United Methodist Church (below) that replaced it cost $123,000. This 1950s view of the church is from the intersection at the southeast corner of the church. This church had a distinctive steeple that, at one time, was even taller (a smaller steeple rose above the crenellated portion in this image). The church would stand until 1976, when it was replaced by yet another, newer structure.

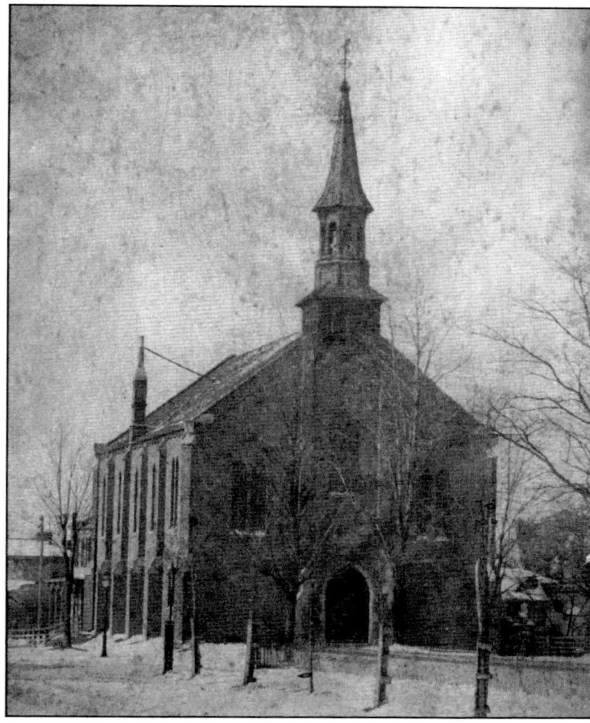

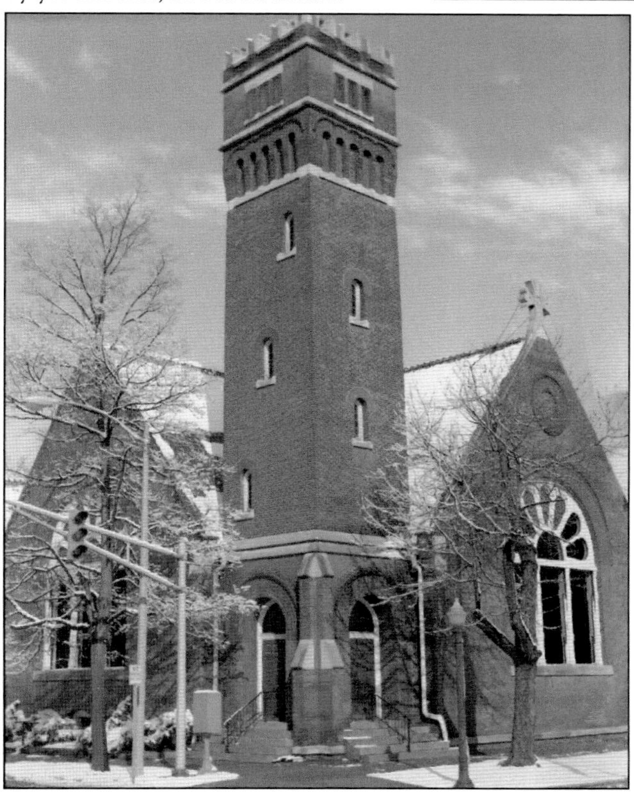

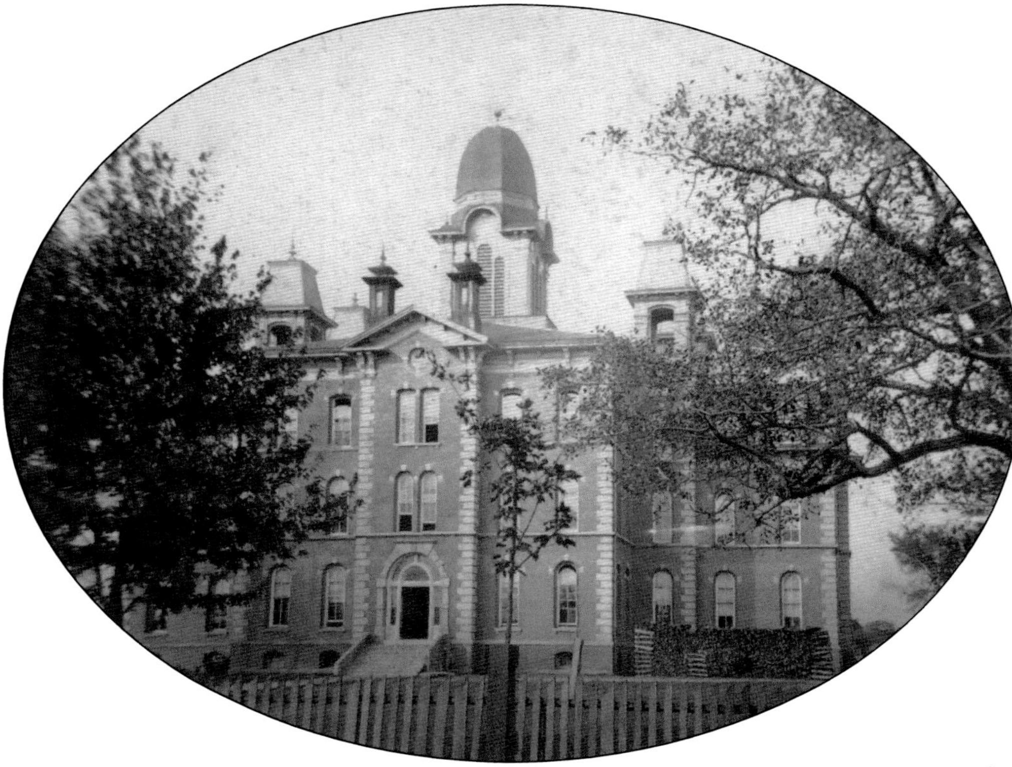

The Central School building was constructed in 1873 on East Jefferson Street to accommodate all public schools in Crawfordsville. Annual commencements began in 1877, but instruction was not organized by department. It was not until after Central School was rebuilt following a fire in 1892 that it was considered a high school.

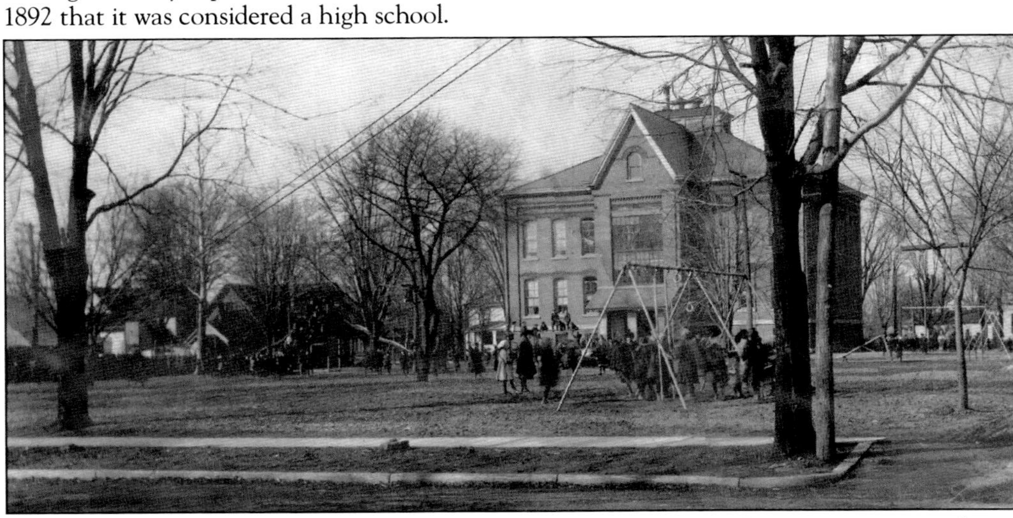

The imposing Old Mills School was located at 801–807 West Main Street; construction began in 1887. In 1908, the *Crawfordsville Journal* donated money to equip the school with swings, bars, and other playground gear. This view looks from Pike Street toward the rear of the school. The structure was replaced in the 1960s by the current building at the same location but with an entrance on Pike Street. (Courtesy Bill Boone.)

The Presbyterian church was organized in Crawfordsville in 1824, but in 1838 doctrinal issues led to a split, and the "new-school" Presbyterians (Center Presbyterian Church) located their church at the corner of Pike and Washington Streets in 1840 (the horses are standing on Washington Street). The church is shown here around 1870 (right). The First Presbyterian Church (below) was built near the corner of Water Street on East Pike Street in 1871, where the city building now stands. This winter photograph, taken around 1905, also shows a private home next to the church where, as written on the back of the photograph, "Abby Curtis and her Aunt Nan Burk lived." The old-school Presbyterians remained here after the 1838 split. This church closed in 1921 when its congregation reunited with the new-school Presbyterians and moved to Center Church (now the Wabash Avenue Presbyterian Church).

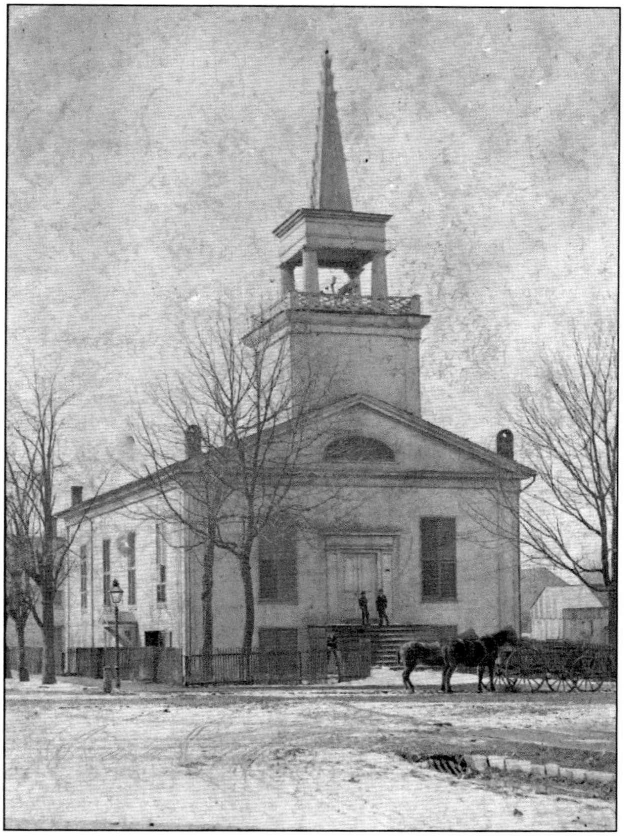

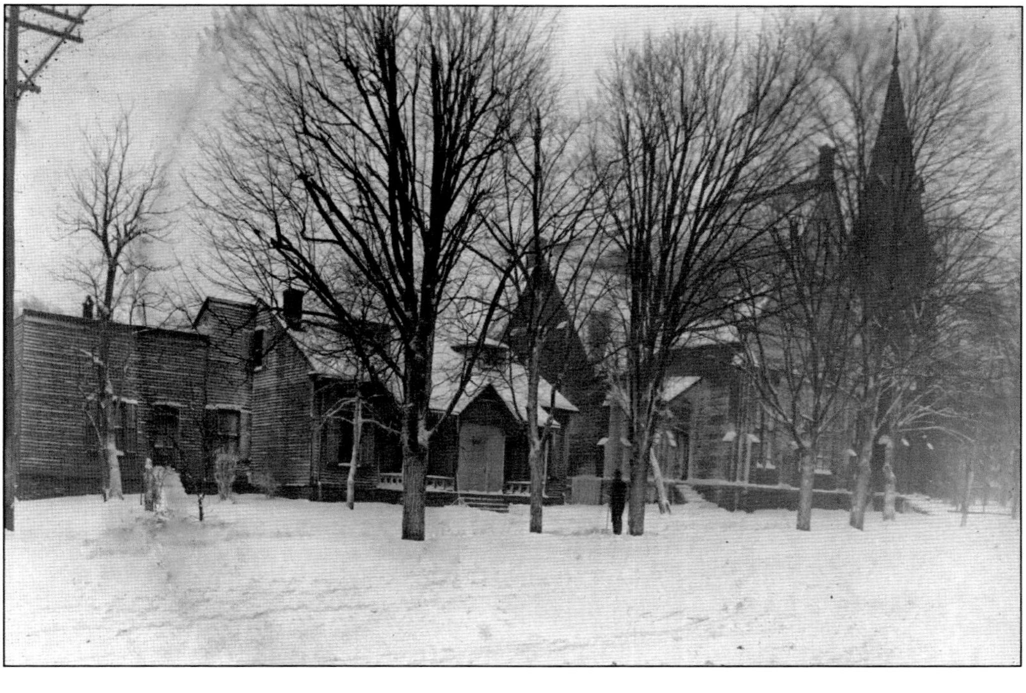

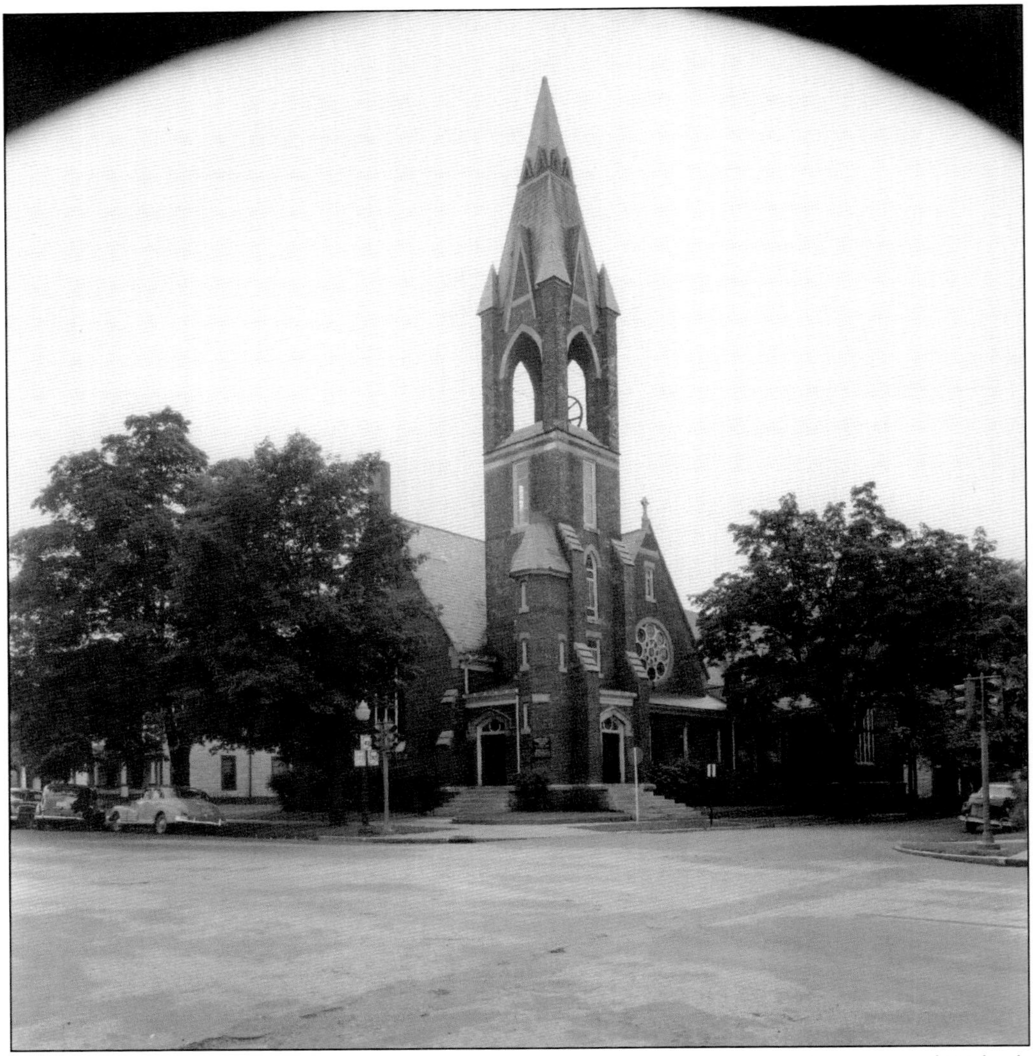

The Center Church was constructed in 1880 at the southwest corner of Washington and Wabash Streets, where it still stands as a familiar landmark for Crawfordsville residents who can easily see its spire from several approaches into the city. In his *History of Montgomery County* published in 1881, Hiram Beckwith observed: "The new building contains all the latest improvements in seating, heating, and lighting, and with its numerous beautiful memorial windows, and graceful contour, is decidedly the finest church edifice in the city." This building later witnessed the construction of two historical buildings on other corners of the same intersection: the Masonic Temple in 1901 and the Carnegie library in 1902, both of which also remain in the same location. Center Church became the Wabash Avenue Presbyterian Church in 1921 when the Presbyterian congregational split was reconciled. It is shown here around 1950 and looks much the same today as it did then, although large trees no longer line the streets on either side of the church. In 1961, a two-story educational facility was added.

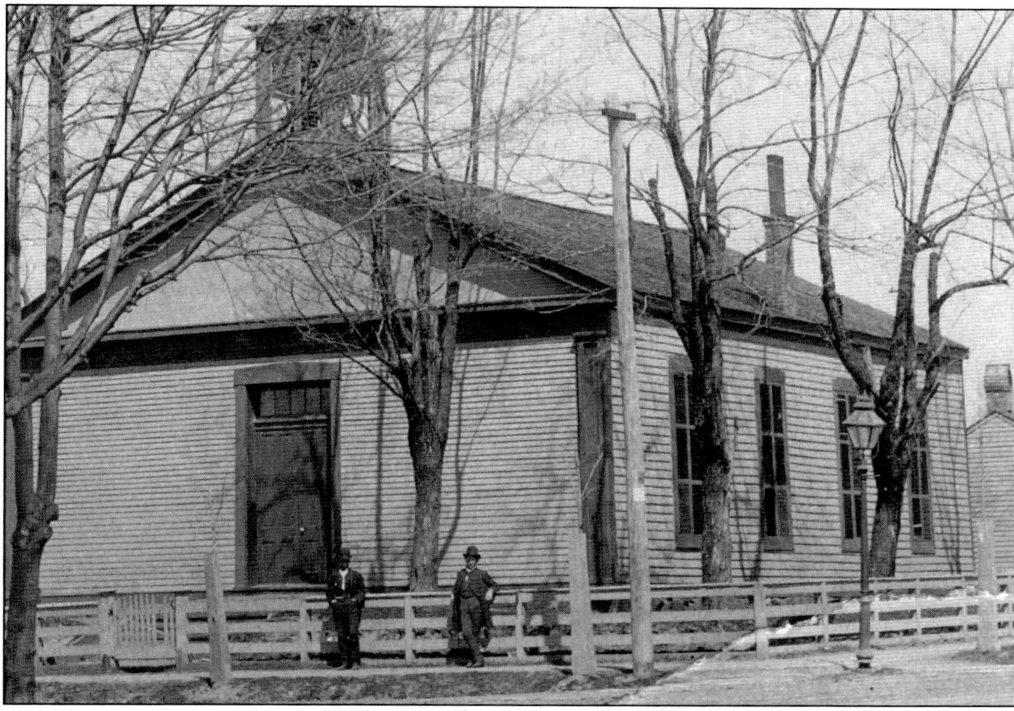

The New Light Christian Church was originally located 4 miles south of Crawfordsville, but in 1833 a newer church (above) was constructed on the corner of Wabash Avenue and Walnut Street, where it became the Christian Church It is shown here around 1870. When it was demolished later to make way for the newer structure, a tombstone was found beneath its flooring. The tombstone was inscribed for a certain Stephen Field, who was one of the county's first homicides in 1835. Field was killed by a man named Bloomfield over a squabble about pastureland. At the time of the discovery, no one knew where Field had been buried, but it certainly wasn't under the church, which was the first building on this site. It remains a mystery how the tombstone ended up under the structure. The First Christian Church, which replaced the Christian Church, was built in 1888 at the northwest corner of Wabash Avenue and Walnut Street on the same spot as the previous building (below). The church is shown here around 1940.

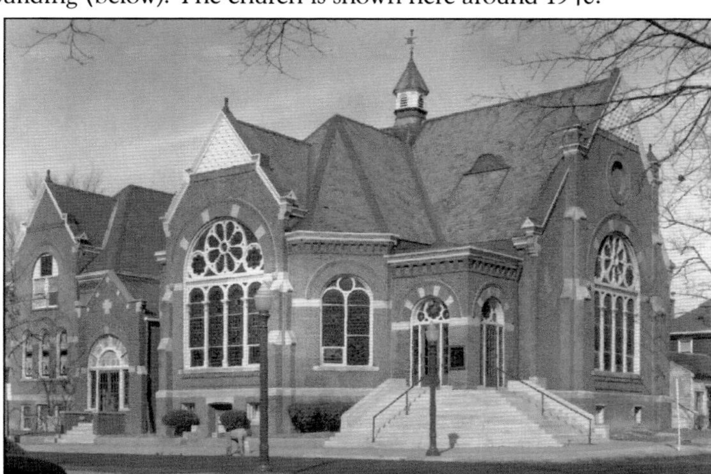

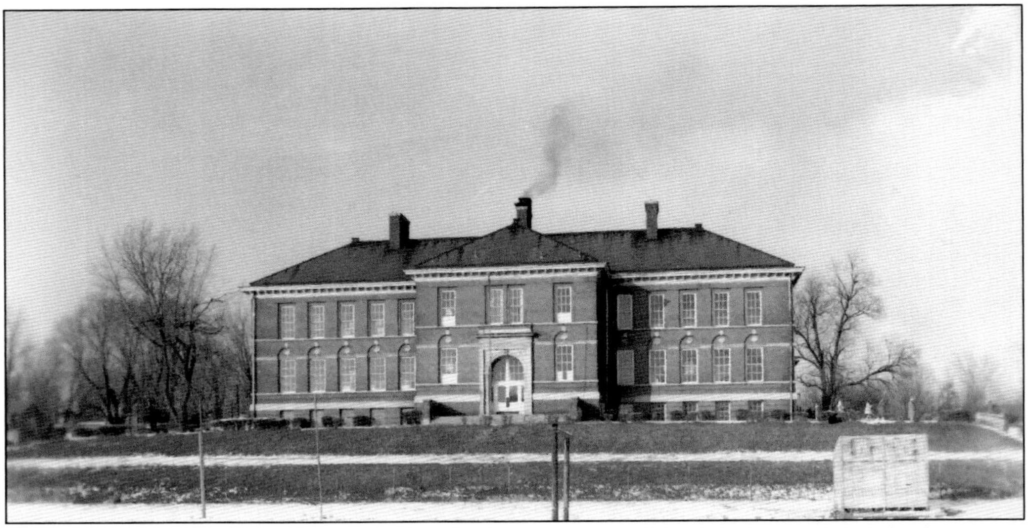

Seen above, the Tuttle Building, as it was known, opened in 1906 between South Elm Street and Wallace Avenue, just south of the Big Four railroad tracks, on a slight hill overlooking a playing field. This multistory brick edifice cost about $20,000 and was equipped with all the modern amenities for its time. By 1911, its 300 pupils were being guided by seven teachers. This view is from the south, near Chestnut Street, where the current Tuttle Middle School field is located. Although the grade-school students of Crawfordsville were segregated for many years, the photograph below shows students from Lincoln School (the African American school) and Tuttle School assembled together on the grounds of Tuttle in 1917. They have been lined up against each other with a teacher supervising a game. Tuttle Grade School would be demolished in 1960 to make way for Joseph F. Tuttle Middle School at the same location.

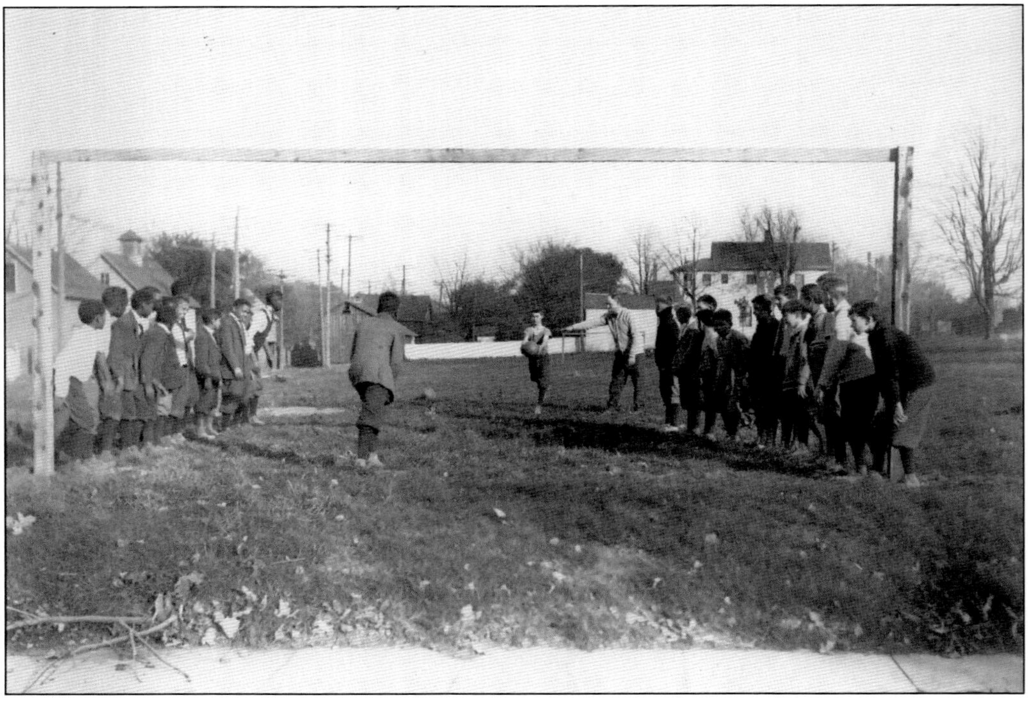

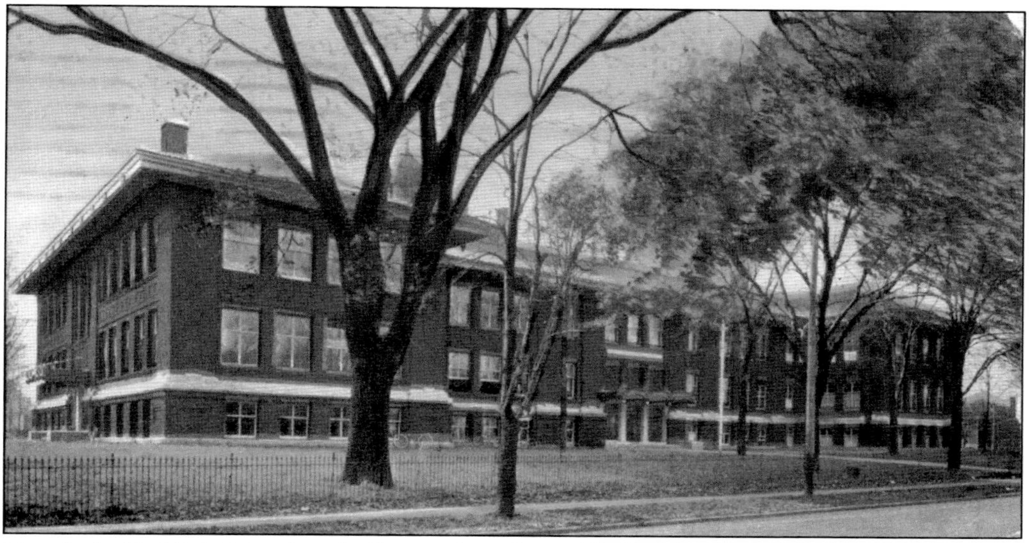

Crawfordsville High School was built to replace Central High School in 1911, which had occupied the same location since 1873. The new two-story building covered nearly an acre and offered amenities, including a telephone system, steam heat, two laboratories, four study halls, three woodworking rooms, four drinking fountains, vacuum cleaners, and five washrooms. Its concrete, brick, and tile construction was considered fireproof. This high school served until a new school was built in 1993.

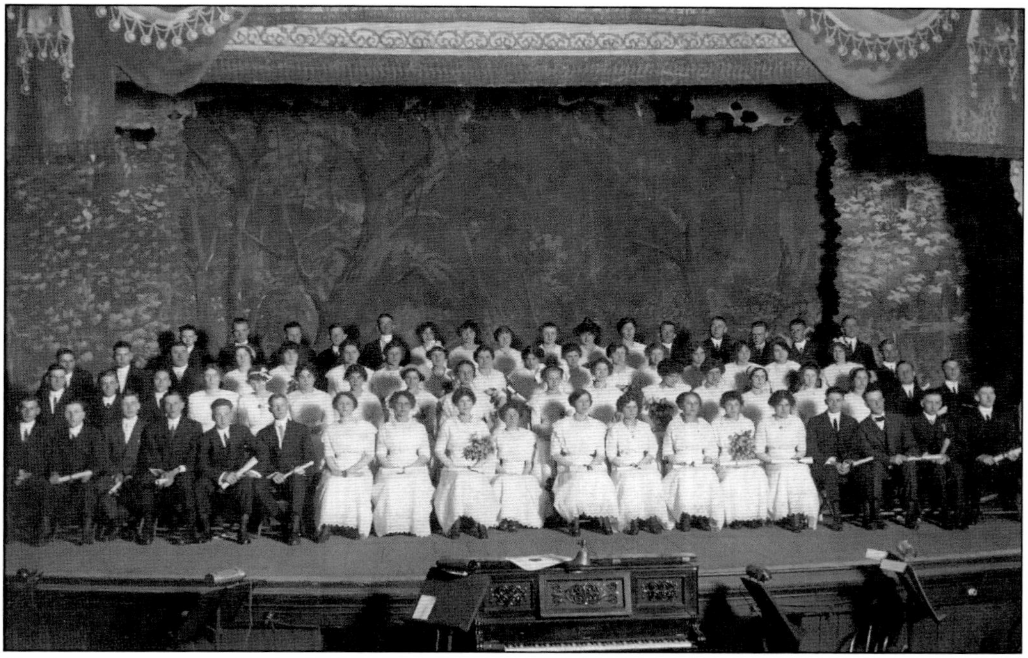

Graduating seniors of Crawfordsville High School's class of 1915 are seated in the Music Hall on 122 South Green Street, just a few blocks from the school (the school would not have an auditorium until 1919). A city pamphlet published at that time boasts: "A remarkably large per cent of its graduates each year enter higher institutions of learning all over the country and the high stand they have invariably taken has justly celebrated the school from which they came."

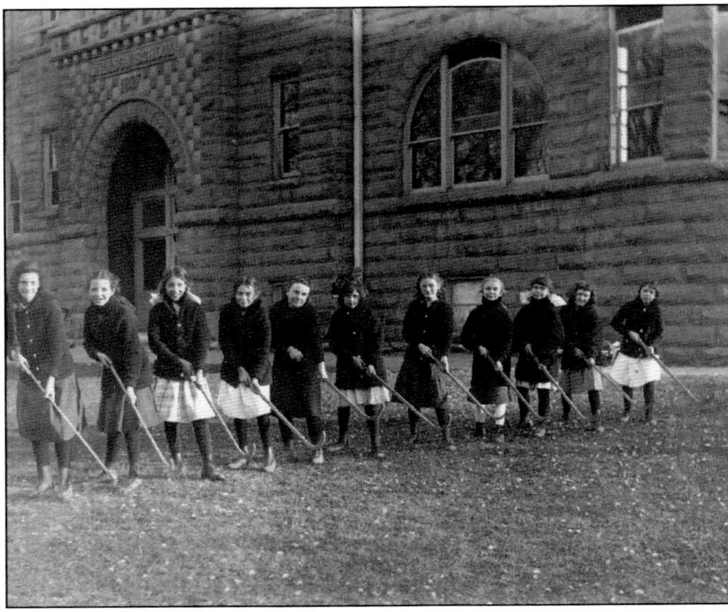

The female field hockey team for Willson School lines up outside the entrance to the school (facing East Wabash Avenue) in 1917. The identified players include Lois Southerd (far left), Mary Iliff (fourth from left), Eliz Mahorney (second from right), Mary Bowers (third from right), and Mary E. Hill (fourth from right). Field hockey was played at the summer Olympics in 1908, which may have added some interest to the sport.

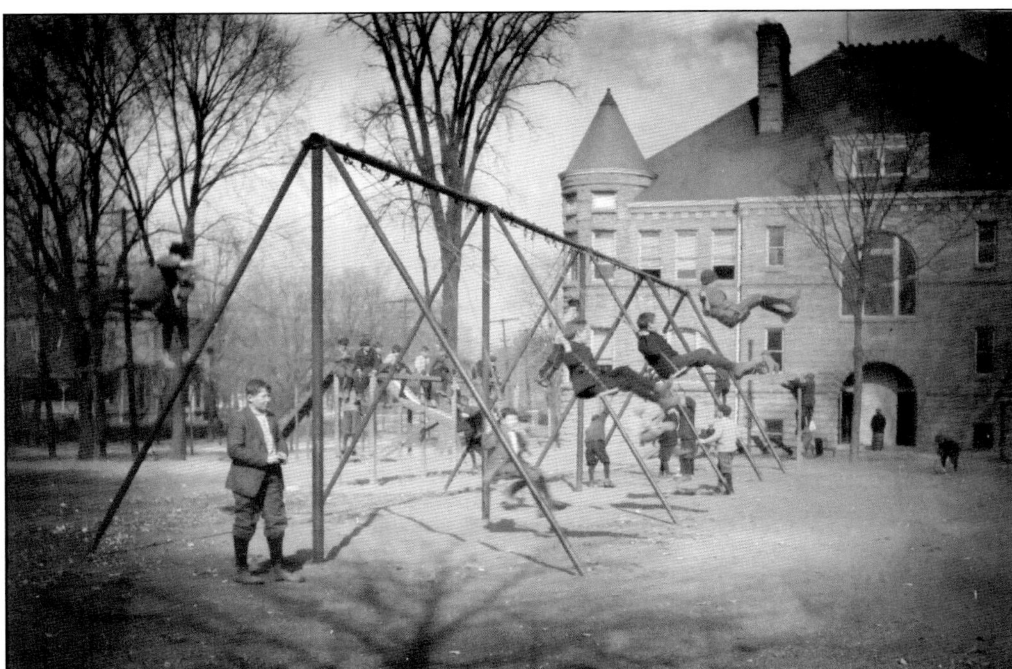

Boys are photographed here around 1916 on the much-admired playground of the original Willson School. A. W. Bowen's *History of Montgomery County* states, "Three hundred dollars in swings, made of steel, traveling rings, giant strides, ladders, see-saws, basket-ball courts and a hundred yard cinder running track, make the grounds one of the best." When Willson School was demolished in 1964 to make way for a modern school, the new structure was built on the playground site (facing Jefferson Street).

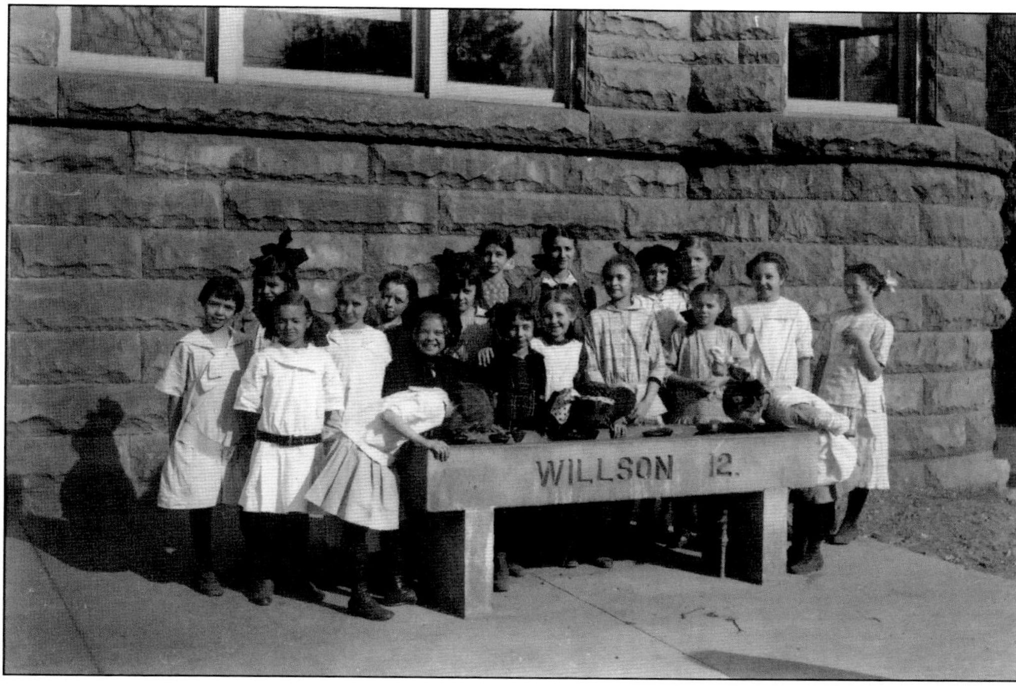

A group of girls (above) gathers near an exterior drinking fountain of Willson School around 1915. Using a tin cup tied to a faucet was a common way for schoolchildren to get water during school or recess. In the early 1900s, however, the drinking fountain was developed to help slow down instances of waterborne diseases. In 1910, for example, there were 13 cases of typhoid in Crawfordsville, and one young woman succumbed to the disease. A young baseball player from a more recent year (below) takes advantage of a renovated fountain from Mills School, which opened after 1887. Mills also had an exterior drinking fountain. This fountain may have been constructed by the same company, or at least at the same time as the Willson fountain, presumably 1912, although it is not clear why the Willson fountain simply had a "12" instead of "1912" chiseled on its side.

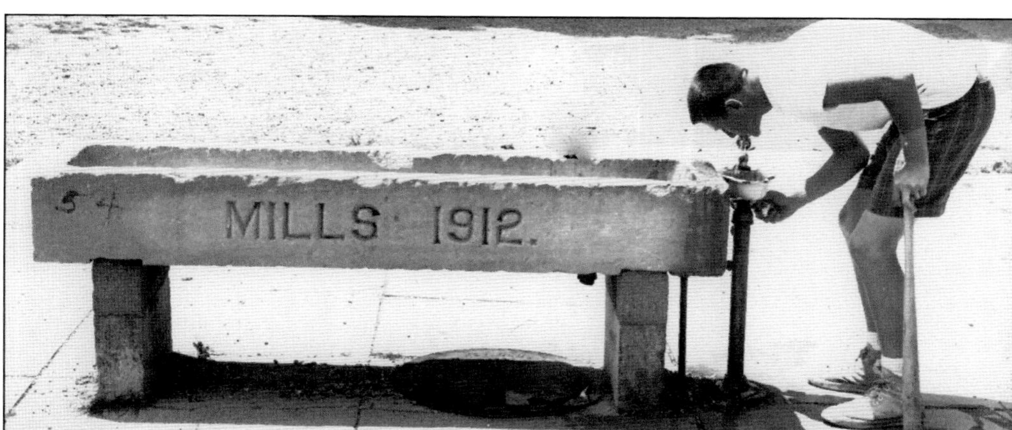

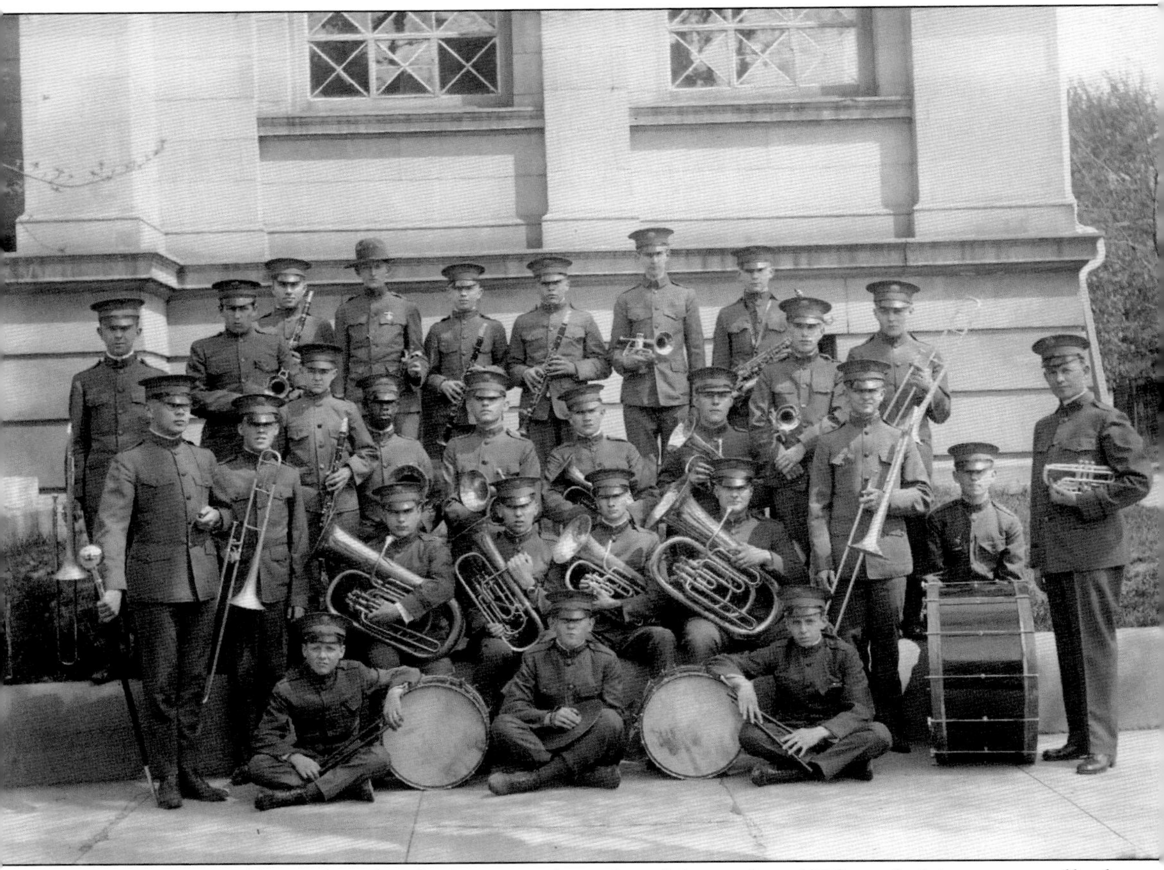

Crawfordsville High School's first marching band formed in 1919, and this group walked a few blocks from school to pose in front of the Crawfordsville Public Library on the corner of Washington Street and Wabash Avenue. The military-like band uniforms had been used by the high school ROTC in 1917 and 1918 during World War I, and the 1919 *Athenian* yearbook labeled the band's picture as the "C.H.S. Military Band." This same yearbook observed that "the band has been of inestimable service to the school" because it brought "spirit and enthusiasm" to every important basketball game and track meet. The band also participated in war loan and war fund campaigns in the area. Leslie Lyons, standing on the far right, was the band director credited with developing this fledgling band into an effective unit. Lyons was the owner of the Lyons Music Company from 1913 until his death in 1955. His obituary in the *Crawfordsville Journal Review* on May 18, 1955, stated, "He had been responsible for the development of many young musicians and music teachers."

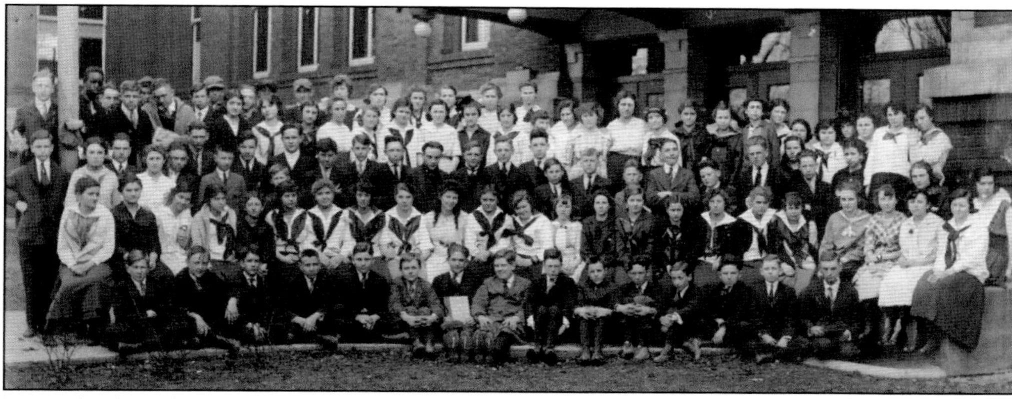

Junior high and high school students have congregated outside the Old Crawfordsville High School building in 1919. The *Athenian* yearbook of 1919 exuded optimism for the future—World War I had ended, and the school was expanding (a new auditorium was finished that year). The editors believed that local money was well spent: "The citizens of Crawfordsville have no reason to feel that the Crawfordsville High School has not been a splendid investment."

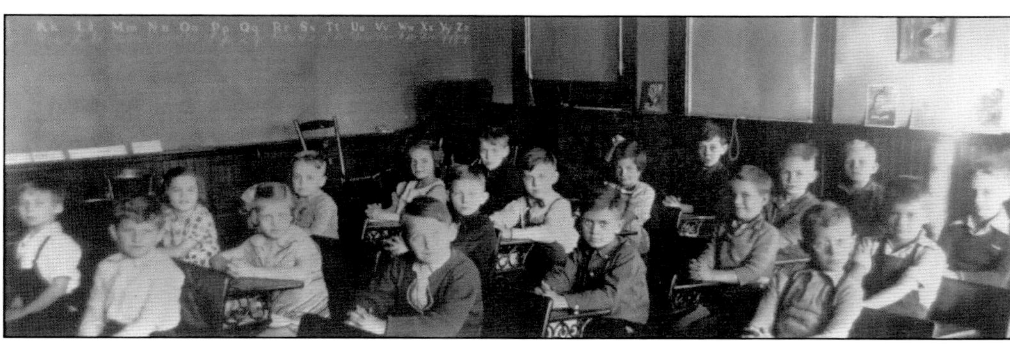

In 1935, Mills Elementary schoolchildren sit at their desks, and more than a few of them were unable to sit still long enough to be captured clearly. The blackboard is lined and ready for cursive writing practice.

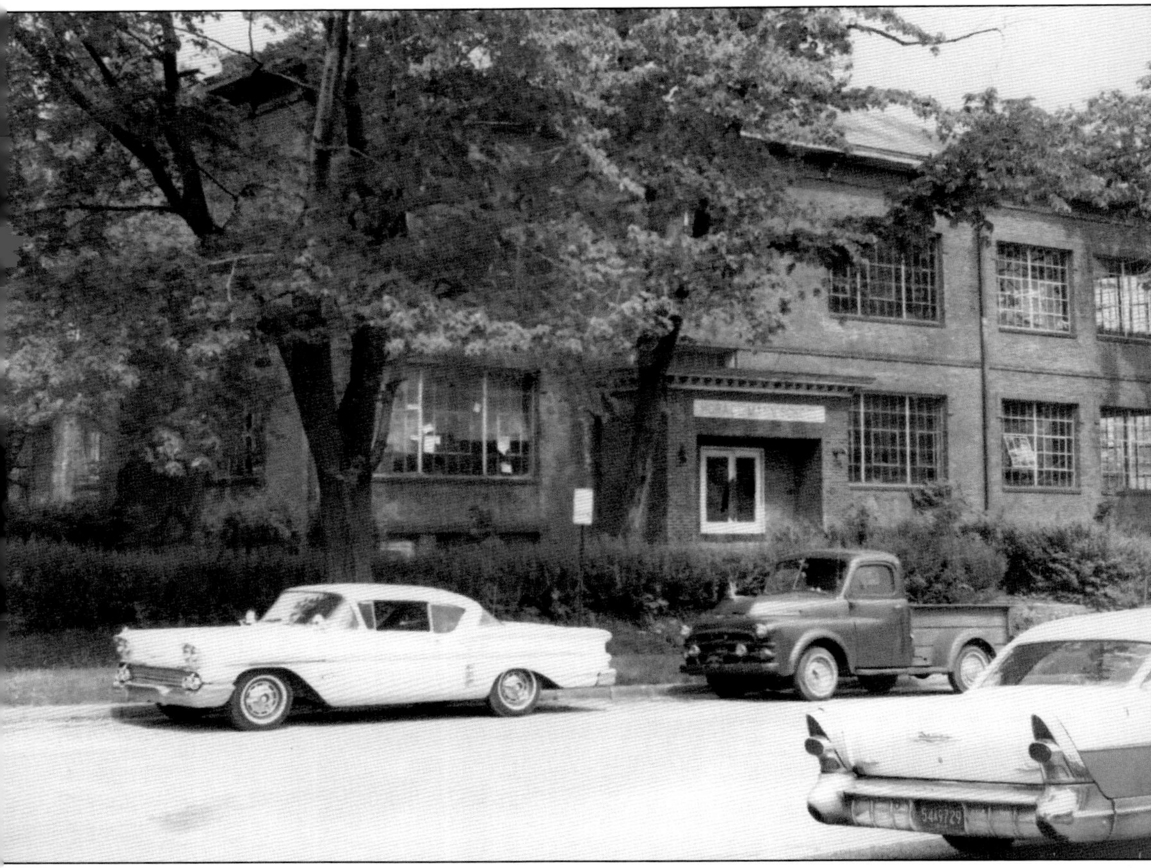

In 1882, Lincoln School was built for African American students at the corner of Spring and North Walnut Streets. Within a decade, however, Crawfordsville was rethinking its policy of segregated schooling because of the very poor retention rate (said to be at 50 percent), higher costs per pupil ($30 per year as opposed to $8 for the other schools), and the difficulty attracting suitable teachers. On the topic of the problems with this school, the *Crawfordsville Weekly Journal* of July 1, 1893, stated, "The scholars learn but little and that little has gone in through their hides." The newspaper further observed that the school board was considering "race co-education" for the grade schools because the surrounding cities had already adopted it. In spite of the board's interest in integration, Lincoln School was not abandoned until 1922, and a new (still segregated) Lincoln School was built on East Wabash Avenue. The old Lincoln School was eventually renovated and reopened as the integrated Horace Mann School (seen here around 1960), which was torn down in 1964.

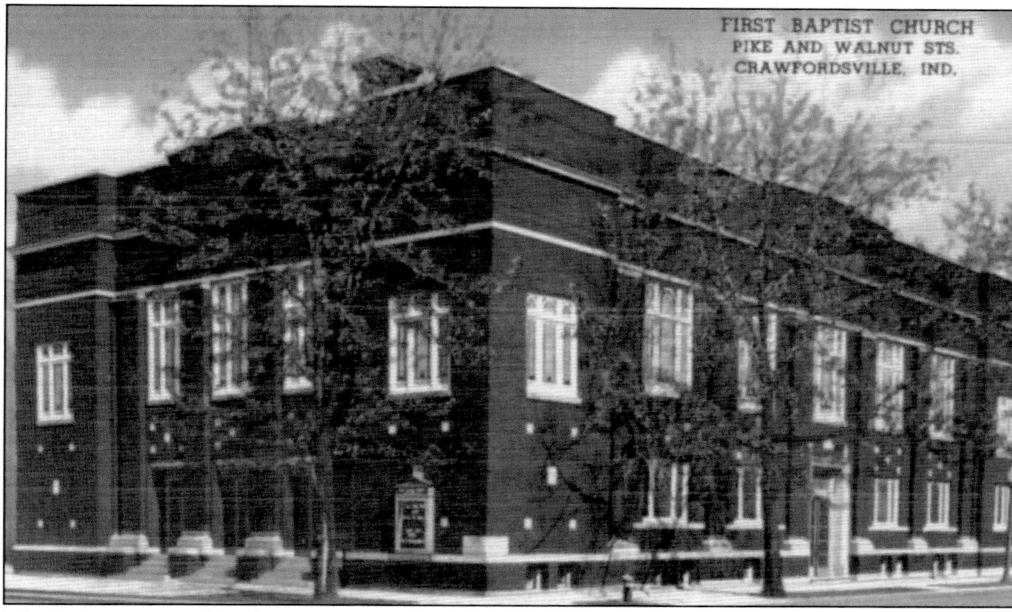

The First Baptist Church was organized in 1838 with 12 members who met on North Washington Street near Sugar Creek. In 1842, the congregation acquired land at the northeast corner of Pike and Walnut Streets and constructed a frame building with two front doors; one was for men and the other for women, as they were not seated together. The present building was constructed in 1925 on the same corner and still stands today, though it no longer serves as a Baptist church.

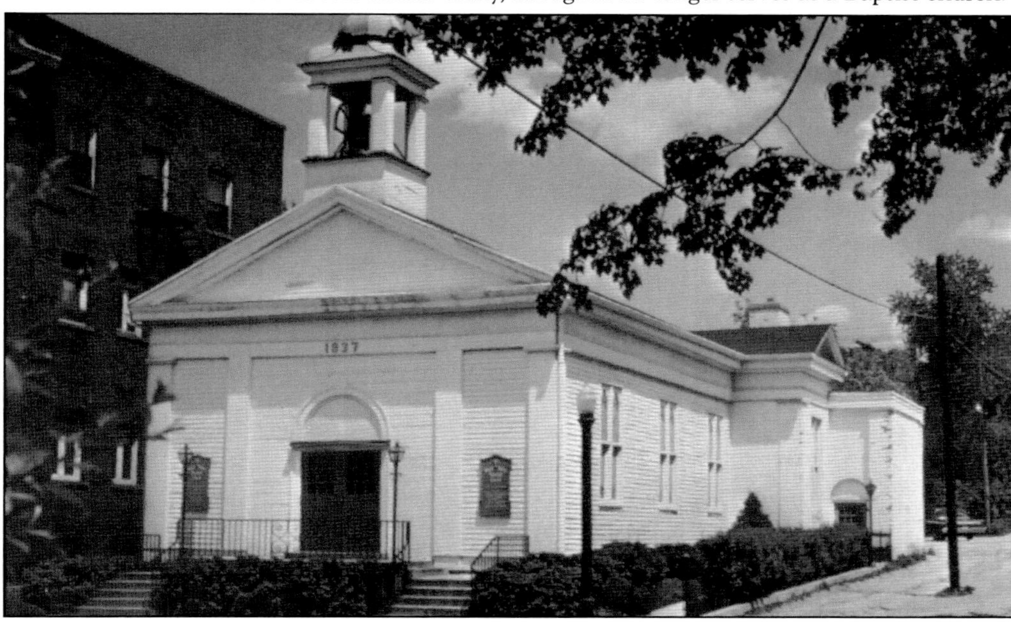

St. John's Episcopal Church, the first Episcopal church in Indiana, was built in 1837 at the corner of Market and Water Streets. In winter 1872, the congregation attempted to move the building to Green Street (near its current location), but the ground proved too soft, and the building was stuck in the street until the spring. The church was extensively remodeled and grew from 4 to 125 members by 1960 when it was featured on this postcard.

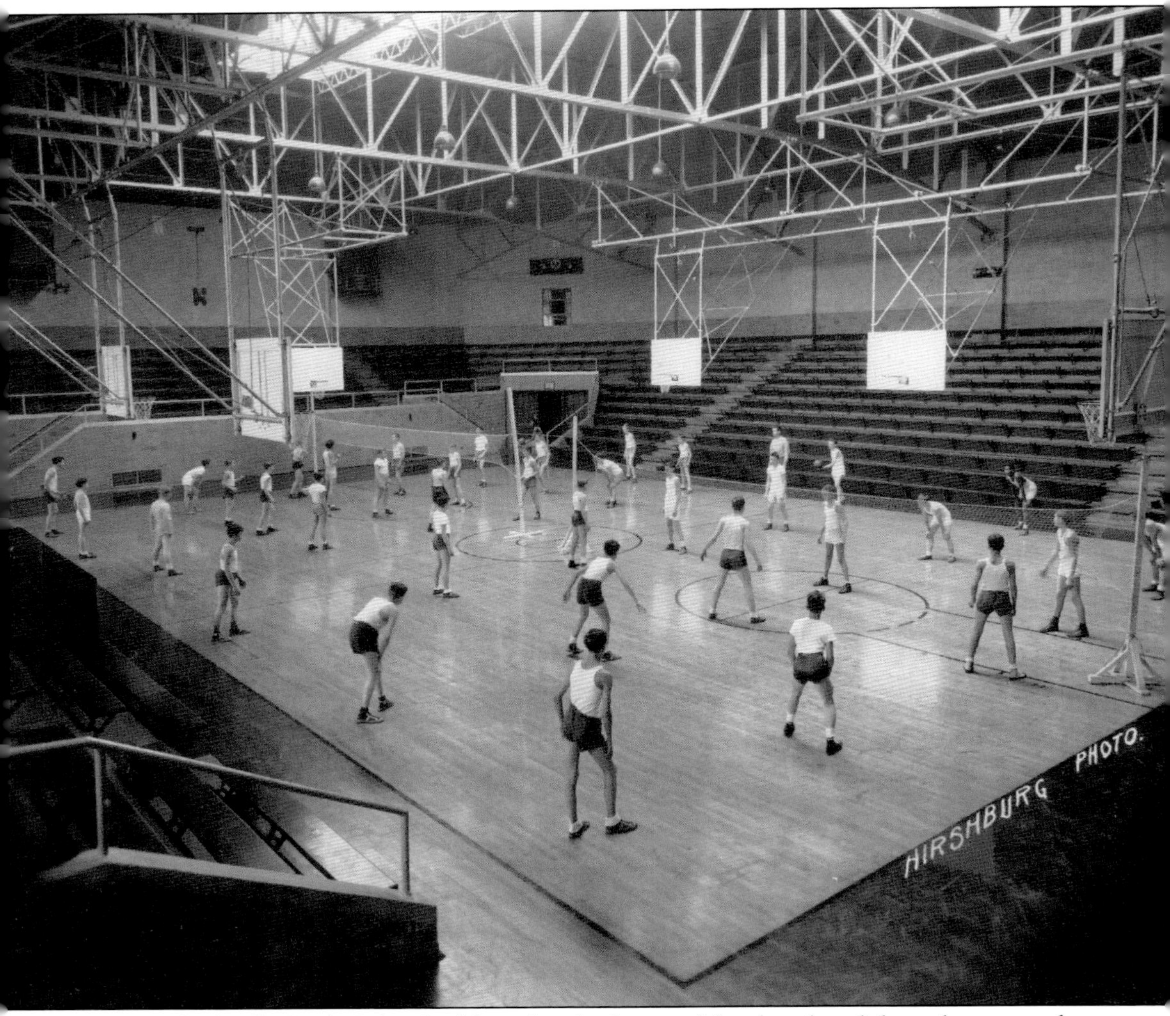

Crawfordsville High School, although it had existed for decades, did not have an adequate gymnasium for its students until 1940. On January 31, 1940, the new gymnasium was dedicated before a crowd of some 2,000 students, teachers, alumni, and townsfolk. The high school band played the "Star Spangled Banner" and then "The Old Gold and Blue" (the alma mater song). After an invocation by Rev. John R. Servies, superintendent Maynard C. Darnall introduced those who were most responsible for completing the gymnasium project. Representatives from various groups then spoke, including Mayor Thomas L. Cooksey. To add solemnity to the occasion, members of the CHS 1911 state championship basketball team were also introduced during the program. This photograph shows students enjoying the new facilities, sometime in the early 1950s, with two volleyball games in progress (notice the two boys serving, between whom can be seen the instructor). The gym still exists as part of the Athena Sport and Fitness Center. (Courtesy Bill Boone.)

Three

THE AGE OF THE INTERURBAN

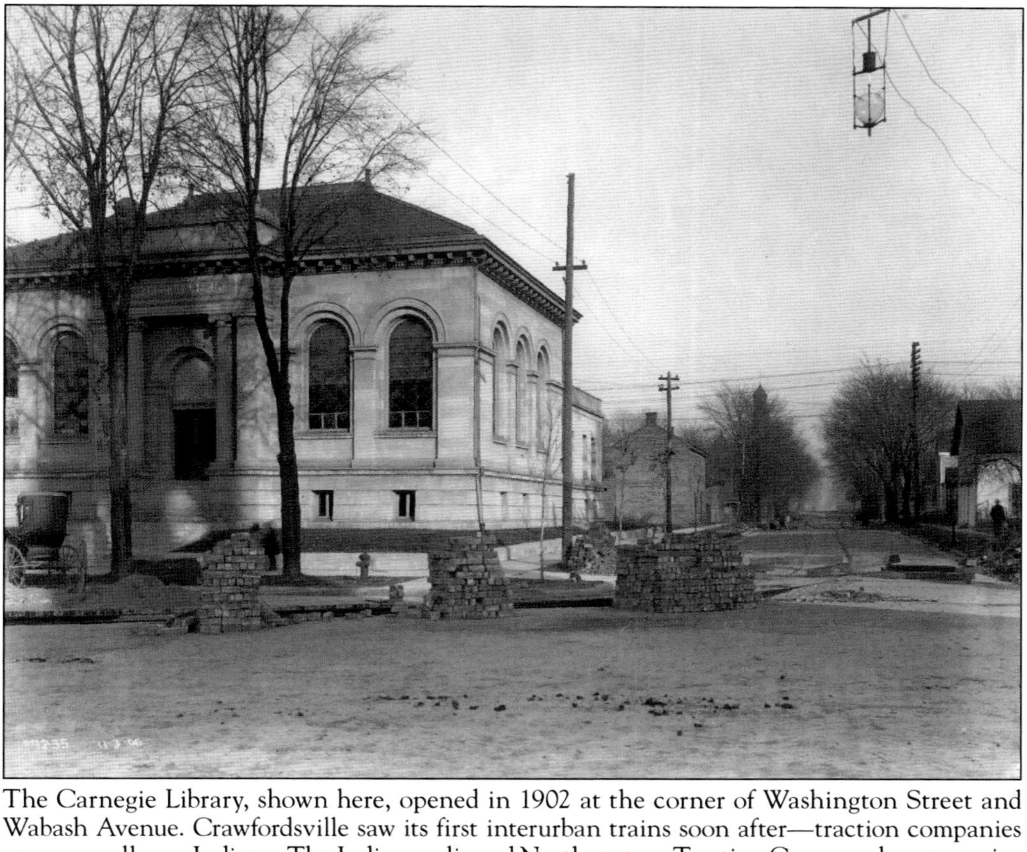

The Carnegie Library, shown here, opened in 1902 at the corner of Washington Street and Wabash Avenue. Crawfordsville saw its first interurban trains soon after—traction companies sprang up all over Indiana. The Indianapolis and Northwestern Traction Company began service to Lebanon and served other cities, including Indianapolis. The Indianapolis, Crawfordsville, and Western Traction Company was created in 1907. This company's line to Indianapolis was eventually named the Ben-Hur route in honor of Lew Wallace's novel. Interurban track was laid just in front of the library. Track continued east on Wabash Avenue to Grace Avenue and then headed south before turning east again toward Indianapolis.

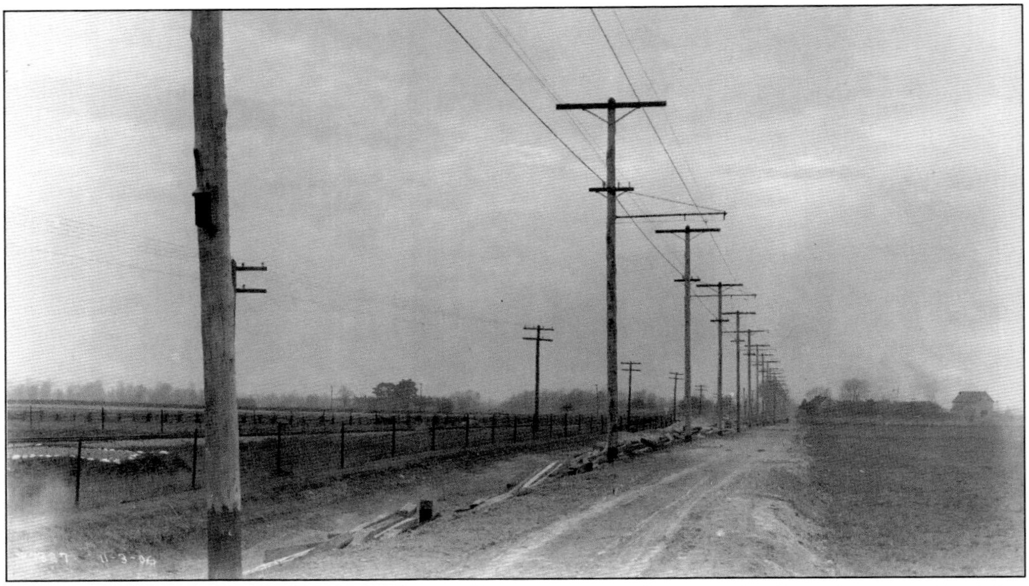

Mules and horses were originally used to pull traction cars along tracks short distances in cities, leaving long distances to steam-powered locomotives. The advent of electrical power, however, was the key to interurban success, and this service provided travelers with an alternative to the railroads. Overhead line construction accompanied the laying of interurban track, as seen in the above c. 1903 view looking west toward Crawfordsville. The Peoria and Eastern Railroad tracks are to the left of where the interurban tracks are being planned. Challenges had to be overcome along each interurban route, of course, and the landscape presented many obstacles to be crossed. Costs for constructing electric interurban tracks were expensive, which already put interurban companies at a disadvantage when revenues did not always meet expenses. The culvert shown below is one of several that any traveler between Crawfordsville and Indianapolis would have encountered.

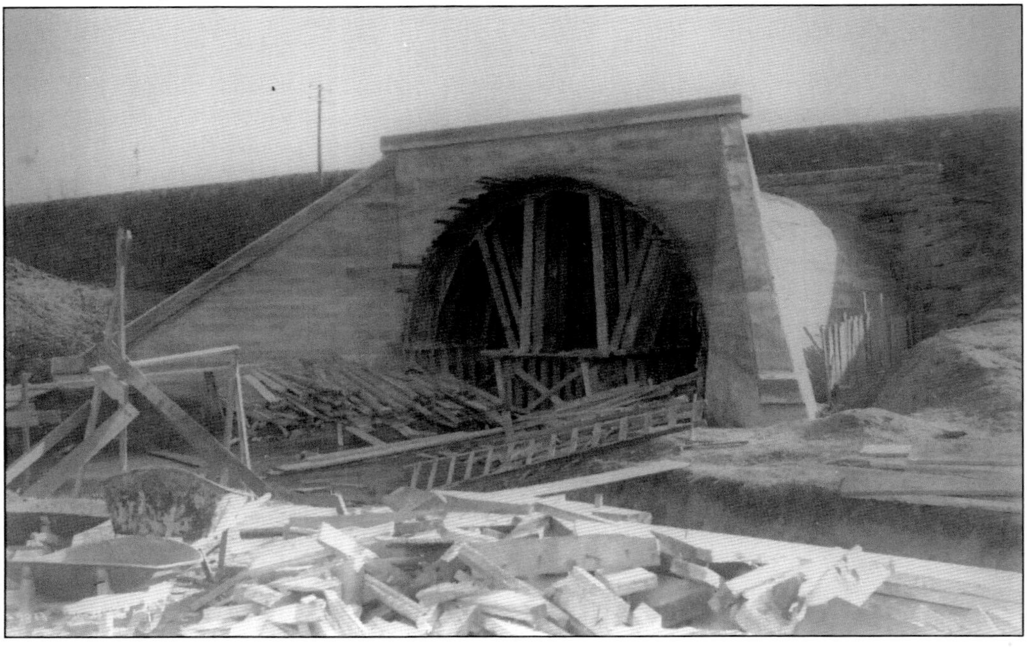

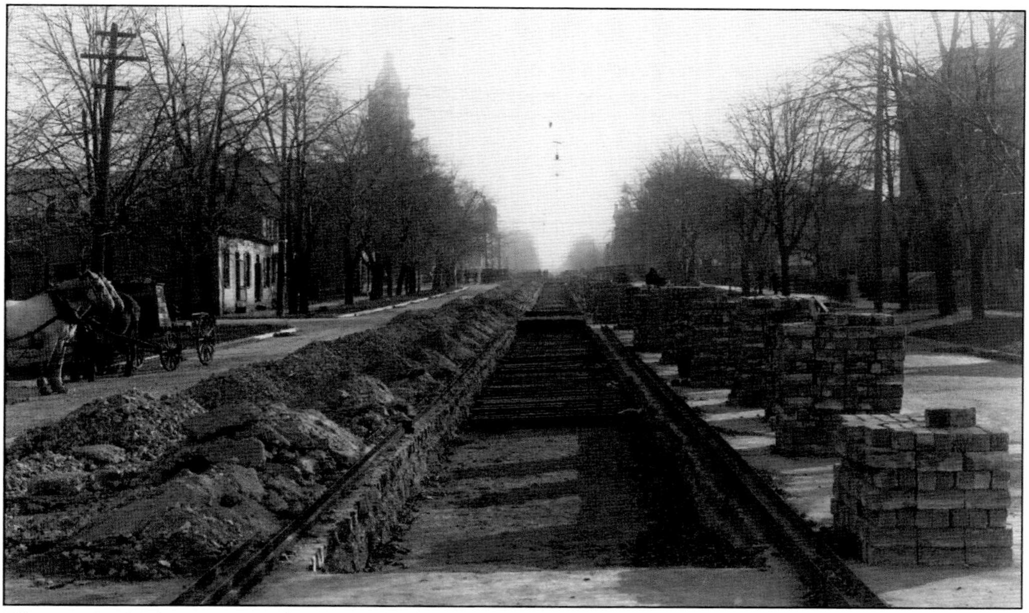

This early 20th century photograph shows interurban track being laid on Washington Street, looking south on what is now U.S. 231, just north of the Market Street intersection. To the right of where the photographer was standing is the Montgomery County Jail (now the Rotary Jail Museum). The courthouse can be seen in the distance on the left side of the road. The distinctive courthouse tower was removed decades later.

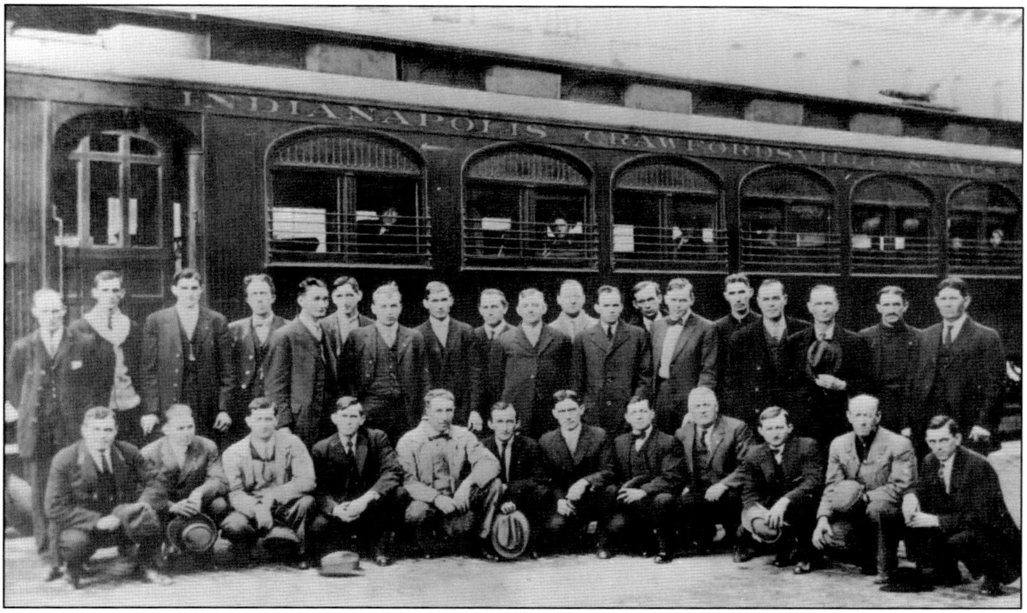

Crew members of the Indianapolis, Crawfordsville, and Western Traction Company pose here around 1912 in front of one of their cars. This company built the interurban line from Indianapolis to Crawfordsville in 1907 and also planned a line to Danville, Illinois. For financial and logistical reasons, however, the company did not complete the line to Danville, which would have required crossing the Wabash River.

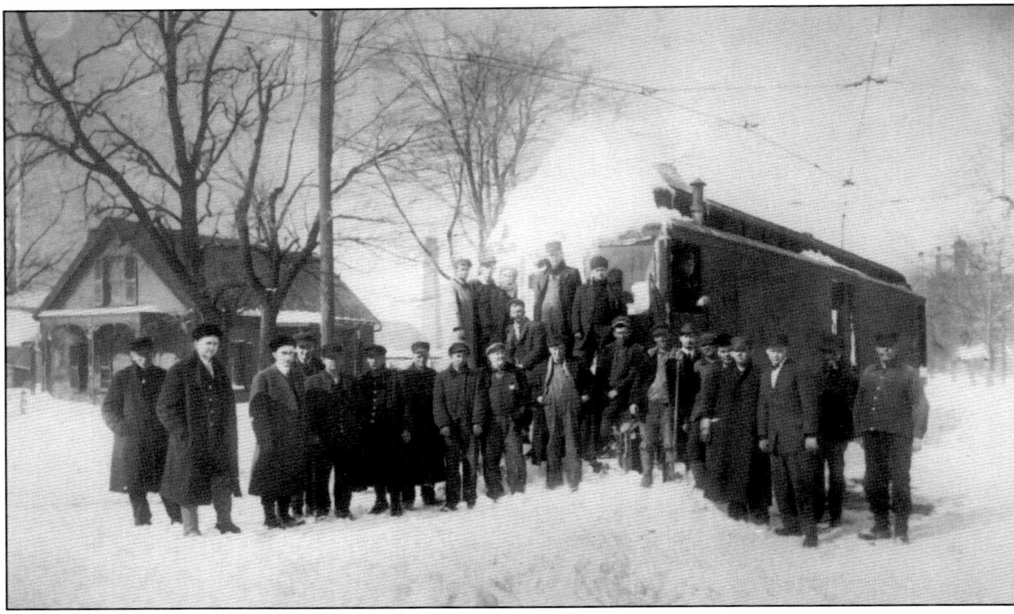

Men gather around an immobilized interurban freight car in winter. In late February 1912, a blizzard dumped nearly 10 inches of snow on Crawfordsville. The wind wreaked havoc, causing severe drifting. Temperatures plummeted to well below zero. Passenger and freight trains were stuck in drifts, and interurban lines had to suspend their schedules.

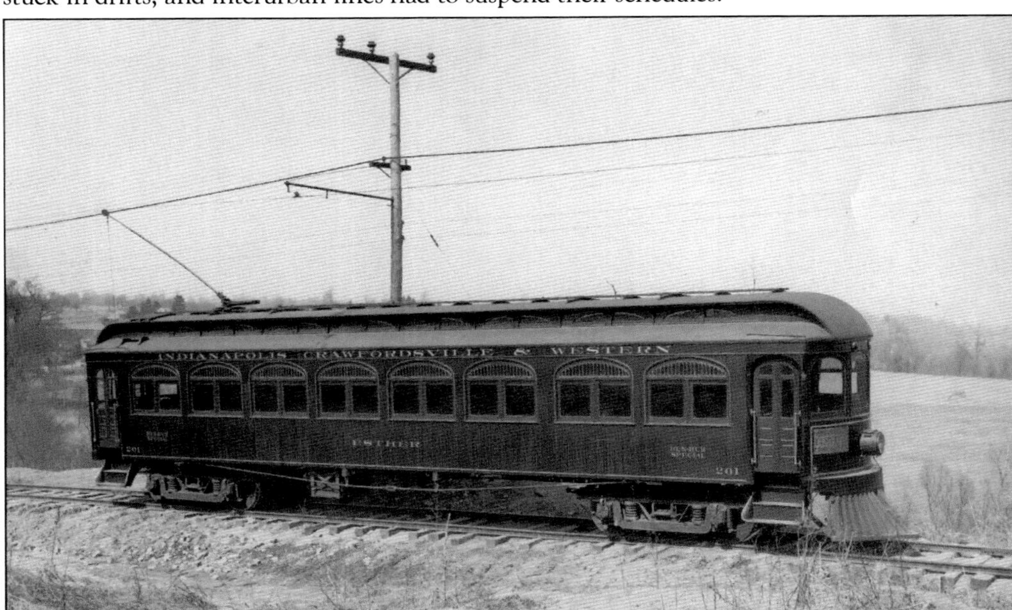

The Ben-Hur special chair car, *Esther*, belonged to the Indianapolis, Crawfordsville, and Western Traction Company. This car is photographed here at the power plant site on Lafayette Avenue. The Terre Haute, Indianapolis, and Eastern Company (THI&E) absorbed the Indianapolis, Crawfordsville, and Western Traction Company in 1912 but continued to run the Ben-Hur special train from Crawfordsville to Indianapolis until 1930.

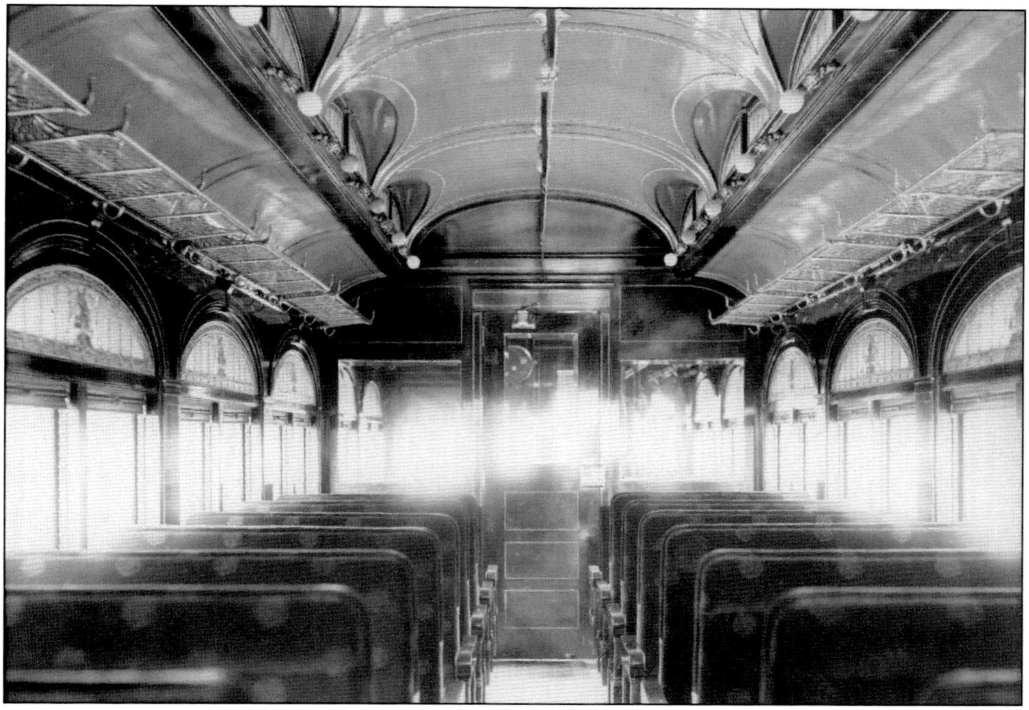

Traveling via the interurban was not necessarily uncomfortable. The Indianapolis, Crawfordsville, and Western line did not seem to spare any expense on its special Ben-Hur cars, *Esther* and *Iras*. The interior of *Esther* (above) reveals an amount of craftsmanship that would not be familiar today to mass transportation users. The *Crawfordsville Journal* of April 4, 1908, reported that for these cars "everything had been done for the convenience of the passengers that ingenuity could devise." Another view (below) of *Esther* shows the plush seats (which were olive green) and the San Domingo mahogany paneling. Art nouveau stained-glass partitions were installed above each window, and silk window curtains would later be added. The company named *Esther* and *Iras* after characters in the Lew Wallace novel *Ben-Hur*.

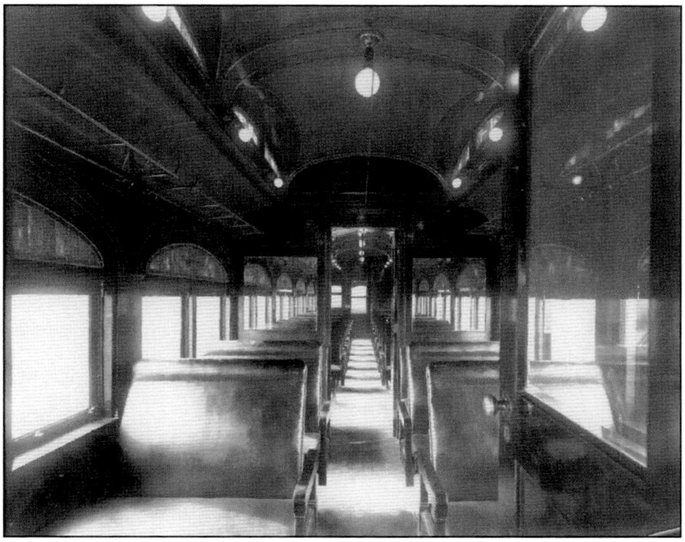

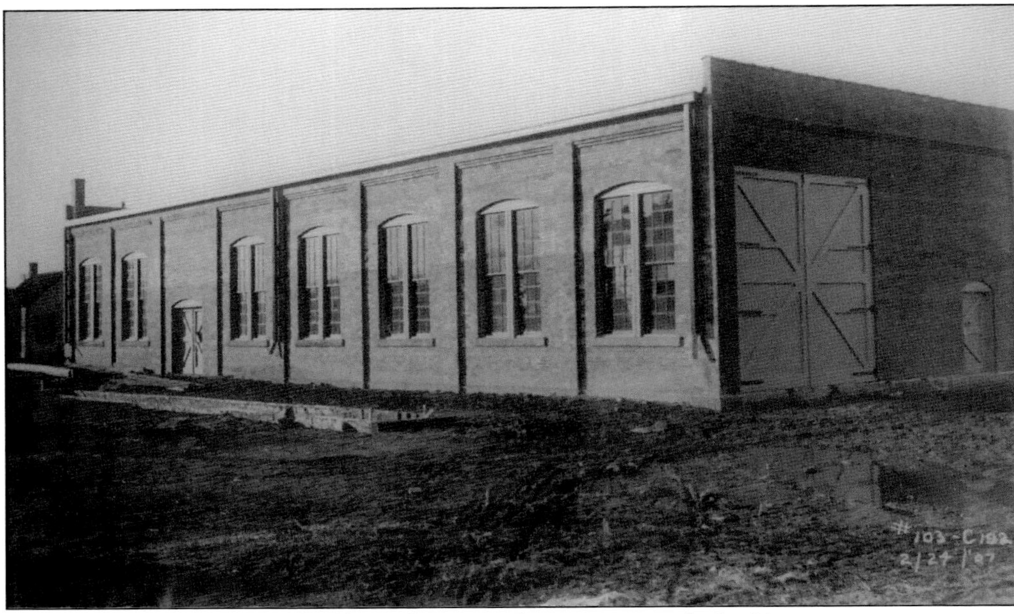

The Indianapolis, Crawfordsville, and Western line constructed a building to service its cars in what was then a convenient location in the north part of the city just to the west of Washington Street, down which its tracks ran. The interurban car barn (above) was located on North Walnut Street, near Harrison Street, northwest of the courthouse. It was a brick and concrete structure about 120 feet long by 43 feet wide. This 1907 photograph shows the repair track on the left side; on the right side is the machine shop. On the inside (below), the doors on the left led to the machine shop. In the general repair shop appears the Ben-Hur special car *Iras*. *Iras* would go into service the next year, with its sister car, *Esther*.

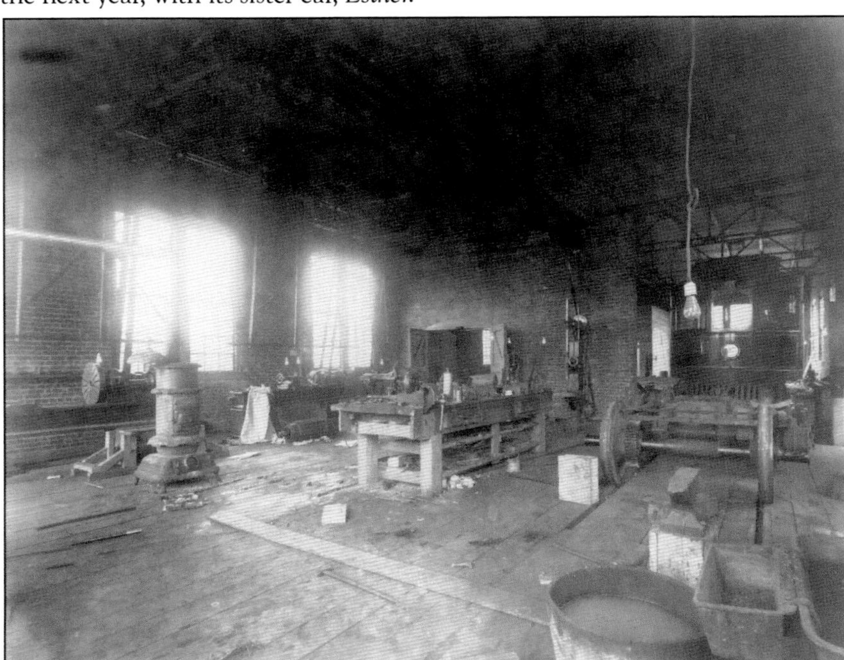

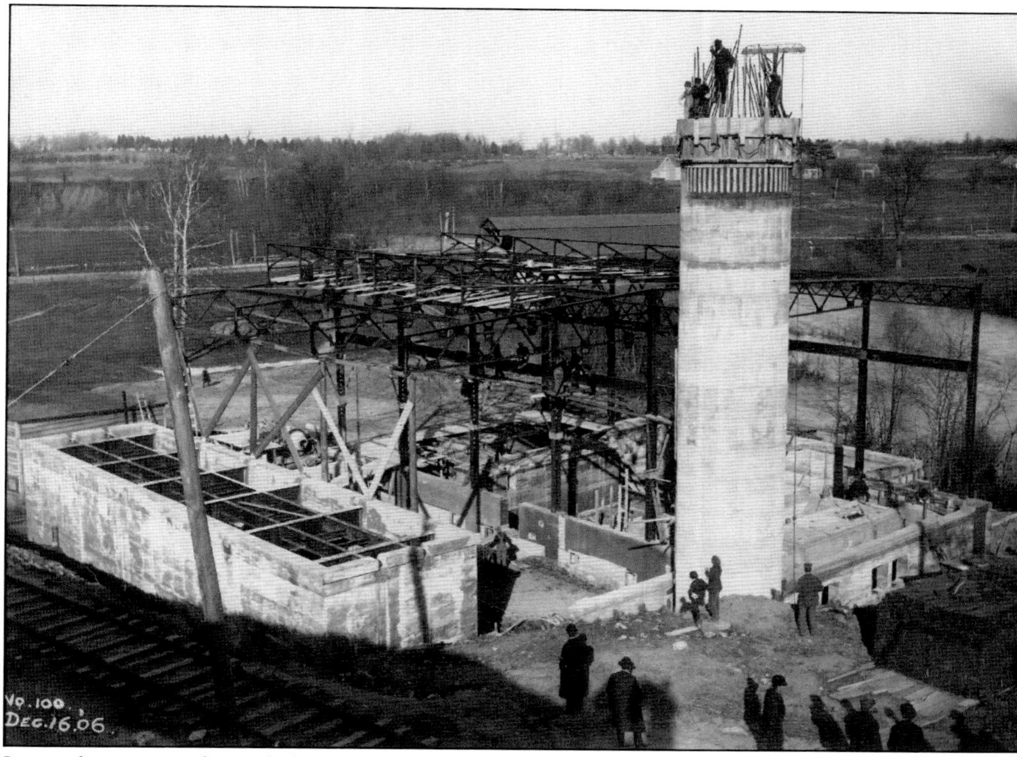

Interurban trains depended on electricity to run, and Crawfordsville constructed a power plant in 1907 to supply the needs of cars on the west end (above). This plant was located near Sugar Creek in what is now part of the Elston Park. In the distance can be seen Lafayette Avenue and the first covered bridge in Montgomery County, the Sperry Bridge, which spanned Sugar Creek until 1928. The interurban power plant had a distinctive 175-foot smokestack as an outlet for the four coal-fed boilers when it was completed (below).

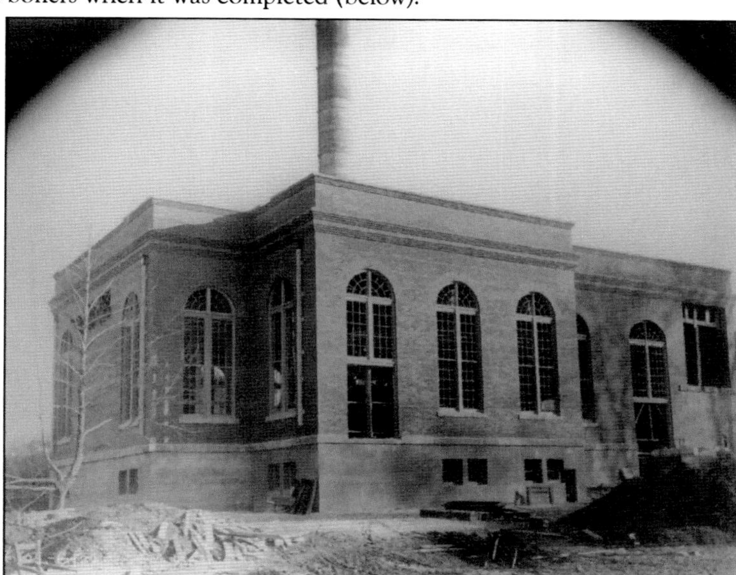

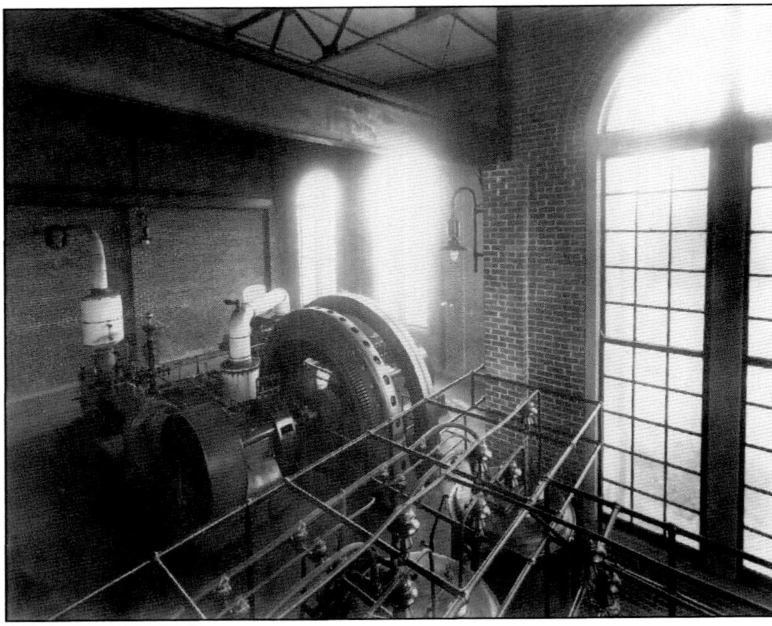

Many present-day residents were unaware of the interurban power plant's original use because it was no longer needed after the early 1930s when the interurban train disappeared from Crawfordsville. It was later converted into a bottling plant for the Coca-Cola Company and came to be called the "old Coke plant." The power plant was torn down in 1993.

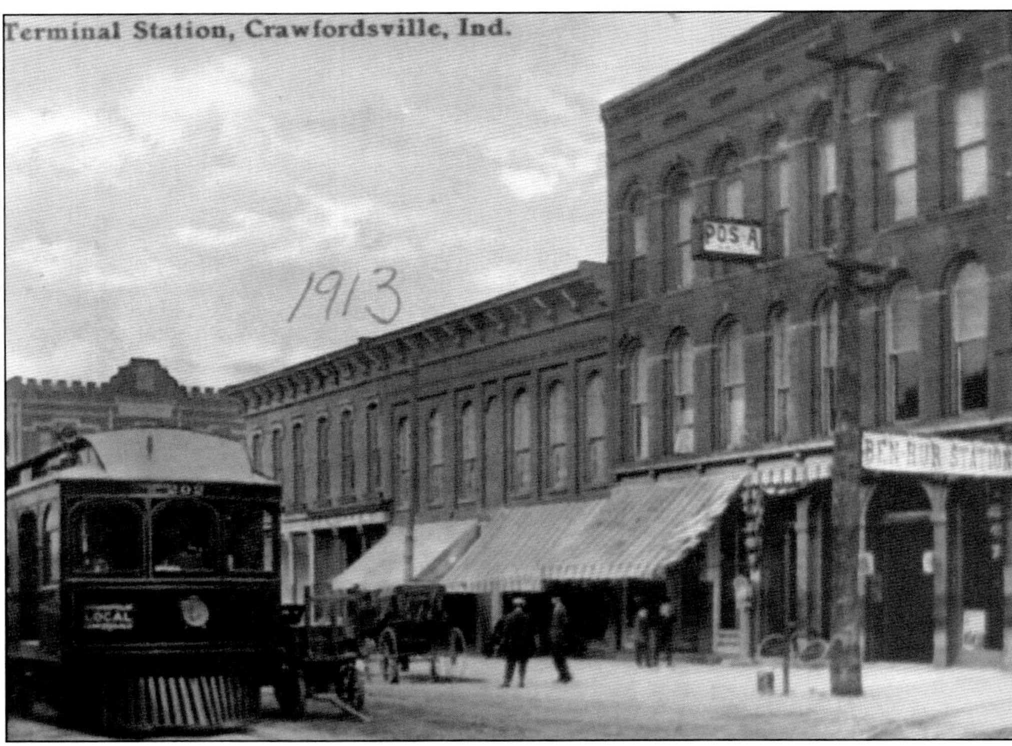

In this 1913 photograph, an interurban car runs south on Washington Street toward Wabash Avenue. Departures left Crawfordsville more than two dozen times daily, arriving in Indianapolis an hour and 45 minutes later via Linnsburg, New Ross, Jamestown, Lizton, Pittsboro, Brownsburg, Clermont, the Indiana Girls School, and Speedway.

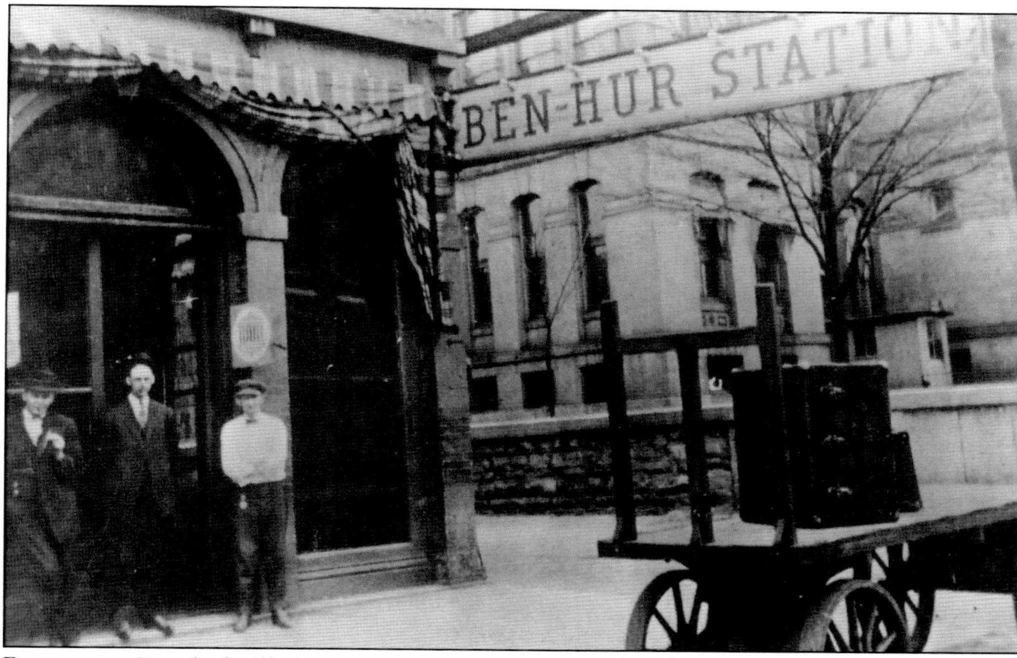

Downtown Crawfordsville became an important hub in the glory days of the interurban train. The Ben-Hur station (above), shown around 1911, was located just north of the courthouse (seen in the background). The Indianapolis, Crawfordsville, and Western line created and ran the Ben-Hur line until it was taken over in 1912 by the Terre Haute, Indianapolis, and Eastern Company. The Ben-Hur station was, of course, a popular gathering place for travelers and residents alike (below). Omer Glover, standing in the back with a bow tie and without a coat, worked for the interurban train from 1908 until it ceased operations in 1930. An empty baggage cart stands on Washington Street. The THI&E moved the station to the southwest corner of Washington and Main Streets in 1914 in what was then the YMCA building.

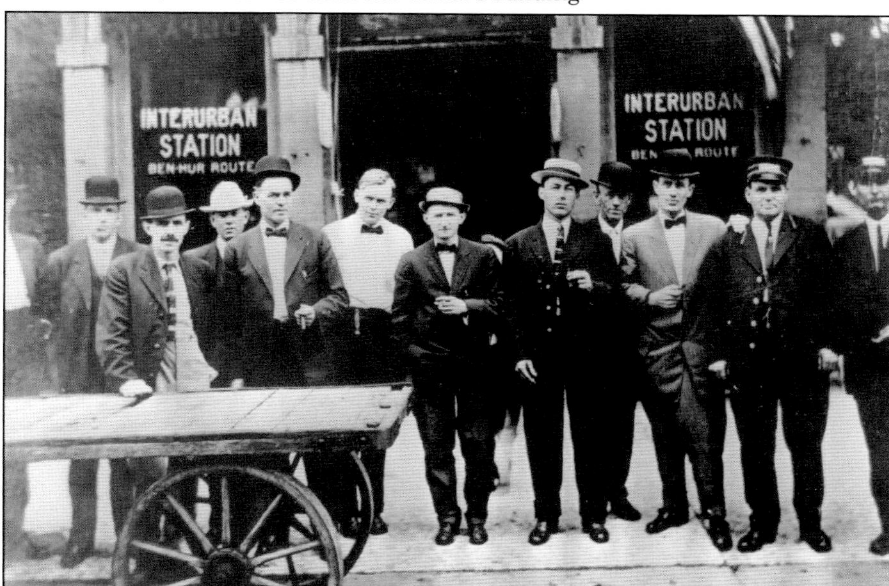

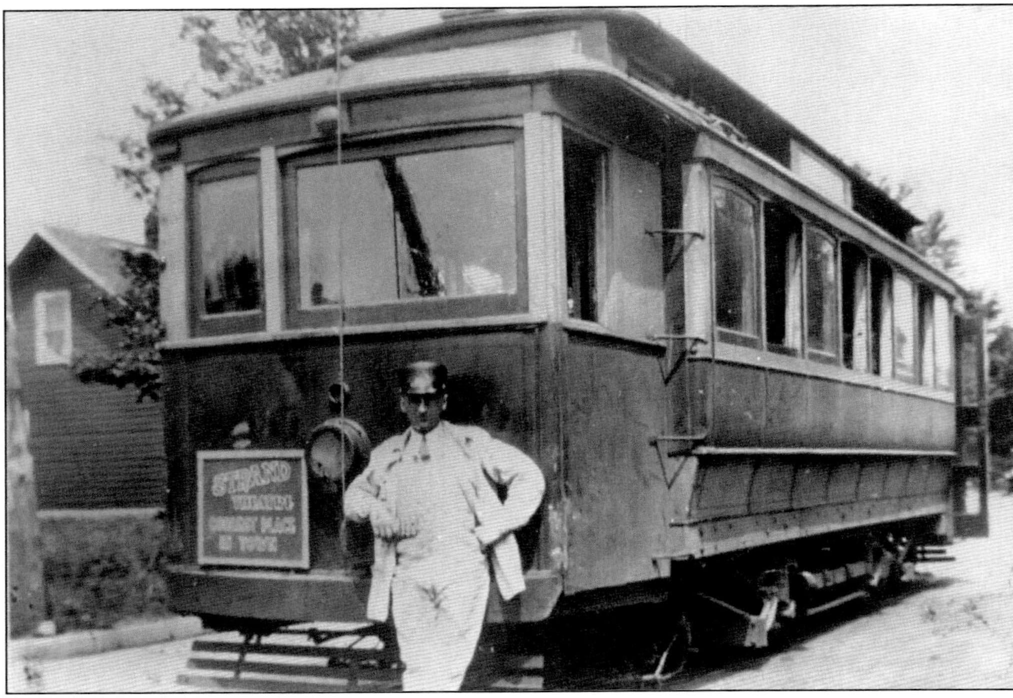

Crawfordsville was also served by trolleys, which began around 1914. A conductor poses in front of his train with a sign that reads, "Strand Theater, the coolest place in town." The Strand Theater was a local landmark, opening in 1919 in the location of the Music Hall at 122 South Green Street and serving the community until January 1999.

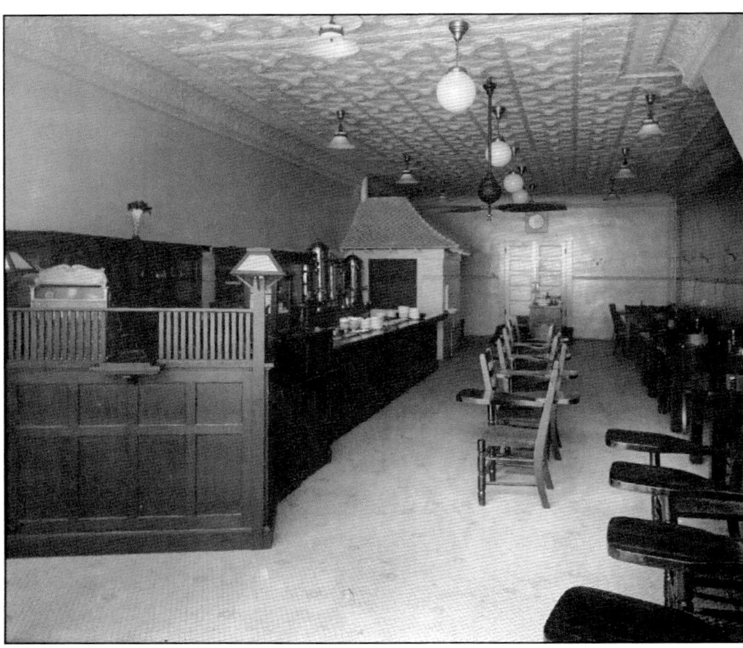

The Ben-Hur Restaurant, shown here around 1912, catered to interurban passengers. Located at 120 North Washington Street, next door to the terminal, the establishment came to be known as the "One Arm" restaurant because customers received their food at the steam counter and then carried it on a tray to one of the seats, each of which had one wide arm to hold the tray.

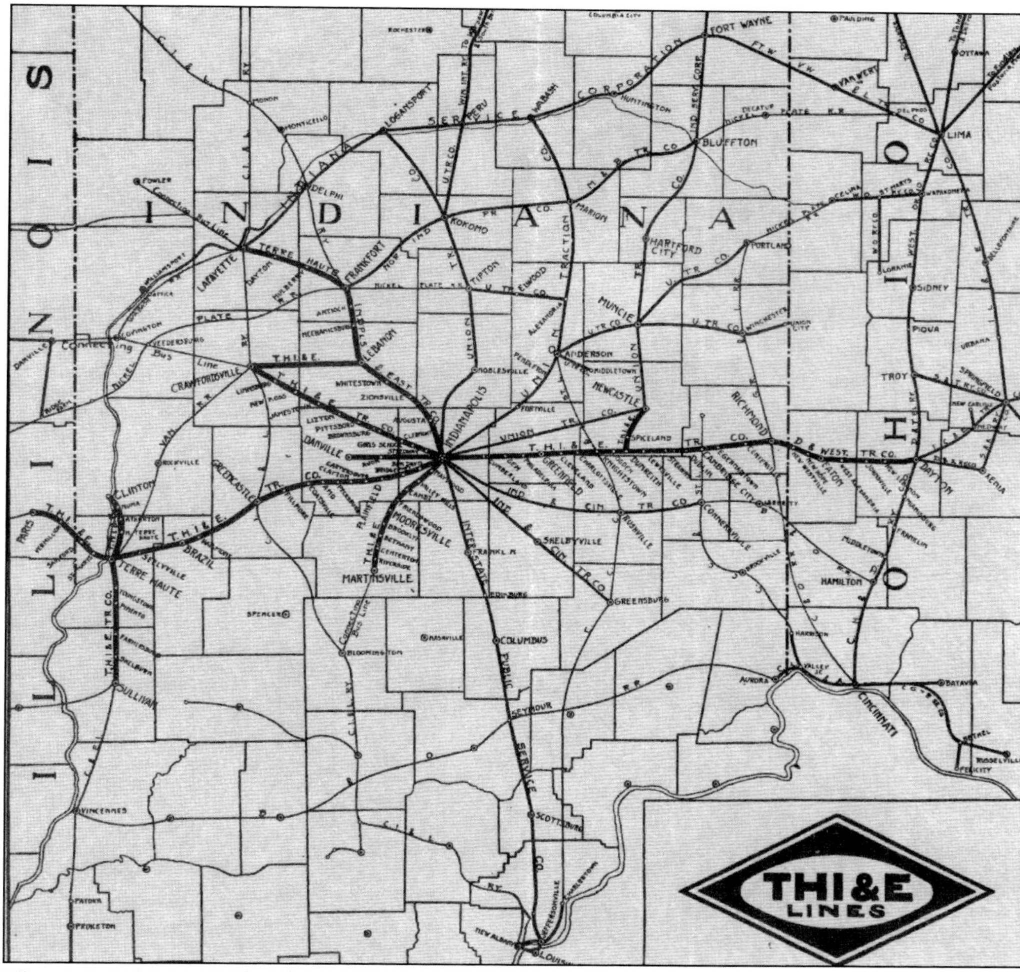

This interurban map for the Terre Haute, Indianapolis, and Eastern Company is from a 1928 brochure. A passenger could travel numerous times per day from Crawfordsville to Indianapolis (with eight possible stops) or to Lebanon. From Lebanon, the Crawfordsville traveler could continue to Lafayette. From Indianapolis, one could continue on the THI&E line as far as Dayton, Ohio. Children under 5 years old traveling with an adult rode at no cost, and those between 5 and 12 were charged half the adult fare. Within any two points in Indiana, 150 pounds of luggage was checked free, but the baggage weight limit was held to 250 pounds. Dogs "provided with properly fitting collar and strong chain" were transported in the baggage compartment at the owner's risk, but the charge was a full first-class rate of fare. Interurban cars could also be chartered for special parties "on short notice at reasonable rates."

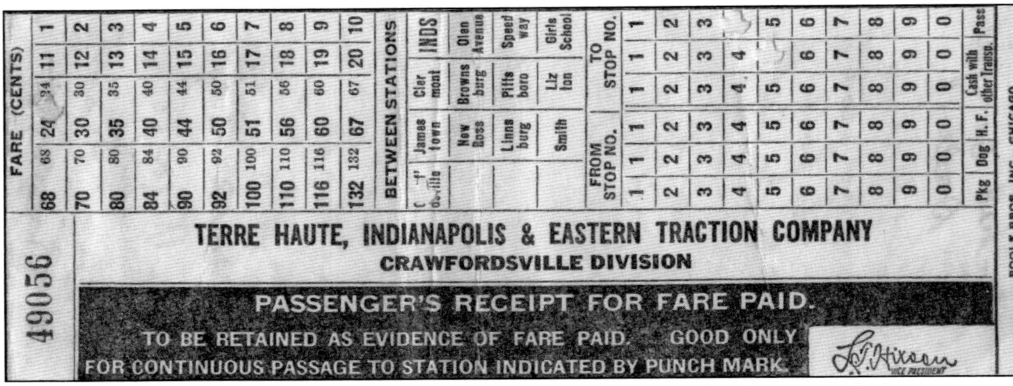

The increased use of the automobile was too much competition for the interurban companies; the Terre Haute, Indianapolis, and Eastern Company lost money through much of the 1920s. The last interurban train to leave Crawfordsville was car no. 51, departing at 10:45 p.m. on October 31, 1930, and heading for Indianapolis. This is the last cash receipt paid for a trip on the THI&E. Dollie B. Harting was a passenger on the first car out of Crawfordsville on the Ben-Hur route and was a conductor on the last car that evening to Indianapolis. Bus service between the two cities began immediately afterwards.

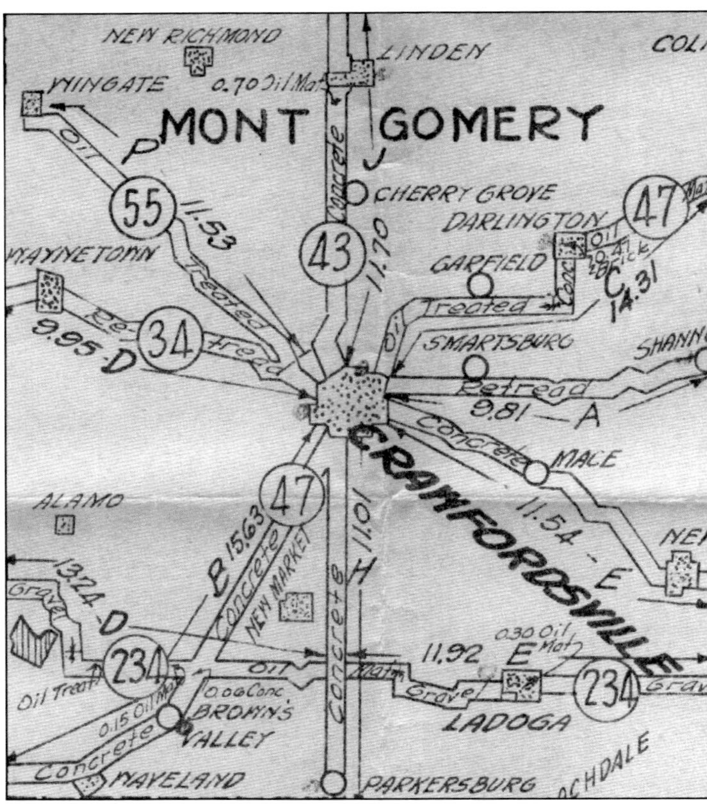

This highway map for west-central Indiana was published on April 24, 1933, and symbolizes the death of the interurban train better than anything. Travel by automobile was not nearly as convenient as today, but it became easier each year as more roads turned from dirt and gravel into concrete.

Four

Celebrating the Indiana Centennial

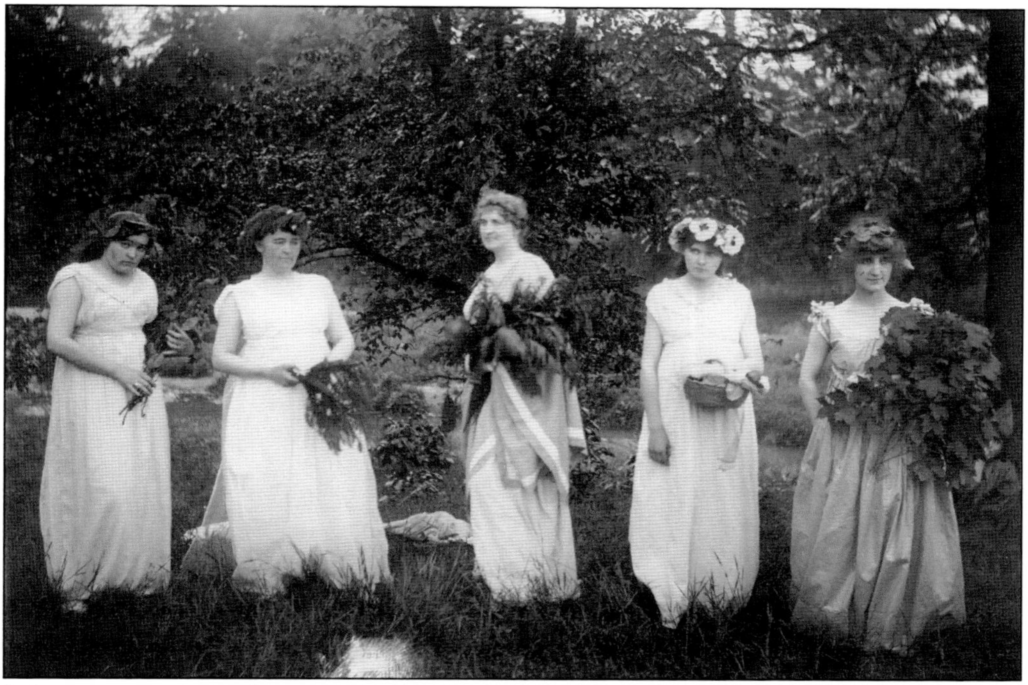

Indiana commemorated its centennial in 1916. Statewide celebrations took place in the summer and fall of that year. Crawfordsville hosted the program for Montgomery County, slated for June 9–14, 1916. The program included an old-fashioned spelling match (restricted to contestants over 40 years of age), screenings of the Moving Picture History of Indiana, historical exhibits, parades, a teachers' reunion, the dedication of the first city park (Milligan), and more. The culminating event was the Montgomery County Pageant, which involved more than 1,000 participants. Mayor William C. Murphy requested that businesses close from 2:30 p.m. to 6:00 p.m. to allow all residents to see the show. Bleachers were erected to hold the more than 3,000 spectators who bought tickets at 25¢, 50¢, and $1. In spite of the fees collected, the pageant lost $800. Lillian Lollis (far right) poses with other dancers.

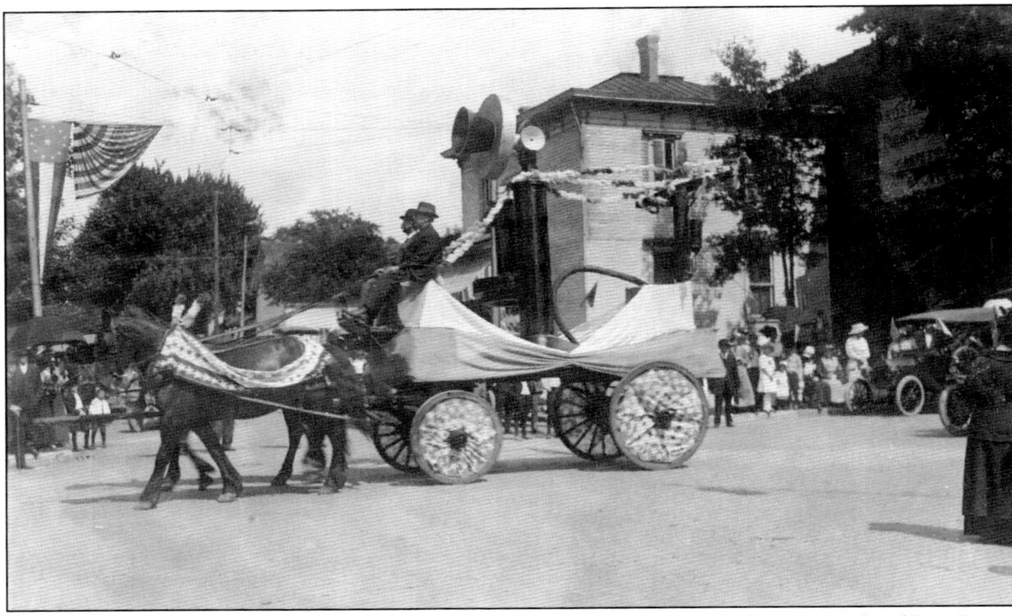

Monday, June 12, 1916, was filled with activities, starting at 6:00 a.m. when a parade of Boy Scouts went through the city announcing the centennial celebrations with bugle calls. A more welcome parade may have been the 2:00 p.m. "Industrial and Civic" parade. Here the Crawfordsville Telephone Company float heads north on Washington Street (above) past the Wabash Avenue intersection. A corner of the Crawfordsville Public Library building (now the Carnegie Museum of Montgomery County) appears to the left in the photograph. On the Art League float (below) can be read "Early Art," and the float contains a woman and girls spinning. The centennial guide for these activities predicted that the parade would be "the largest demonstration of the kind in the history of Montgomery County." Witnesses estimated that the length of the parade was more than 2 miles long.

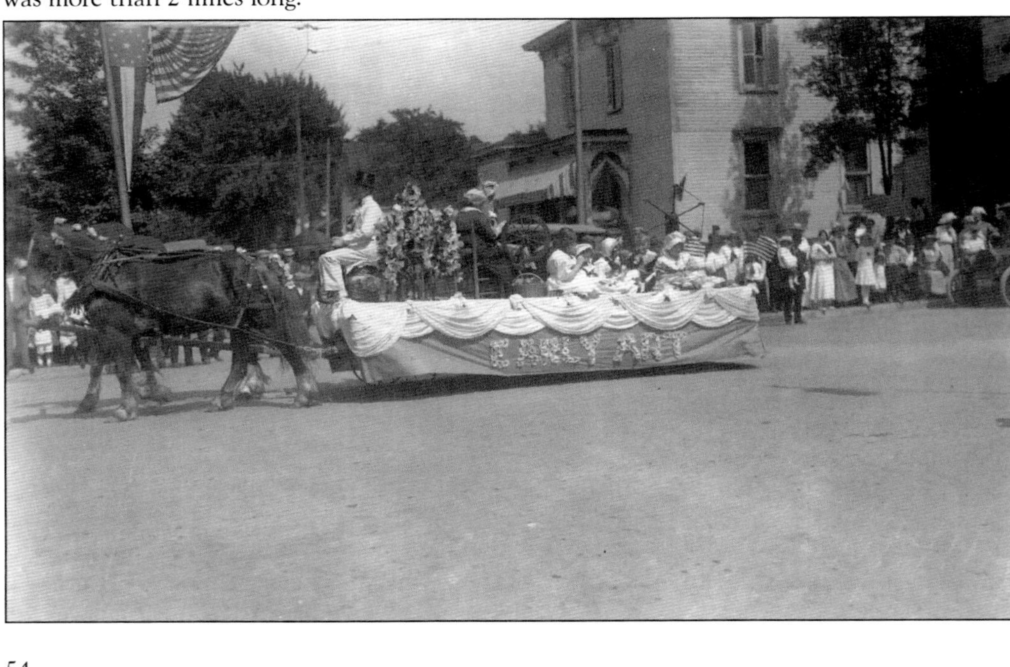

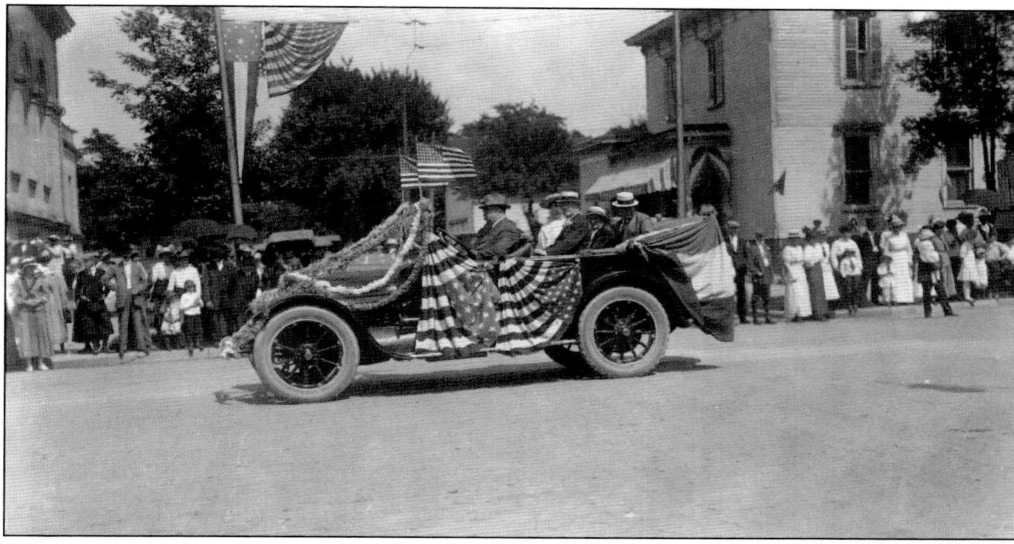

Motorized vehicles also participated in the parade, and the leading automobile, driven by its owner Charles Gregg, contained some of the celebration's VIPs, seen above. Linneas Neal Hines (president of the Montgomery County Centennial Association) rides in the front seat; in the middle seat are Mayor William C. Murphy and Mrs. James Waugh (Montgomery County Centennial Association, executive committee); and in the rear seat are Lew O'Bannon and Miss Charity Dye from the Indiana Historical Commission. The parade started promptly on time and reportedly took at least an hour to pass one point. The photograph below shows one of the several automobiles that were decked out with flowers and bunting, followed by a motorcycle rider. Many merchants preceded the line of motorized vehicles with horse-drawn wagons to pull displays of their exhibits, and evidence of the horses' passing is still apparent in the street.

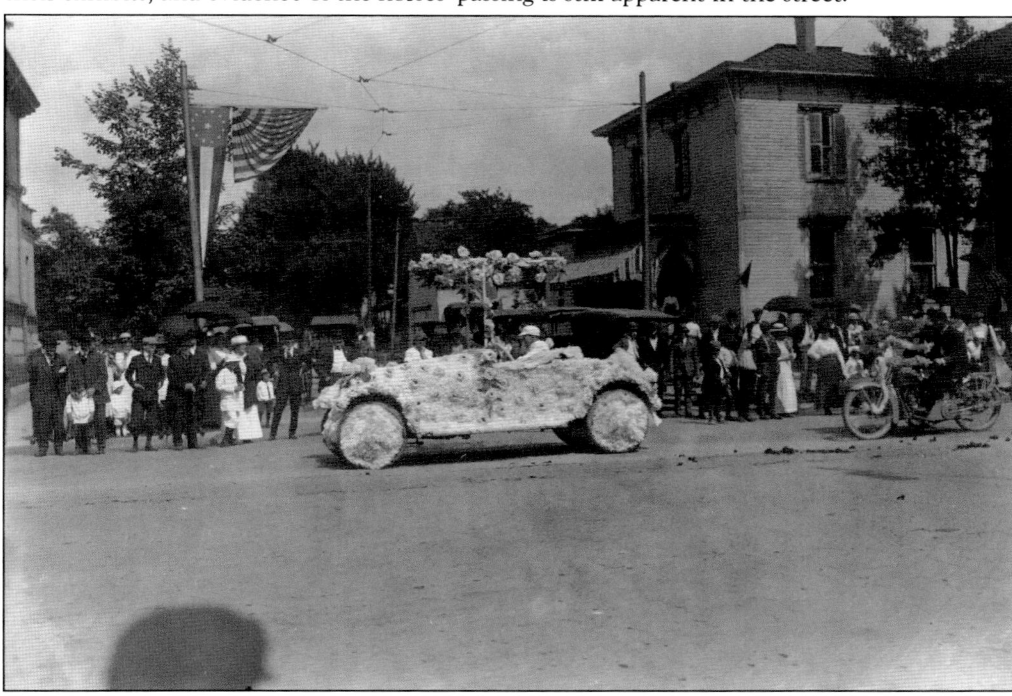

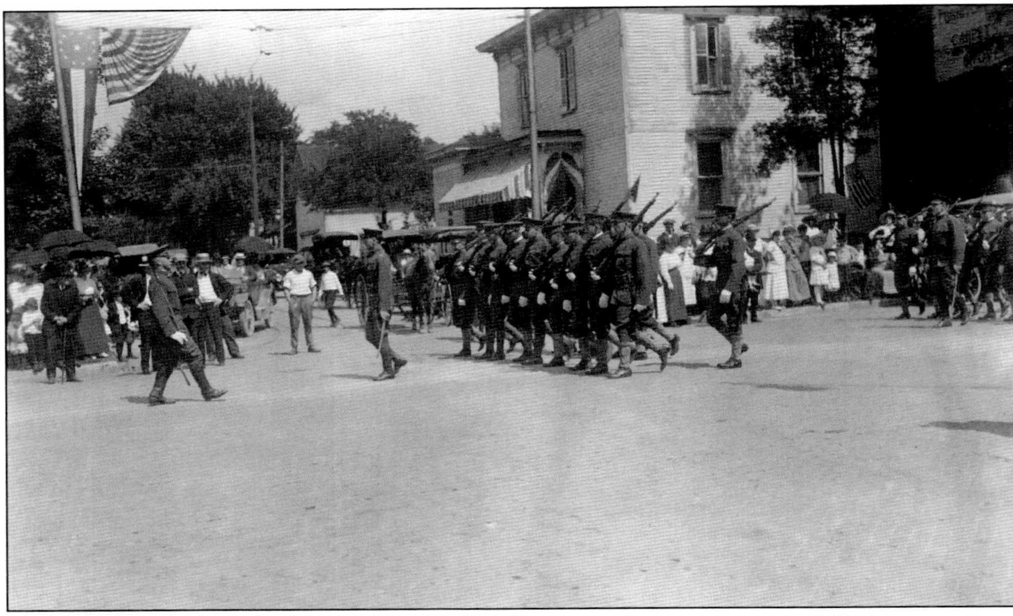

Company C of the 2nd Indiana National Guard crosses the intersection of Washington Street and Wabash Avenue as spectators lining Washington Street look on. The interurban tracks at the intersection can just be seen. Within a week, Pres. Woodrow Wilson would call out the National Guard, including Company C, to reinforce the regular U.S. Army and secure the Mexican border.

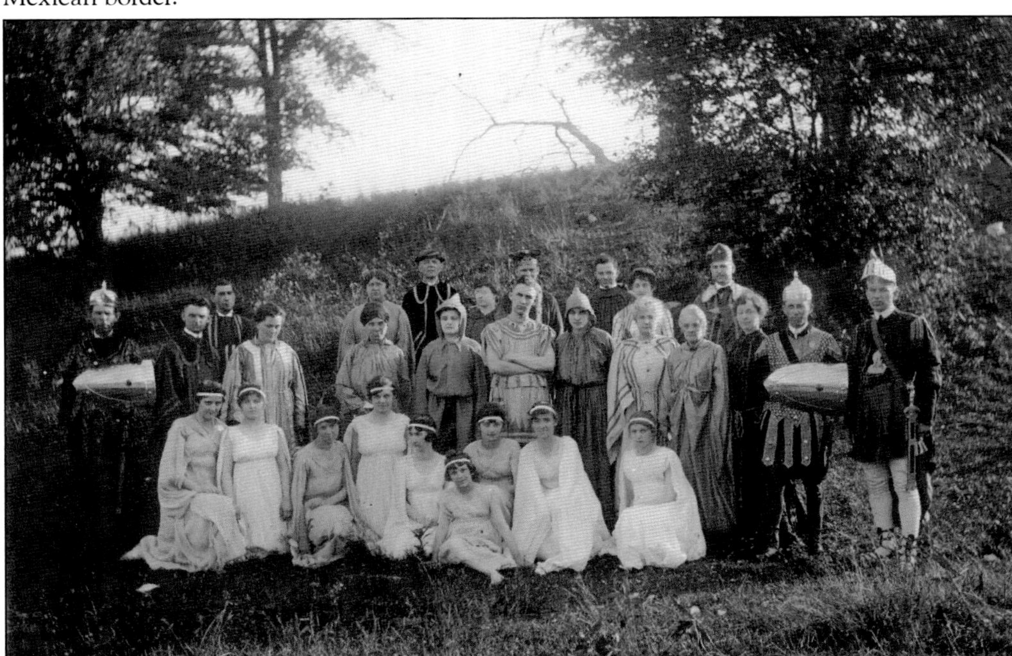

Episode V, scene 1 of the Montgomery County Pageant ("Later Days") showed Lew Wallace composing *Ben-Hur*. The scene had Wallace writing at a table, with the novel's various characters appearing before him.

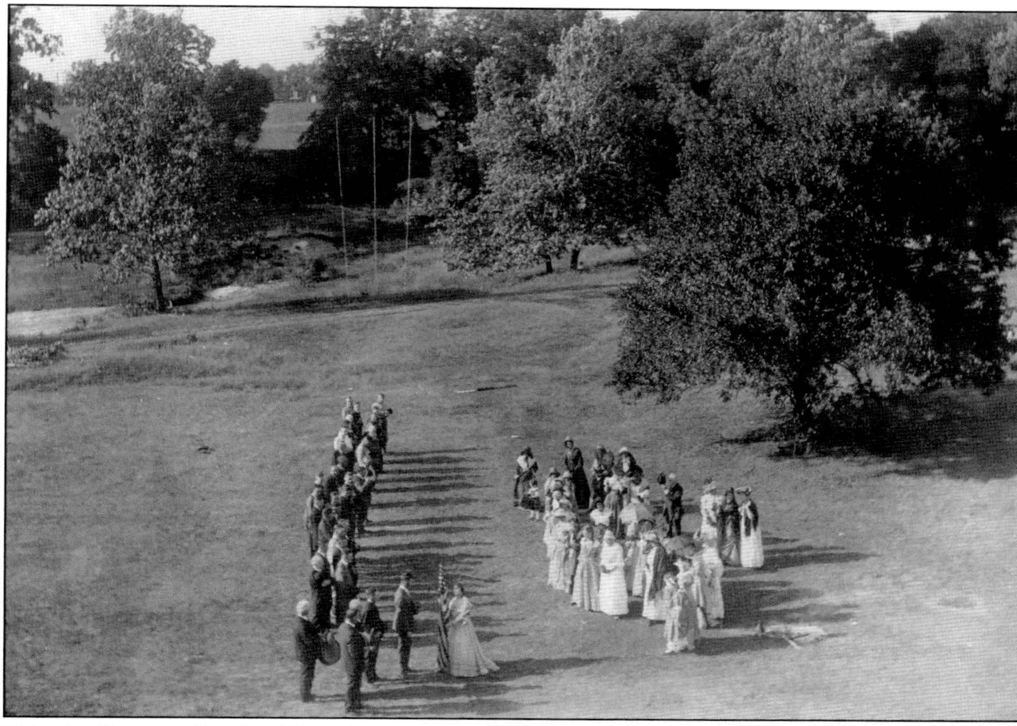

Episode II opened with "The Mexican War." Eleanor Ristine holds the flag playing the role of Mrs. H. S. Lane. Mrs. Lane's husband, Henry Lane, a state representative (and future U.S. congressman, governor, and U.S. senator), became captain of a group of Indiana volunteers. Before their departure in 1846 for Mexico, the volunteers congregated outside the Lane's home, where Mrs. Lane presented them with an American flag.

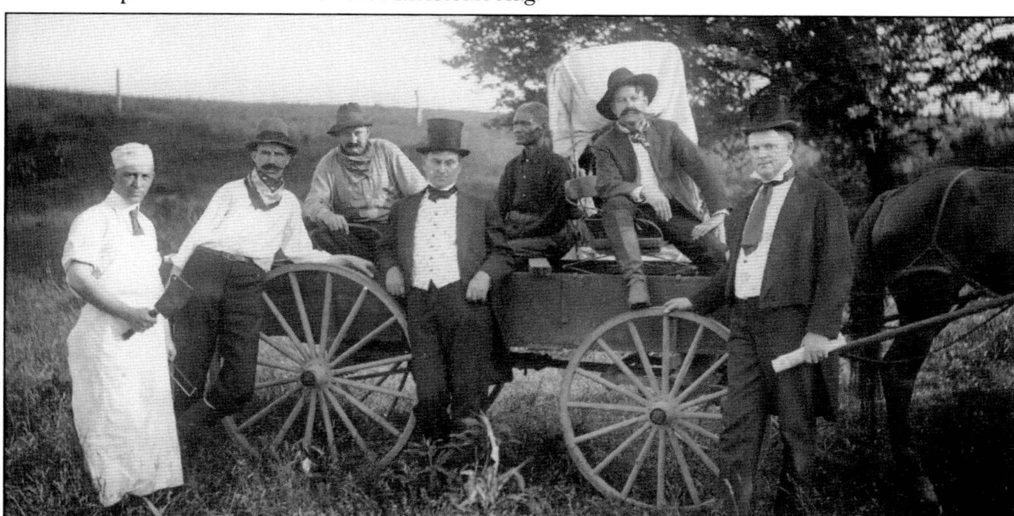

Episode III, scene 3 portrayed the days of the Underground Railroad. From left to right are Fred Vance, W. A. Collings, H. E. Biddle, S. P. Templeton, Robert Hopkins, Harry Michael, and George F. Leonard. Hopkins, who portrayed the runaway slave, was actually born a slave in Kentucky but escaped during the Civil War to enlist in the Union army.

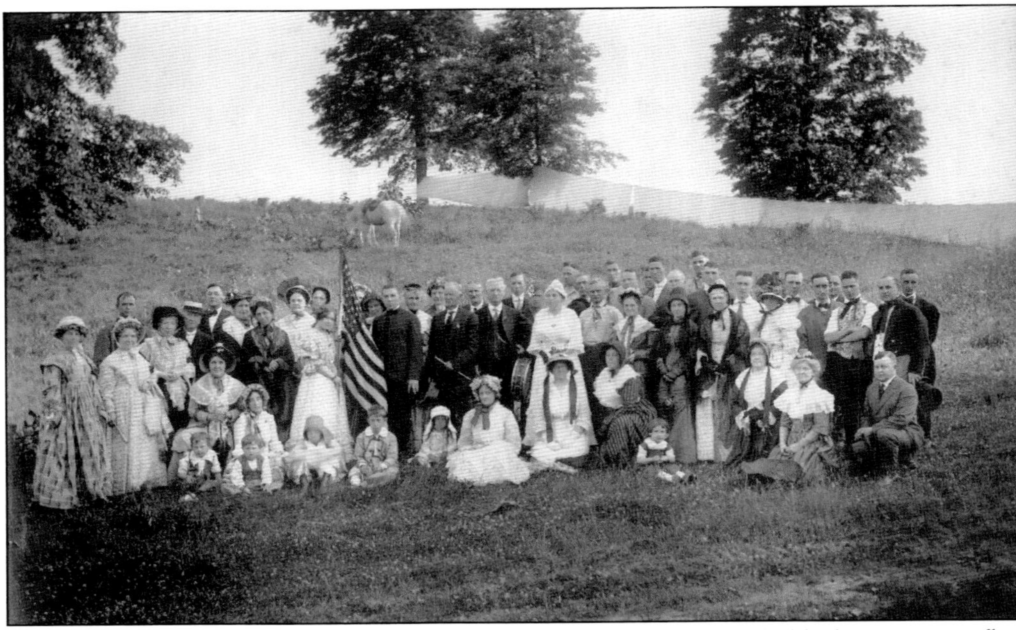

Participants and spectators gather for a group portrait. Eleanor Ristine holds the American flag. A pageant horse grazes in the background near the 8-foot canvas wall that was erected to prevent nonpaying customers from viewing the activities.

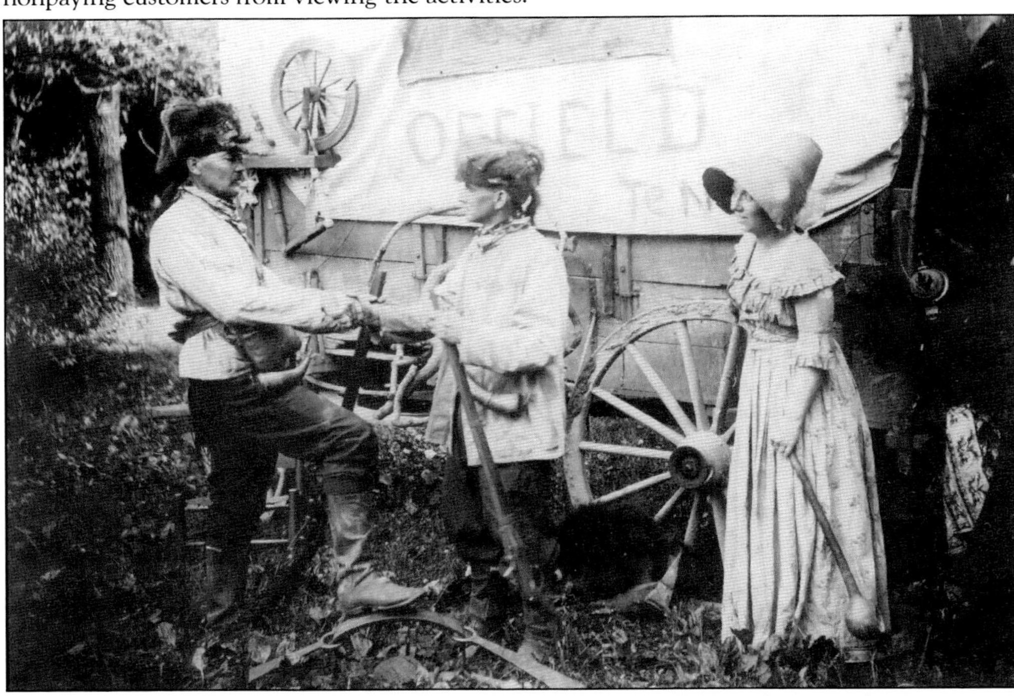

"The Coming of William Offield" reenacted the arrival of the first settler to reach Montgomery County in 1821. Edgar A. Rice (center) played Offield, and Elizabeth Cowan portrayed his wife. Dumont Kennedy took the role of Offield's companion. Cowan was the daughter of Edward Cowan, the last surviving Civil War veteran from Montgomery County.

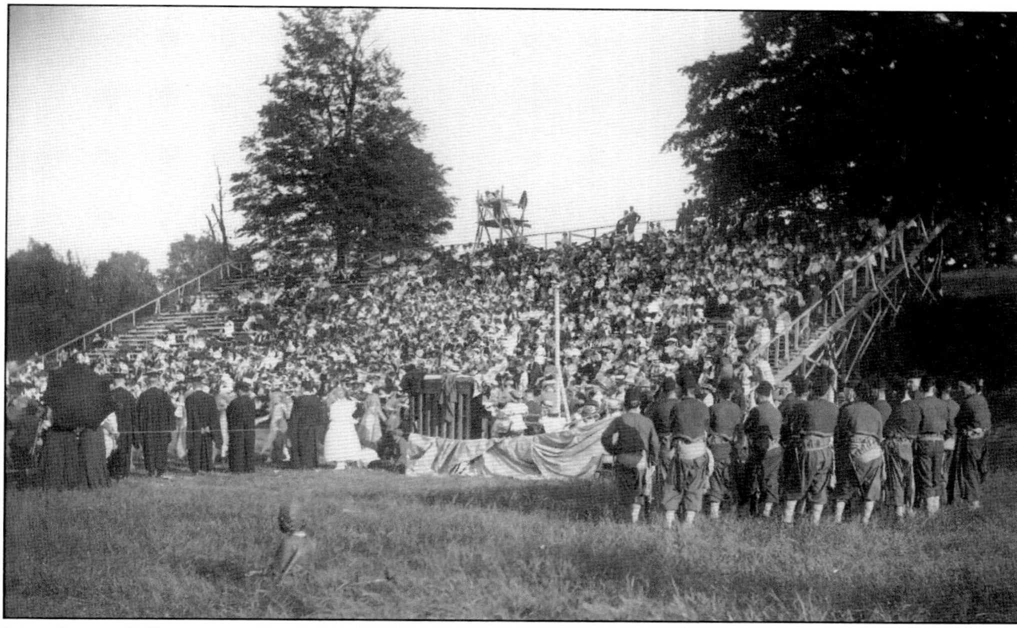

Members of Company C of the 2nd Indiana National Guard dressed as Zouaves to represent Gen. Lew Wallace's company when it enlisted in the Civil War. The costumes did not arrive in time for the first production of the pageant on June 13, but the Zouaves were fully outfitted by the time of the June 15 production. Rain forced cancellation on June 14.

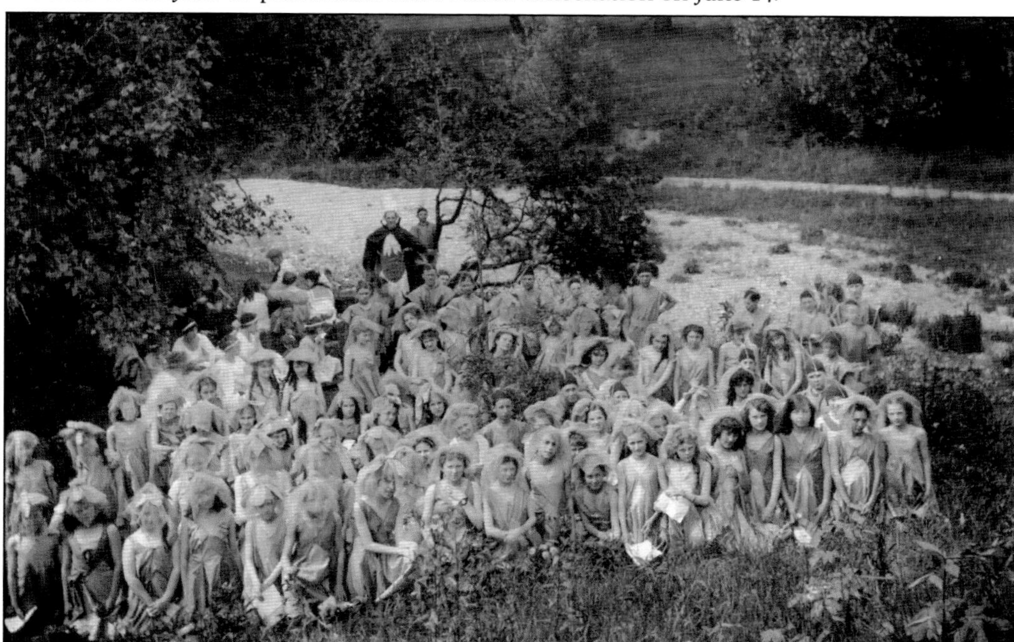

Costumed children participate in one of several interlude dances separating each episode of the Montgomery County Centennial Pageant. One hundred boys and girls symbolized the fertility of the fields in a performance entitled "Dance of the Corn and Wheat." Dry Branch flows in the background; the stream still flows through Crawfordsville today.

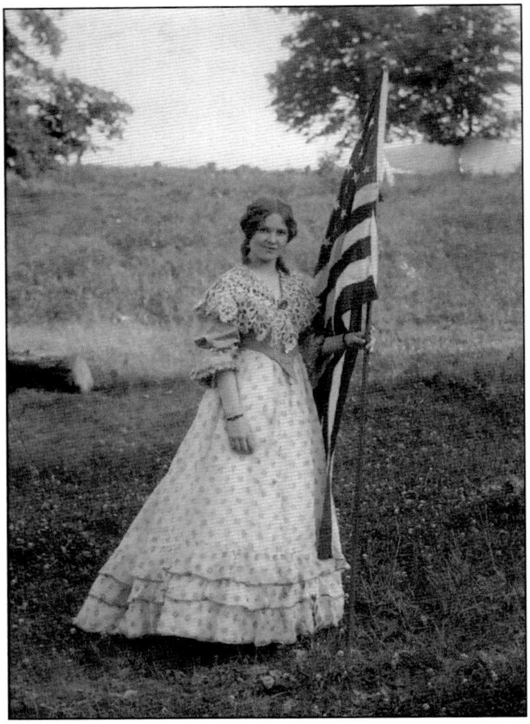

Eleanor Ristine held a prestigious role in the pageant, playing Mrs. Henry S. Lane. (Henry Lane was instrumental in securing Abraham Lincoln's nomination for the presidency.) Ristine wears the waist that Mrs. Lane wore at Lincoln's inauguration and the wedding dress that Susan Elston used for her 1852 marriage to Lew Wallace. Ristine graduated from the Carnegie Library School in Pittsburgh and later worked at the Crawfordsville Public Library and then the Wabash College Library.

The weather was ideal for the opening of the Montgomery County Centennial Pageant on June 13, 1916. The program began with a symbolic masque of Montamin, an American Indian creation legend. Children playing wood nymphs descended, dancing from the hills and accompanied by music to invoke the aid of the spirits of corn and wheat. Kitchemonda, the Great Spirit, was portrayed by S. C. Campbell, who is seen here standing against the tree.

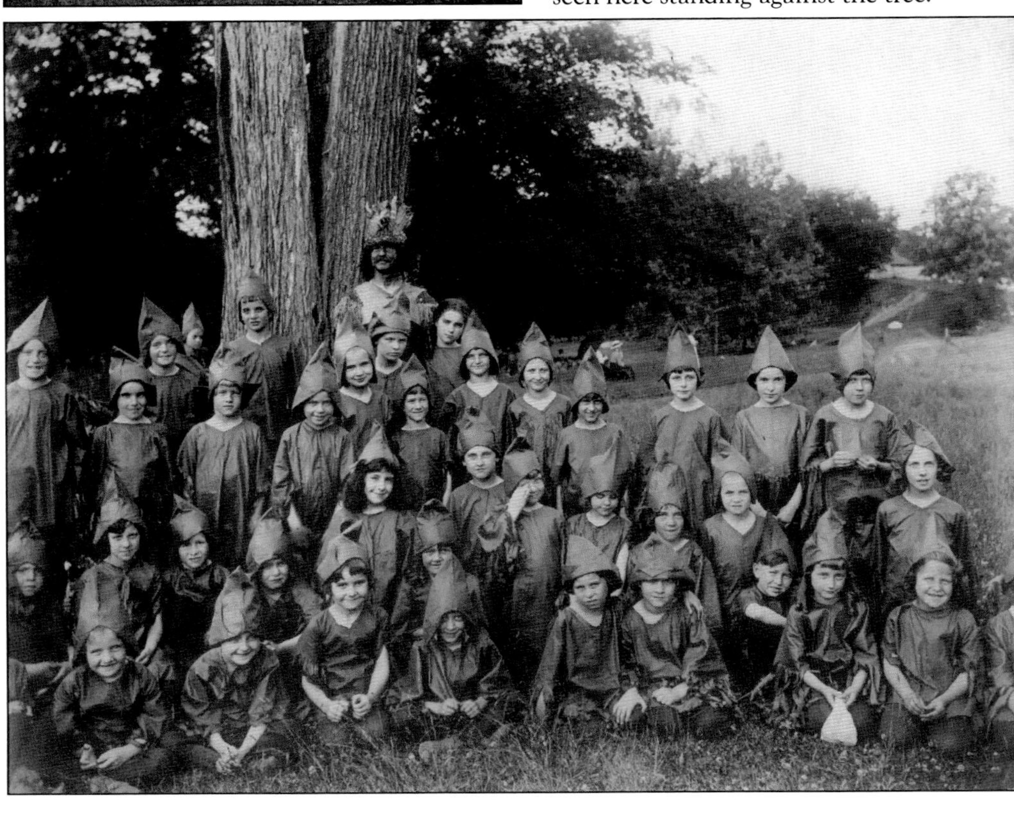

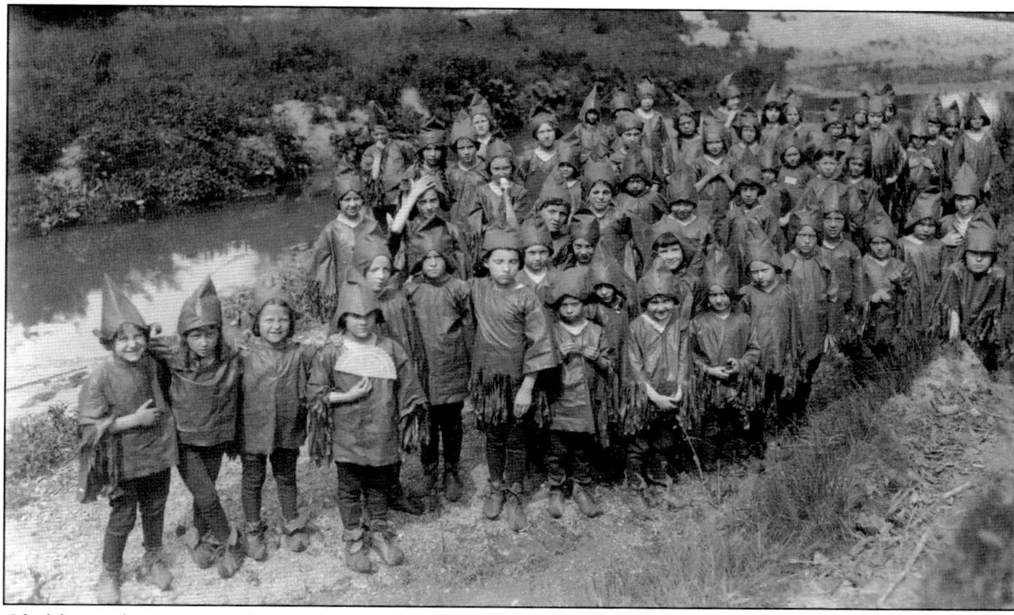

Children playing wood nymphs for the opening masque of Montamin pose by the edge of Dry Branch, a stream that crossed Crawford's Woods. Harold Watson and Kenyon Nicholson, Wabash College students, wrote the script for the Indian creation legend that opened the pageant. Nicholson went on to a minor literary career, with at least one Broadway success in 1927 (*The Barker*). Watson was killed during World War I in 1918.

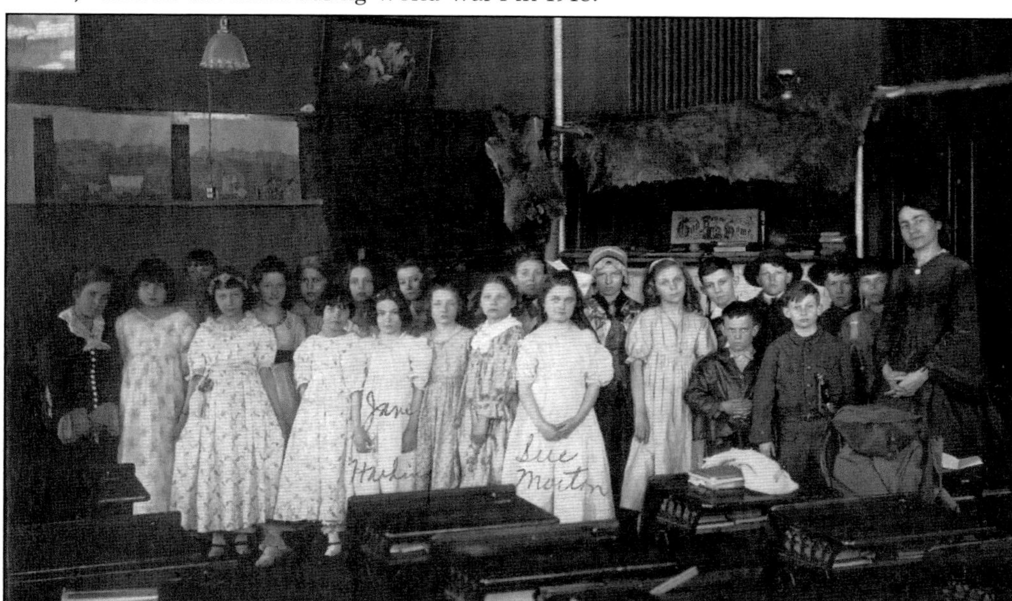

The Montgomery County Centennial Celebration was a countywide affair: each township contributed to the success of the weeklong celebration. More than 1,000 residents participated. Local schools began the celebration several months earlier, in March 1916, with an observance day. Students from Elizabeth Winter's (standing, right) sixth-grade Mills School class dressed in period costumes and played as extras in the pageant episodes.

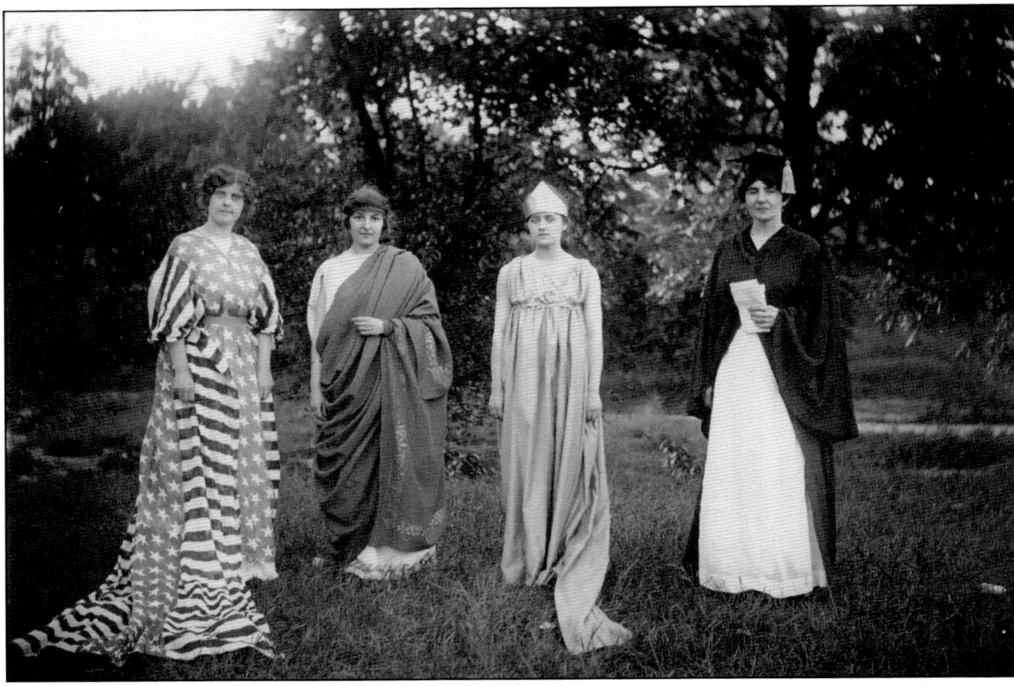

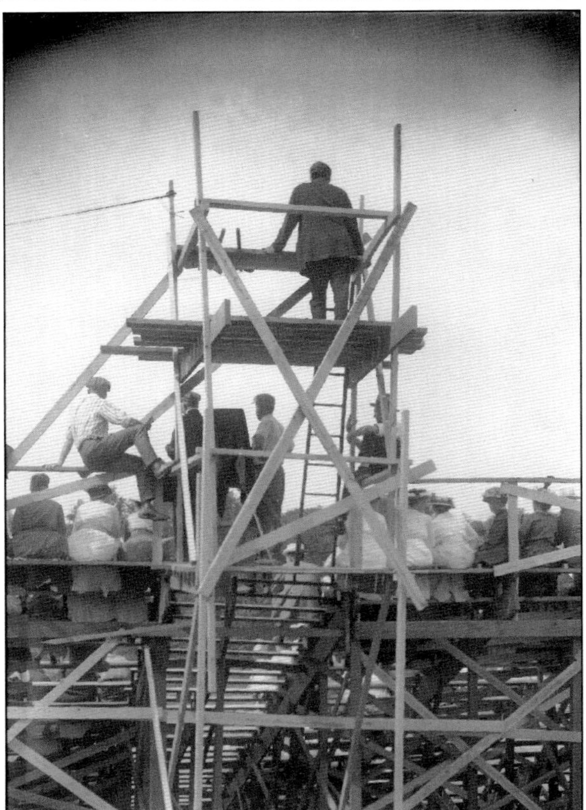

Allegorical roles for the finale included Columbia, the Spirit of Literature, Indiana, and the Spirit of Education. Natalie Quick portrayed Indiana (third from the left), and Mrs. Fred Turner (in cap and gown) was the Spirit of Education. Progress in agriculture, excellence in education, unsurpassed patriotism, and local contributions to national literature were the four themes that were interwoven throughout the episodes to characterize the life of Montgomery County.

Professor Daniel D. Hains of Wabash College was the Pageant Master, and he was able to direct the proceedings from high above the bleachers using colored flags to signal the actors far below. He also took advantage of an electric buzzer to cue the 25-piece orchestra. Hains, a Wabash graduate, taught Greek at the college from 1895 to 1916 and directed many Greek plays as well as community pageants.

Georgia Potter (at right) of Chicago was the director of the dances in the Montgomery County Centennial Pageant. The *Crawfordsville Journal* reported after the first representation of the pageant on June 14, 1916, that "Miss Potter is a graceful dancer and it was largely thru her efforts that the pageant was a success since she had direct charge of the training of all the dancers." Although Potter was in the area for just a short time, she was of such community interest that when she married the next year in St. Joseph, Missouri, the *Journal* announced the event and stated that she had "acquired a large number of friends and admirers" during her time in Crawfordsville. Four of the girls Potter directed in the "Dance of the Corn and Wheat" stand in their costumes during a break in the festivities (below).

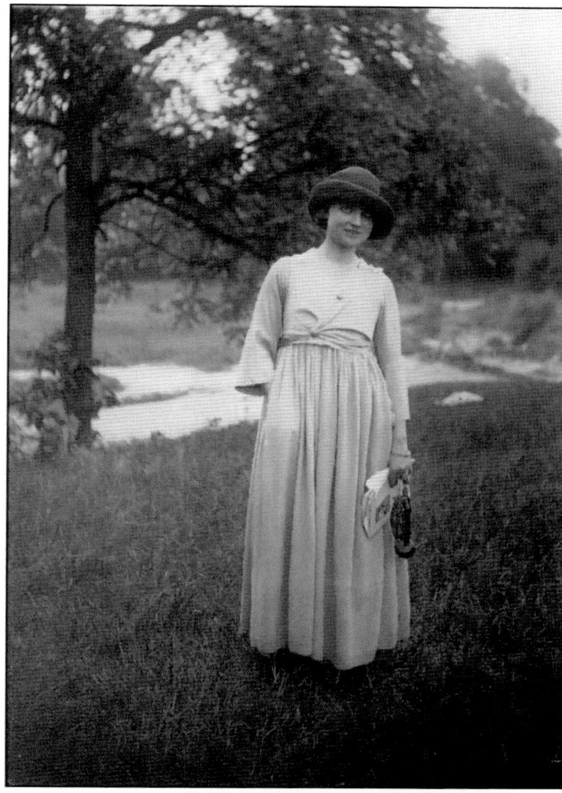

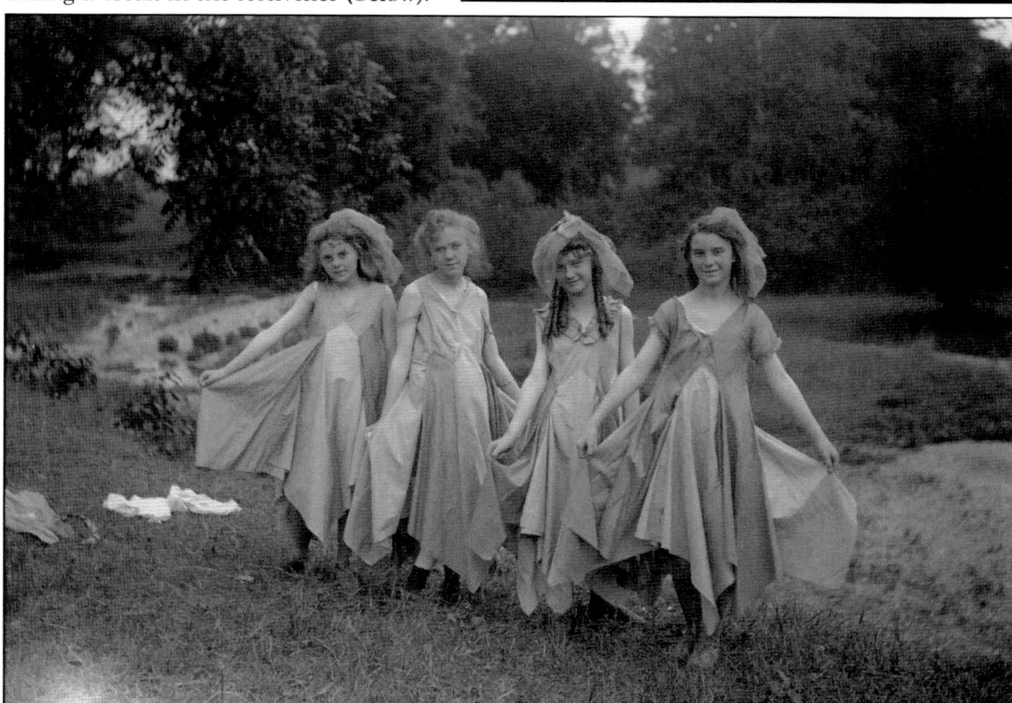

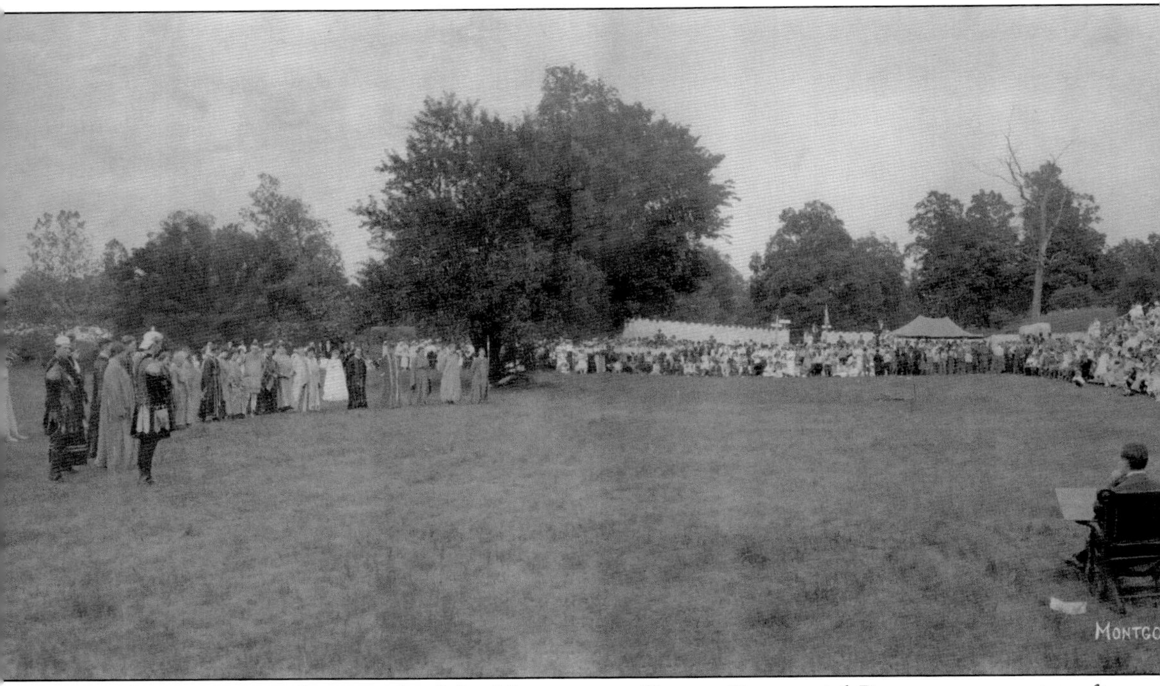

This panoramic photograph of the Montgomery County Centennial Pageant was cut into five different pieces and stored in the public library's archives for years as separate images until just recently when they were recognized as one shot. In the chair may be professor Daniel D. Hains, directing from the stage instead of from his regular perch above the bleachers. The scene being

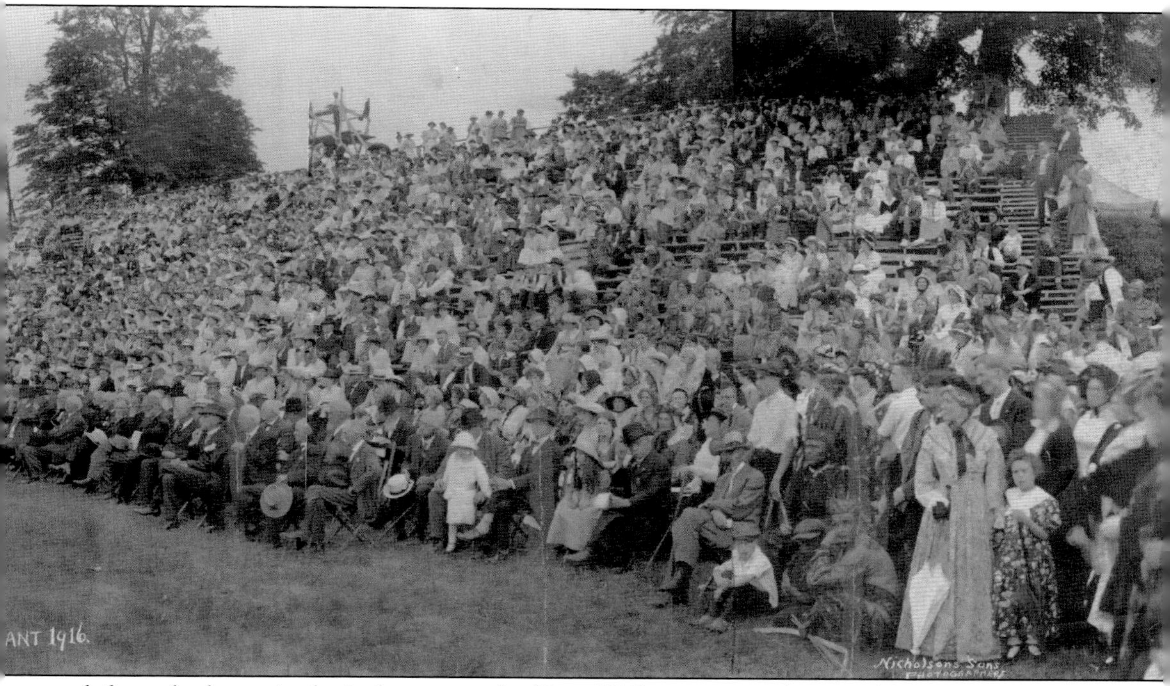

acted, from the last episode, is the portrayal of Lew Wallace creating his novel *Ben-Hur*. Many of the pageant participants are visible, still in costume, in the bleachers, including many of the wood nymph children who have rejoined their parents. GAR veterans have honored seats in front of the bleachers nearer to the action.

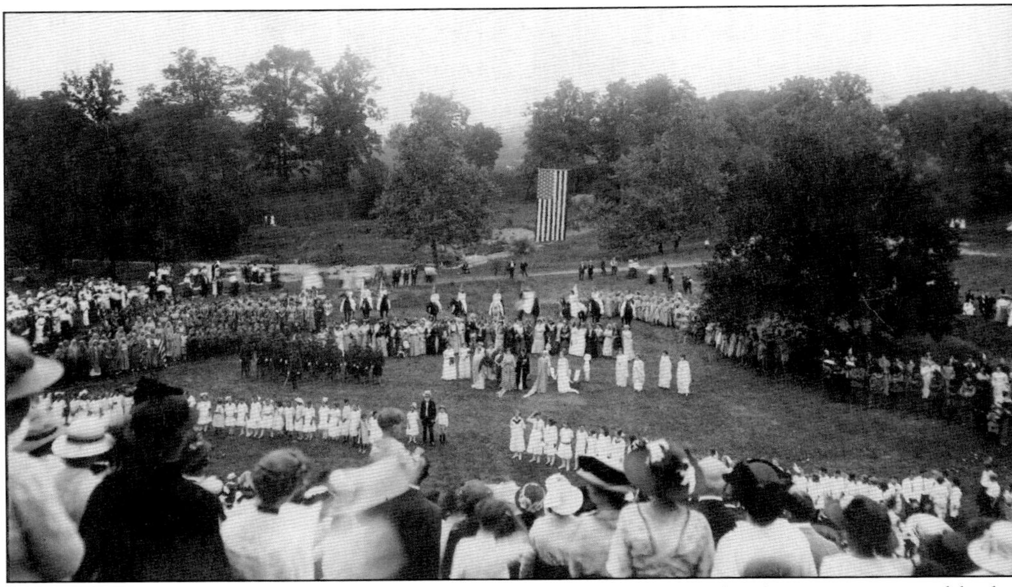

In the finale of the Montgomery County Centennial Pageant, Columbia, accompanied by her "spirits of advancement," comes forward, followed by Indiana and her crowning as a state. A group of schoolchildren came next, symbolizing "Past Achievements and Future Promise." Next, the Spirit of Montgomery County arrived with its 11 townships, portrayed by girls on horseback. Finally, as the entire cast congregated on stage, the audience rose and sang "America."

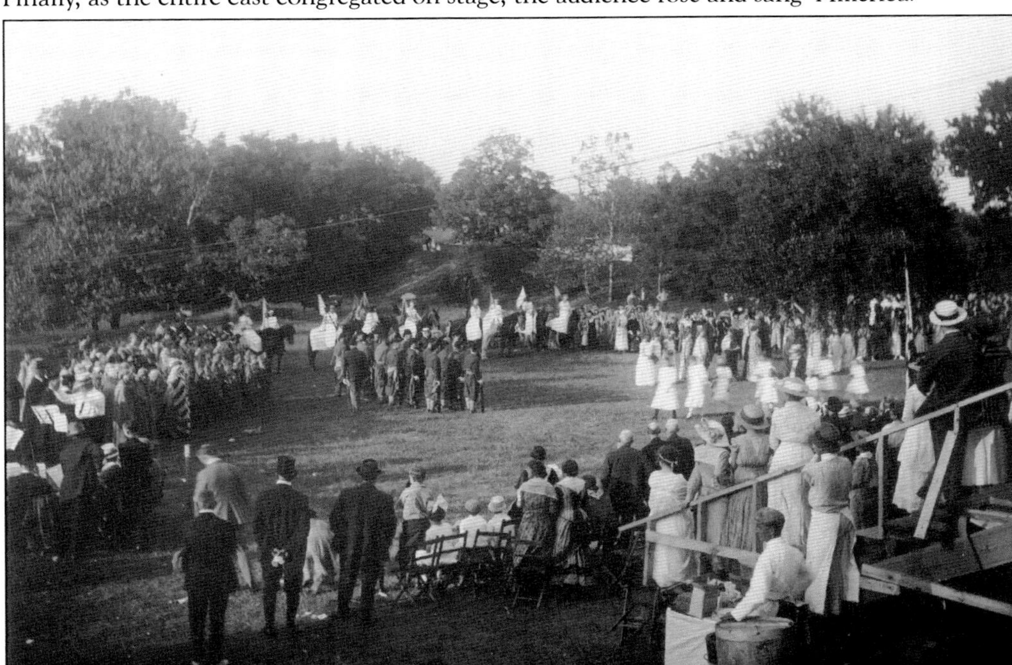

Spectators at the finale of the Montgomery County Centennial Pageant were able to see the entire cast on the grassy stage. A group of schoolchildren meant to symbolize "Past Achievements and Future Promise" arrives in the center of the activities.

Five

Crawfordsville at Work

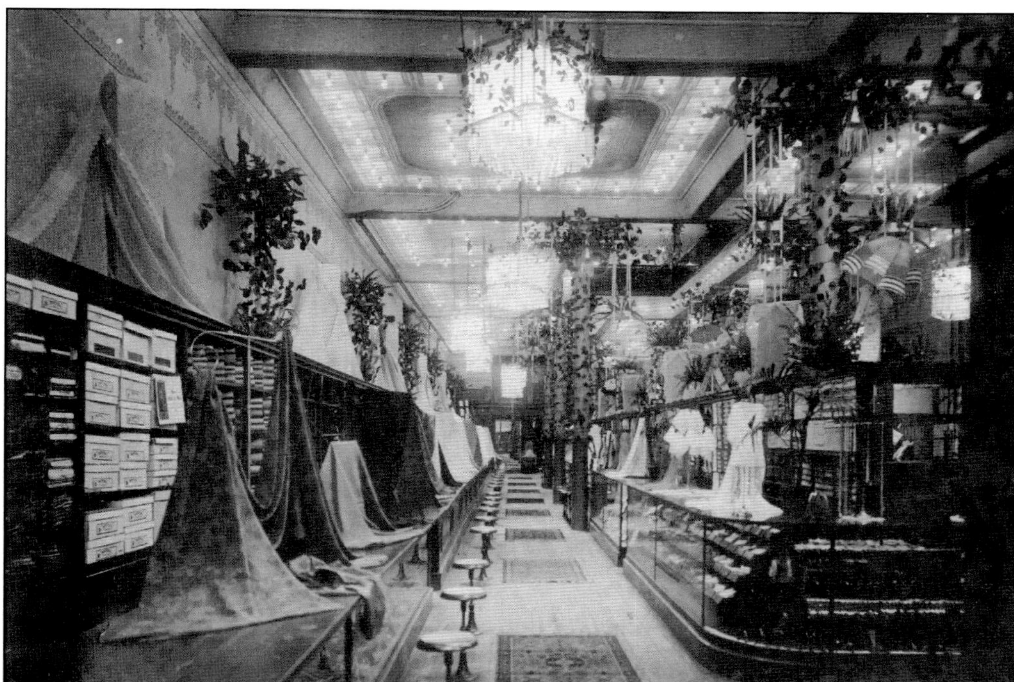

Louis Bischof came to Crawfordsville from Terre Haute at the age of 17 and became a partner of Jacob Ferber in a store located at the corner of Washington and Main Streets. In 1882, Louis Bischof bought Ferber's interest. Bischof's career as a storekeeper spanned three decades. He built a four-story building on the corner of Main and Green Streets in 1899, and in 1907 this establishment became Bischof's Big Store. The store was a cooperative, with more than 3,000 area stockholders earning annual dividends. Bischof was a lifelong bachelor and natural salesperson who wore a red carnation every day for more than 40 years. The first floor of Bischof's Big Store, shown here in the early 20th century, was used for fabric, which could be fitted on the fourth floor. In May 1906, when a circus was in town, the Big Store advertised in the *Crawfordsville Weekly News Review*: "Especially for circus day we have arranged a special bargain sale of rich, pretty silks that you'll want for your summer waists and dresses. . . . You are heartily welcome whether you want to buy or not."

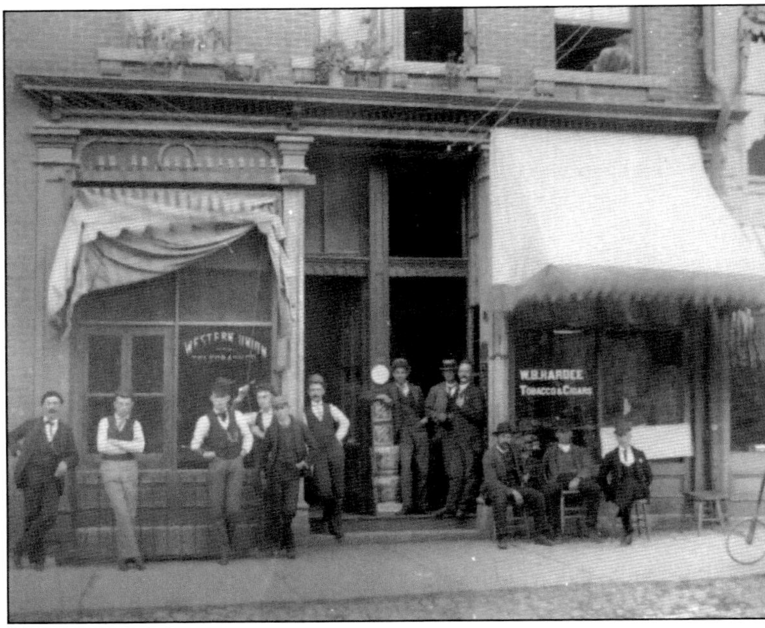

Seen here around 1890, William B. Hardee's Tobacco and Cigars store was located at 104 South Green Street next to the city's Western Union telegraph office. Tobacco was big business in Crawfordsville; at the time, five cigar manufacturers were listed in the city directory. William Hardee sold his store in August 1896 and died in a suspicious hunting accident a few months later.

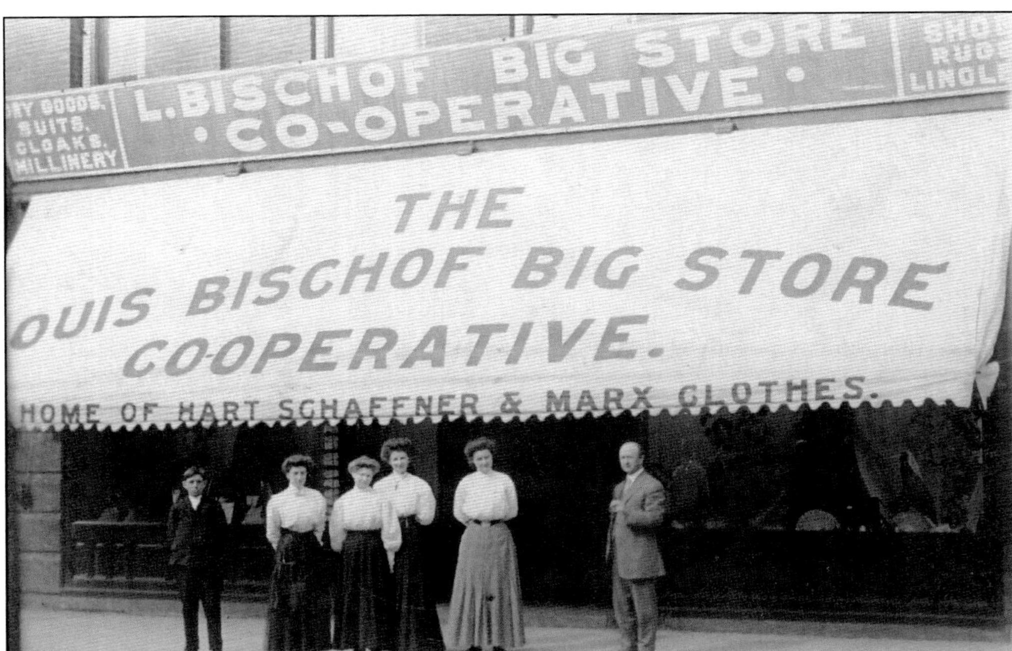

Louis Bischof of Bischof's Big Store was known for philanthropy and kindness, and his employees were proud to work at his establishment. In 1909, several employees had a postcard made of them standing outside the store. At its height, the Big Store employed some 100 workers. It was a landmark in town, day or night (when it was brightly lit), and prospered until it was bought by Goodman's in 1925. The building burned to the ground in 1933 in one of Crawfordville's most disastrous fires.

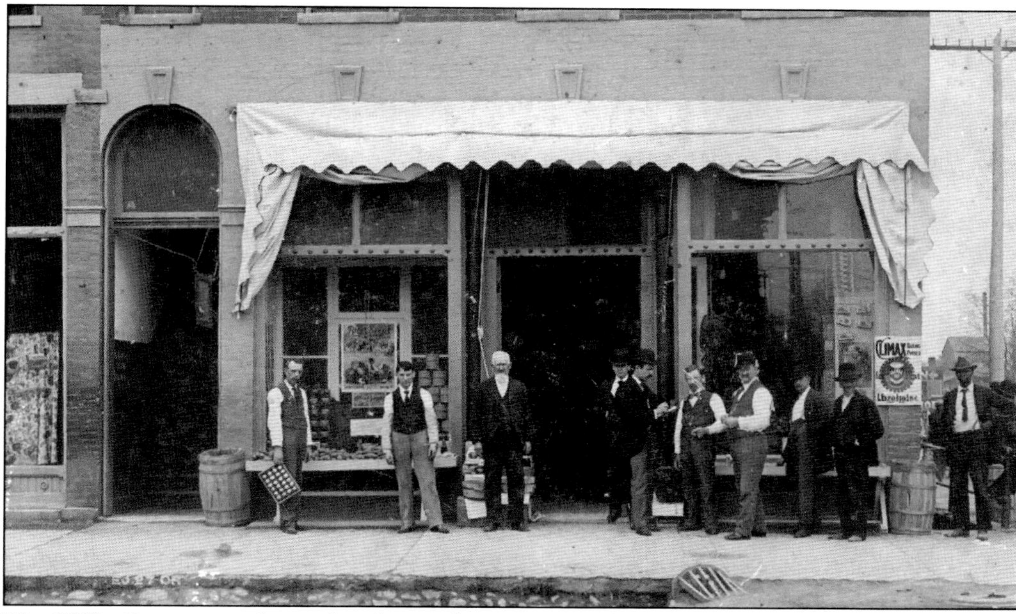

The Willis Grocery was located at the southwest corner of Market and Washington Streets when this photograph was taken around 1910. Mead W. Willis was the proprietor from 1907 until his death in 1919. His wife, Ada Dunn Gerard, then ran the store until the mid-1920s, when it became the Francis and Mount grocers.

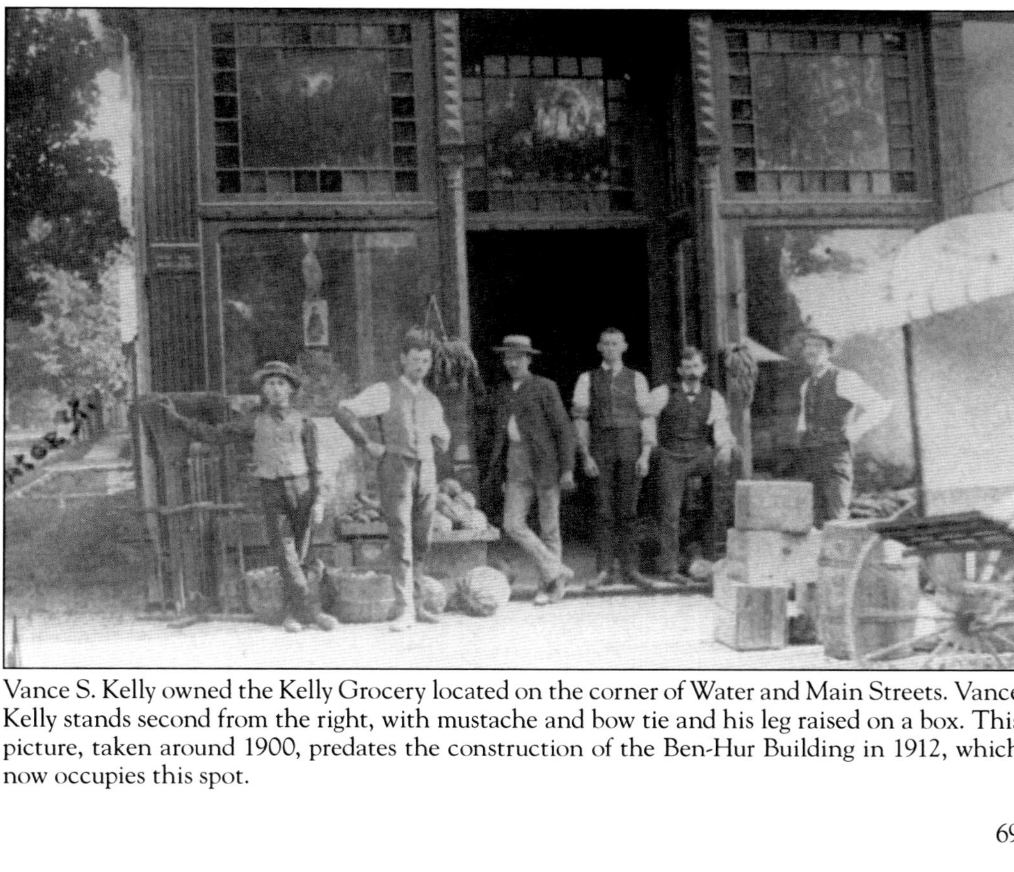

Vance S. Kelly owned the Kelly Grocery located on the corner of Water and Main Streets. Vance Kelly stands second from the right, with mustache and bow tie and his leg raised on a box. This picture, taken around 1900, predates the construction of the Ben-Hur Building in 1912, which now occupies this spot.

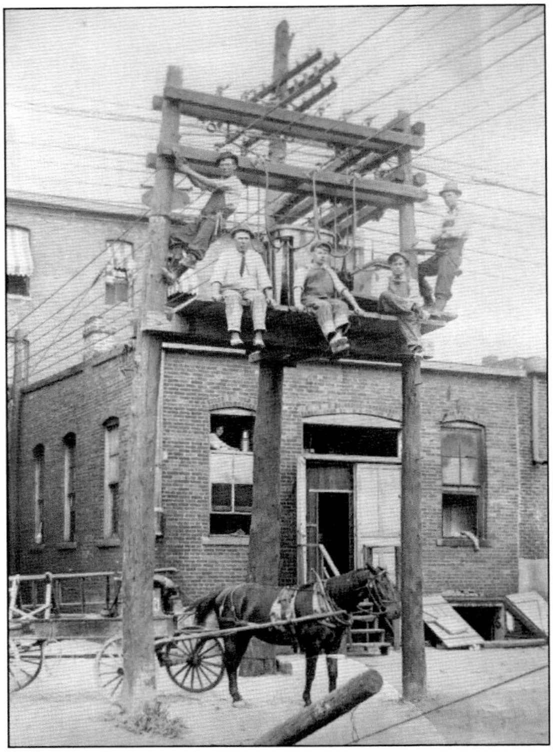

In 1890, the Crawfordsville City Council voted to maintain its own electric light plant, and by the next year the city's first electric light and power plant was built on the corner of Washington and North Streets. In this photograph, line superintendent Peck Lyons and his crew pause in the alley between Market and Main Streets and Green and Water Streets. By late 1891, the city's elected officials considered Crawfordsville the best-lighted city in the state.

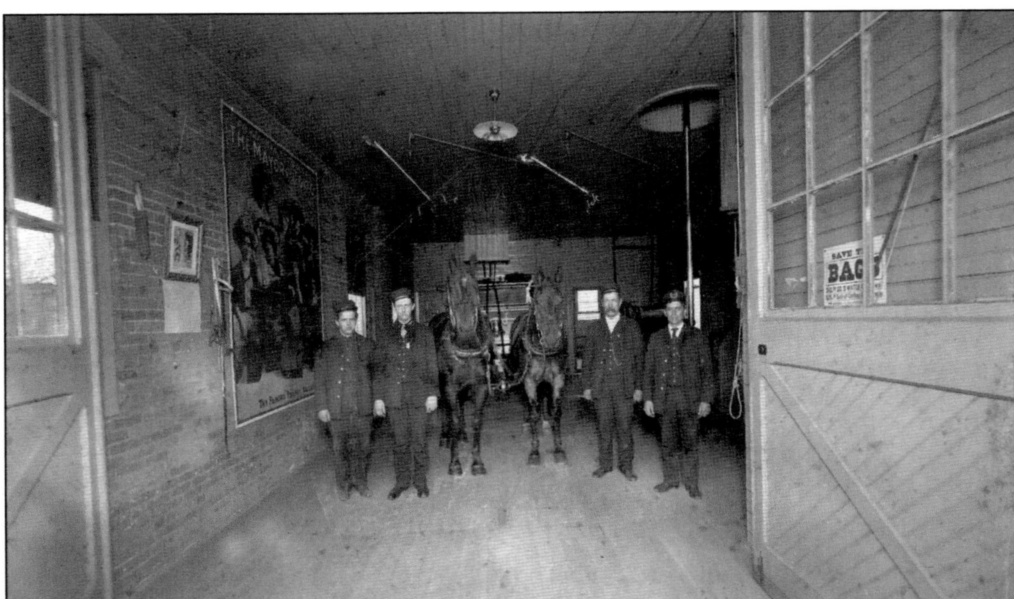

Crawfordsville organized a volunteer fire department in 1869. By 1900, seven men (and several horses) were employed. On June 7, 1906, (from left to right) employees Ike Hayes, Harrison Young, Charley Ayers, and Clarence Williams were photographed at their station. Williams was the first firefighter killed on duty. On August 7, 1914, the fire wagon he was riding was struck by an interurban car at the intersection of Pike Street and Woodlawn Avenue.

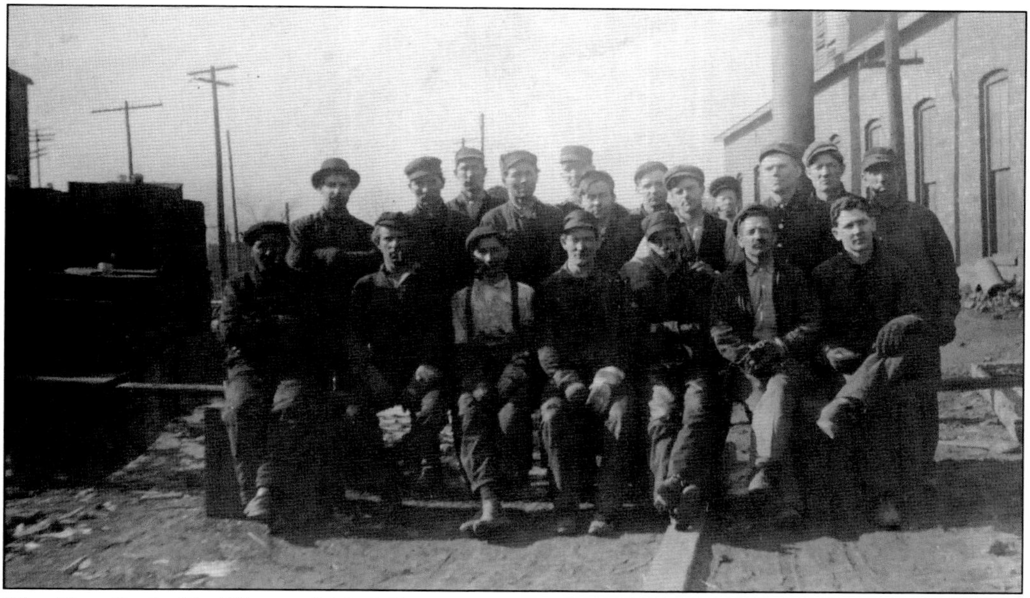

The Crawfordsville Wire and Nail Company opened in 1901 near the junction of the Monon and Big Four Railroads. The company manufactured all types of metal products: nails, fence wire, barbed wire, fence staples, and more. By 1910, when this photograph was taken, six rail cars carrying materials were going in and out each day. The factory, which then employed more than 150 workmen, evolved into Mid-States Steel and Wire Company after the original company was purchased in 1929.

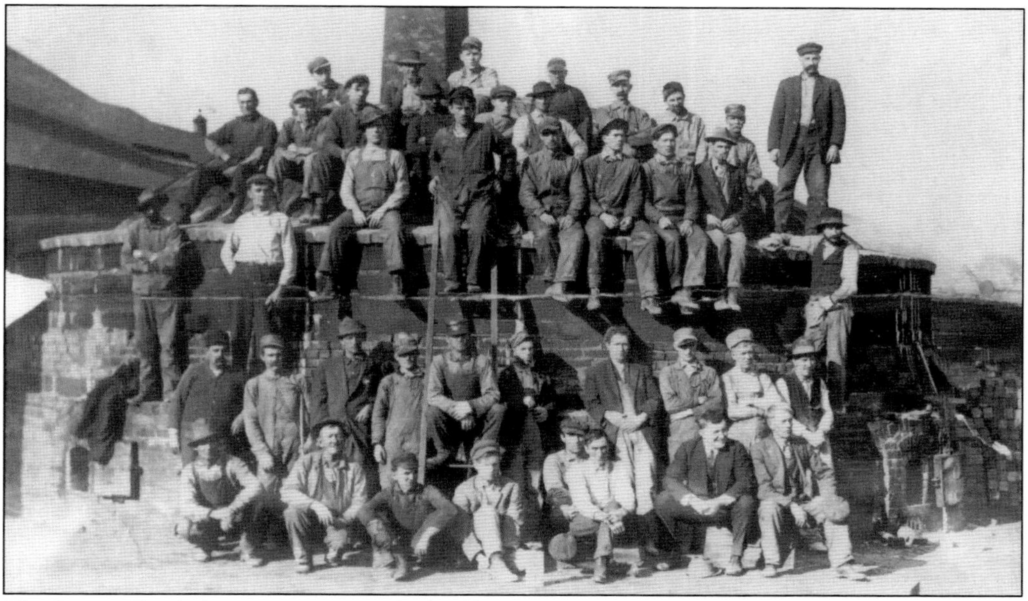

The Poston Brick Company in Crawfordsville opened to the west of present-day Poston Drive in 1901. The company made paving brick and soon began to manufacture face brick. The Poston Brick Company produced a high-quality product with a national reputation. Employees pose around 1910 in front of one of the large kilns, which had a monthly capacity of 600,000 bricks at that time.

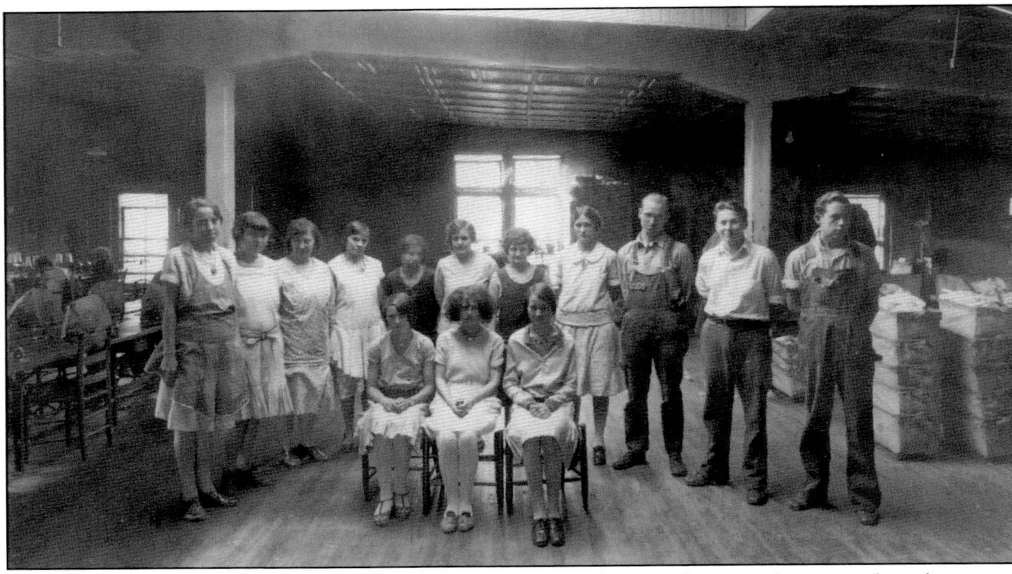

The Gregg Glove Company incorporated in 1911 to manufacture gloves and mittens, later becoming the Boss Manufacturing Company. The Crawfordsville factory was located at 211–213 East Main Street but moved to 112–116 East Pike Street. The home office was located in Crawfordsville, and the company also had factories in nearby Frankfort and Lebanon, employing about 400 workers total. Crawfordsville employees are photographed here in a factory workroom in the late 1920s.

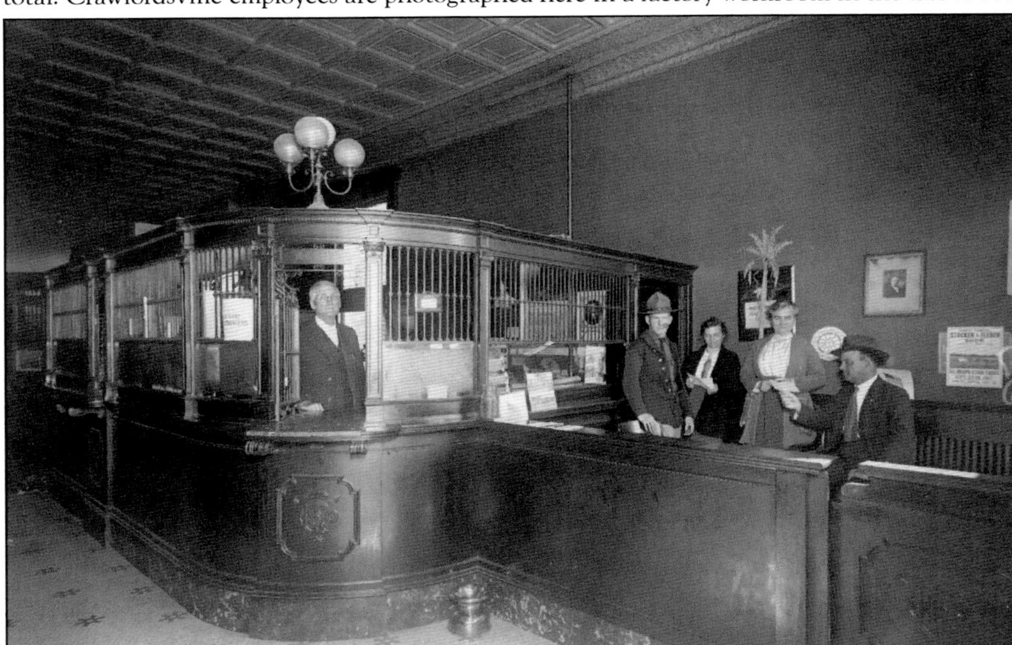

On September 15, 1917, when this picture was taken, the Crawfordsville Trust Company stood at 132 East Main Street. Walter Breaks, a prominent businessman and political figure in the county, sits to far right. A Spanish-American War veteran, he served on the Purdue University Board of Trustees from 1919 to 1921. The teller's counter is shown to the left, and a spittoon for customer convenience is located near it on the floor.

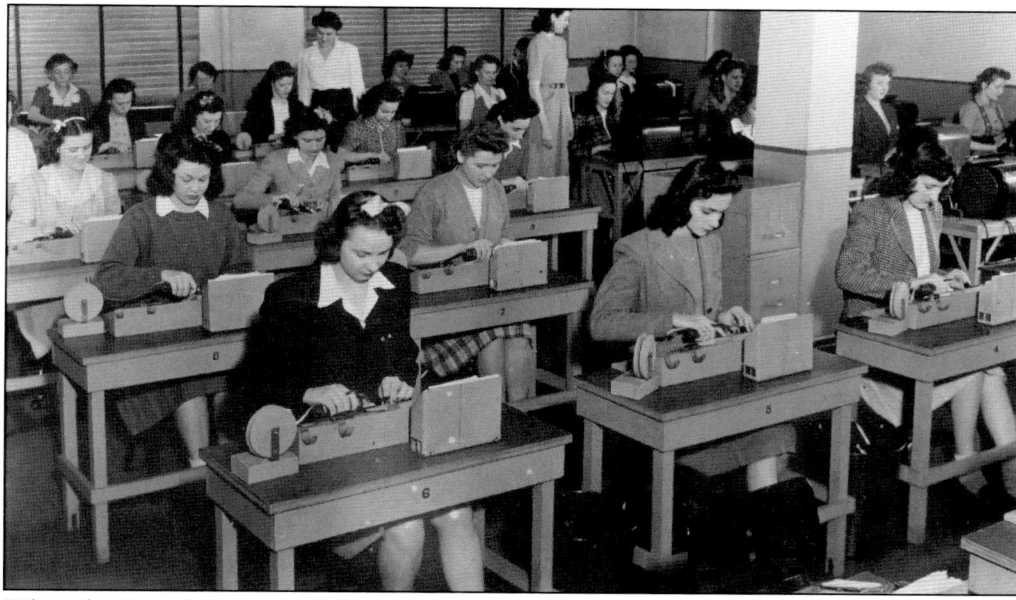

When the United States entered World War II in 1941, Western Union opened a Teletype school on the fifth floor of the Ben-Hur Building. Young women were recruited to attend this school, and these Western Union Girls (WUGs) came from 10 surrounding states (including Indiana) to master the telegraph machine in nine weeks. The school survived until 1961, when the telephone eventually rendered Teletype skills obsolete.

The Stephenson Crane Cigar Store on 107 South Washington Street was also a pool hall from the 1920s through the 1940s. The store was owned by William E. Crane and James F. Stephenson (Crane's father-in-law). Although the building still stands, no early photographs have been found. As was common practice, the Stephenson Crane Cigar Store produced trade tokens that were good for different amounts. These tokens are valued collectibles today.

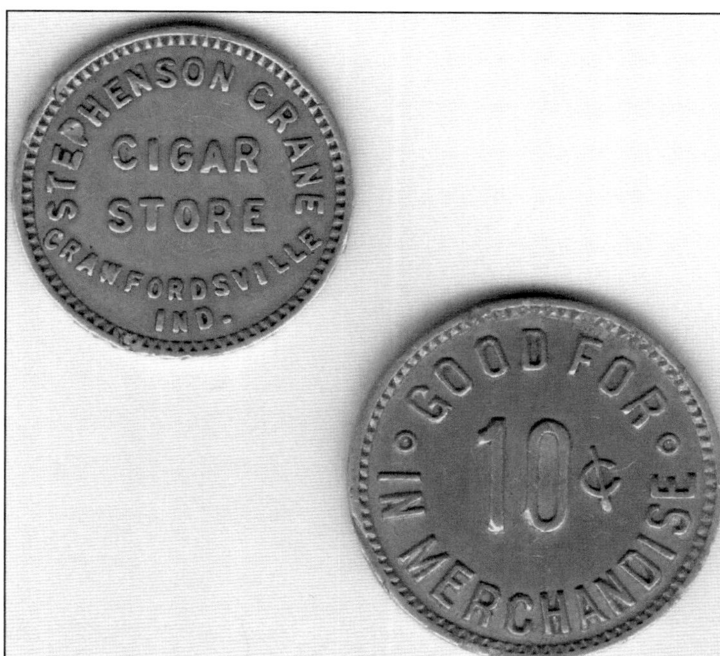

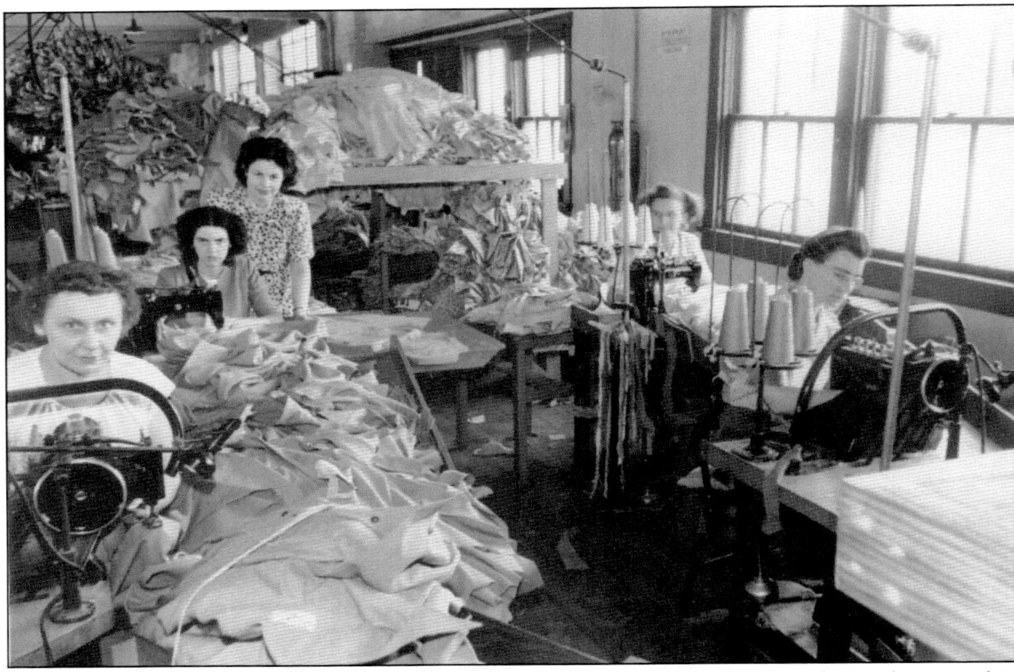

The Wilson Brothers Company, founded in 1864 in Chicago, soon found a niche as a shirt manufacturer. Success led to expansion, and by 1937 a Wilson Brothers shirt factory was constructed in Crawfordsville at 1002 Lane Avenue. The entire process was conducted on-site, from cutting to sewing as well as inspecting. This 1940s view of a sewing room shows (front to back, on the left) Maxine Lyons, Ruth Tanselle, and Imogene Gardner surrounded by piles of shirt pieces.

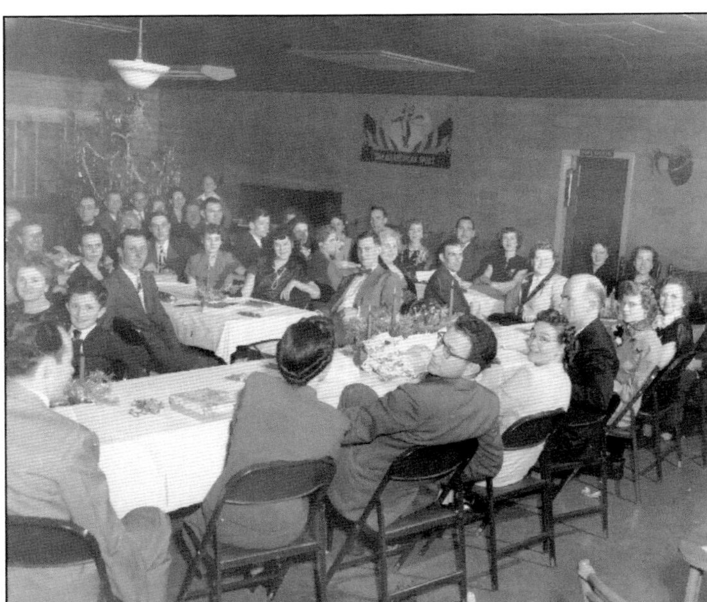

The Wilson Brothers shirt factory held annual Christmas parties for employees and their families. The company was a popular employer due to good conditions and camaraderie among the workers. Employees and family members pose during a Christmas party held in the Crawfordsville Municipal Clubhouse in the 1940s. The factory operated for 20 years in Crawfordsville, disappointing many when it was sold in 1958 and relocated to another state.

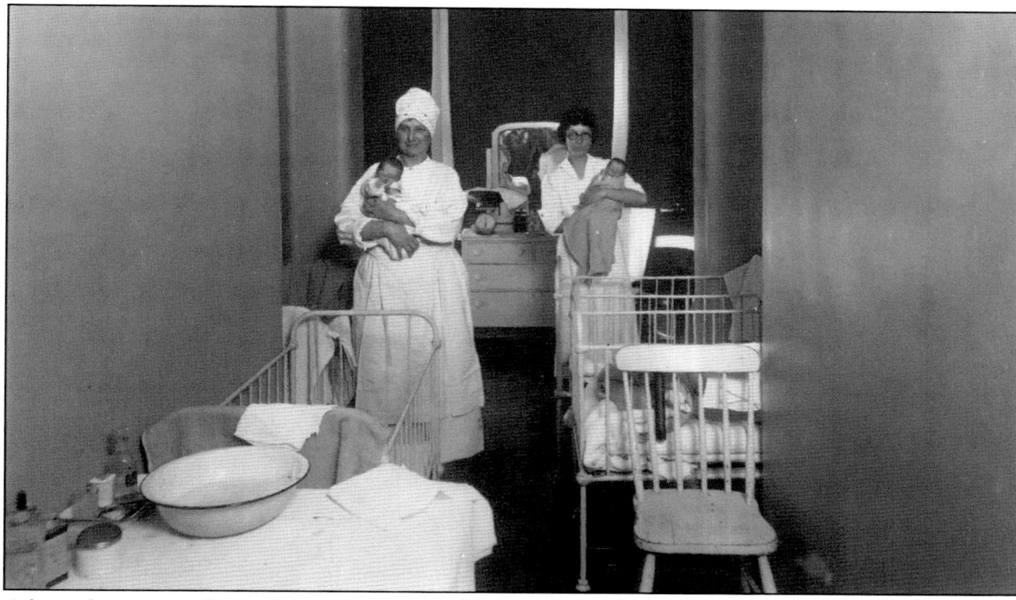

After a long struggle to obtain support and funding, Culver Union Hospital eventually opened in 1902 on Binford Street (above). In this photograph, two nurses hold newborns in what was considered a very sanitary facility (to keep dust down, no upholstered furniture or hanging pictures were allowed, and room corners were rounded). When the hospital opened, the nursing staff included one trained nurse and two student nurses. The second Culver Union Hospital replaced the original institution in 1929, and it could accommodate 48 patients—a new addition to this building, finished in 1942, nearly doubled the capacity, but by the end of the decade the hospital was again straining to serve an expanding community. Three nurses pose (below) with newborns in March 1948, and an incubator holds another in the foreground. This structure was used until 1984, when AMI/Culver Hospital (now St. Clare Medical Center) was completed north of Crawfordsville.

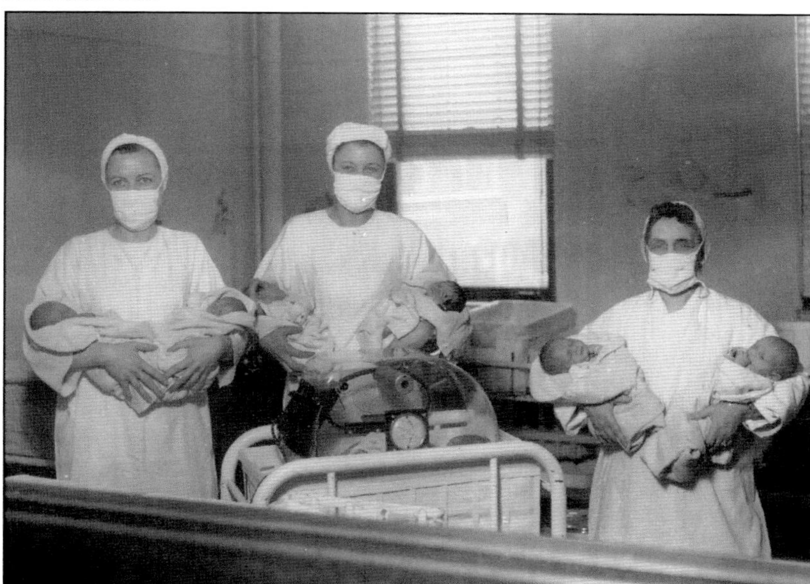

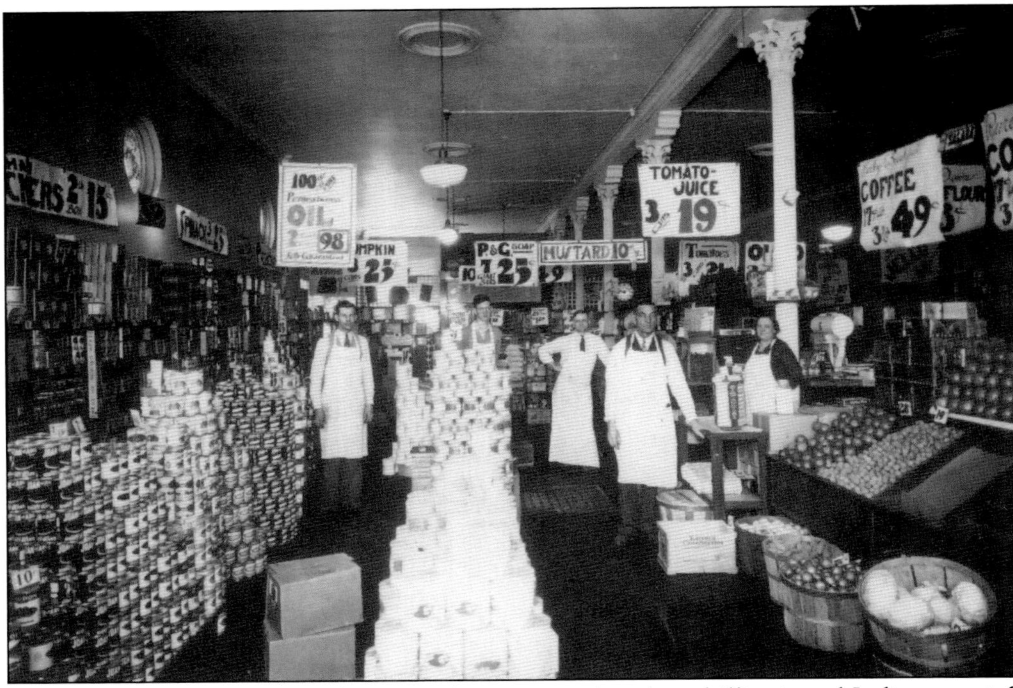

Grab It Here was a chain of about two dozen stores that dotted Illinois and Indiana, mainly from the 1930s until the 1980s. Employees at the Crawfordsville Grab It Here store (at 109 East Market Street) pause from their duties a moment for this photograph in 1937. From left to right, these employees are Leonard Shelton, Fred Whittington, Howard Abney, Earl Keller, and Ramona Keller.

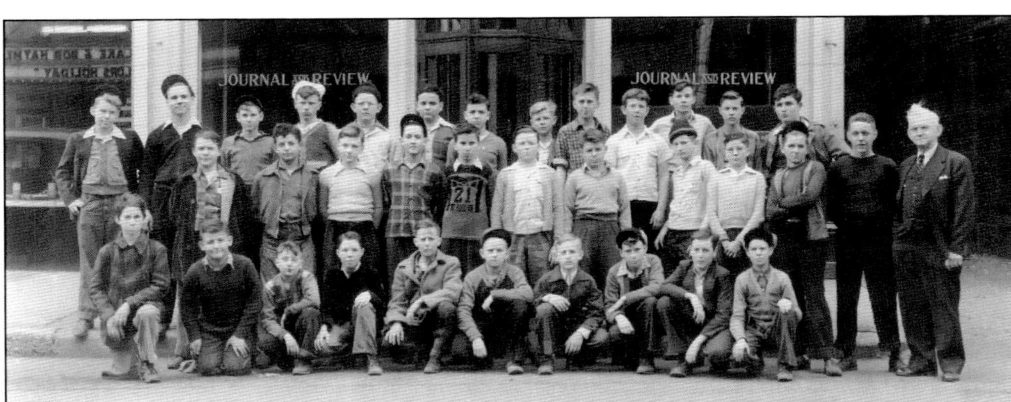

Newspaper carriers for the *Crawfordsville Journal Review* line up in front of the paper's building at 119 South Green Street on March 15, 1944, after raising money for the American Red Cross at the height of World War II. Many of these boys had fathers or brothers in the service, and they gathered a fund of $30.

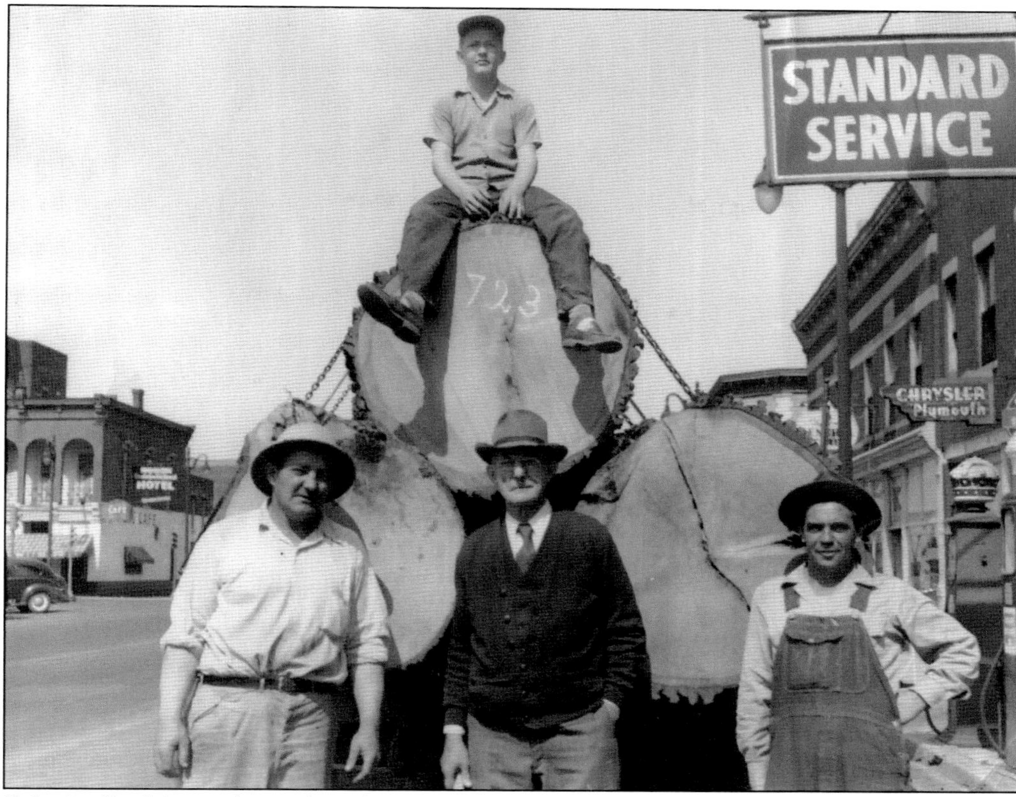

Odis Stafford (center) stands with two men and a boy on East Market Street behind a truck loaded with logs in the late 1950s. This view looks west on Market Street, and a Standard gas station with pump is just to the right. The Otto Schlemmer Building at the corner of Green and Market Streets is visible to the left.

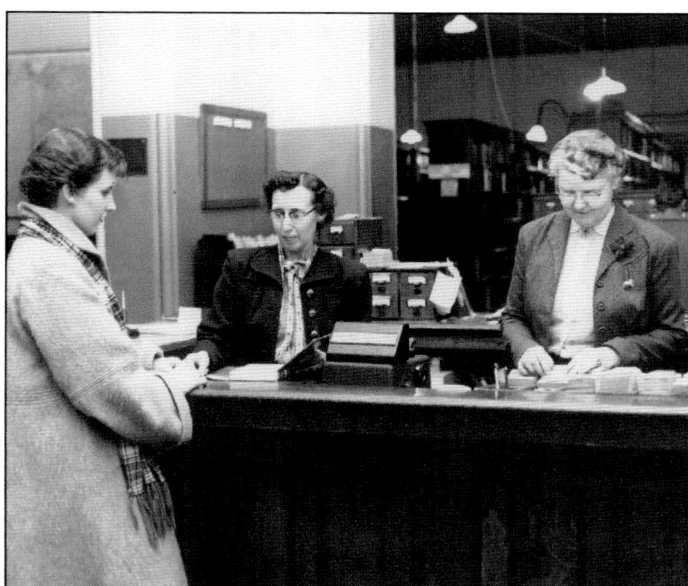

Louise Graham (center) and Marie Ward (right) help an unidentified patron during a winter evening at the Crawfordsville Public Library in the mid-1950s. Behind them are the stacks and the books that made up most of the library's collection. Keeping track of book circulation using paper was a labor-intensive task. Ward is looking through the cards containing patron and book information while Graham is inserting a due-date card in a book's pocket.

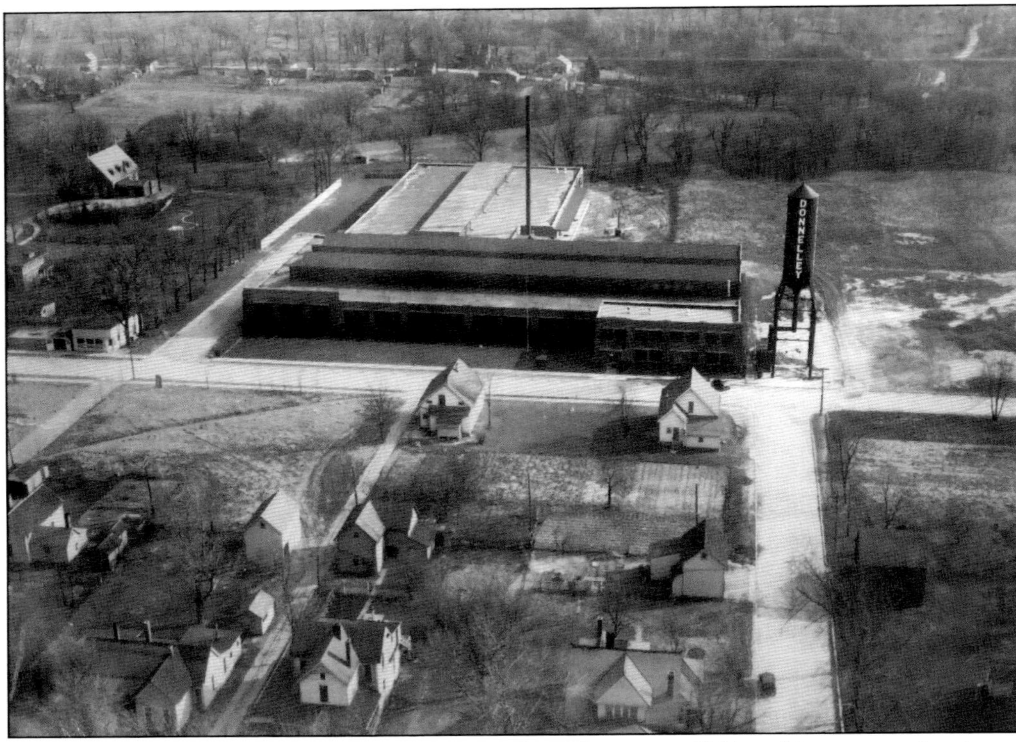

R. R. Donnelley and Sons Company was started in Chicago in 1864 and became an important printing business before expanding to Crawfordsville in the early 1920s, which was when this aerial view of the new plant was taken. By 1927, the company employed at least 250 residents, becoming the largest commercial enterprise in town and a major employer since. The water tower was used as an emergency water supply. R. R. Donnelley and Sons Company greatly expanded in the 1940s (below), when this picture postcard was produced (viewed looking west on Sloan Street). The plant, which hid its water tower inside the brick tower, became the book manufacturing center for the company. R. R. Donnelley and Sons enjoyed great success with its Crawfordsville plant, the source of many printing innovations. Donnelley constructed another plant in Crawfordsville in 1964 (the south plant). (Above, courtesy Anna Pennington.)

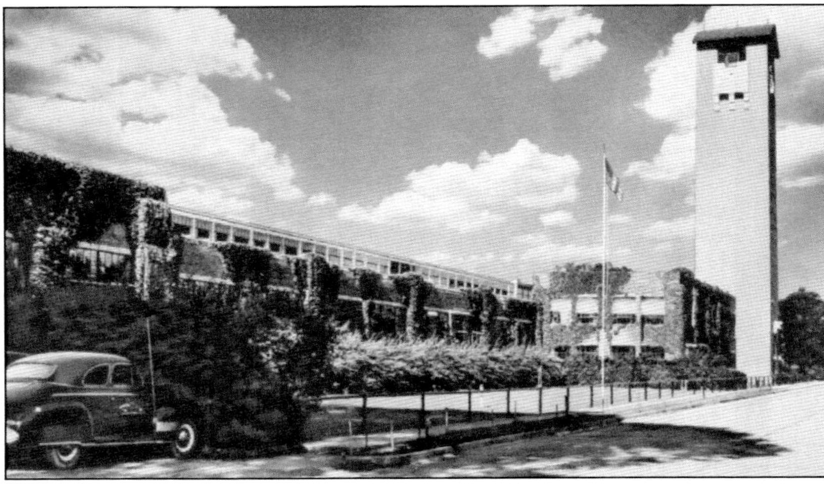

Six

Crawfordsville at War

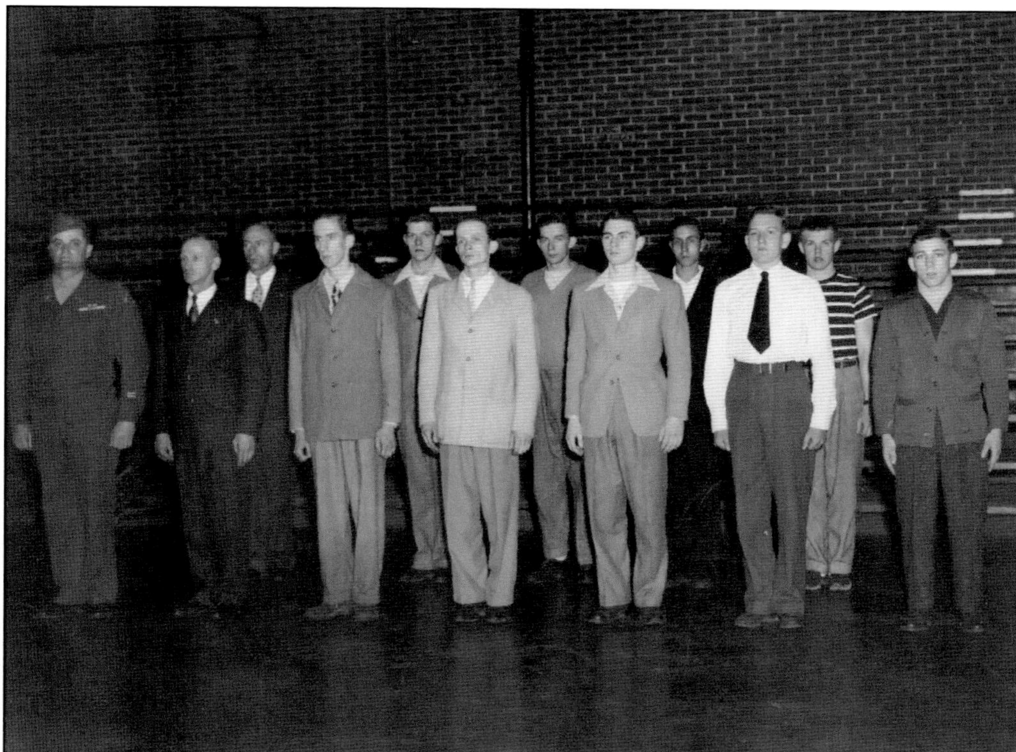

In 1942, a group of men lines up in the National Guard armory (on Green Street) for induction into the service. In the first row, third from left, stands Wabash student Robert Lee Pugh. As a private in Company B of the 409th Infantry in the 103rd Division (7th Army), Pugh was sent to Europe in October 1944. His parents received word that he was missing in action on December 1 of the same year. Pugh's company was attacked by German troops, who killed all but 13 of his fellow soldiers. Pugh was taken prisoner, but his parents did not learn that he had been captured and was a POW in Germany until March 1945. From Stalag IIIA (Luckenwalde), 30 miles south of Berlin, Pugh wrote to his parents, "Don't worry, we are treated all right and I am in good health. Although it is pretty cold here, I have plenty of warm clothes. . . . So far, we haven't had to work and I'm finding difficulty to know what to do." Pugh remained a prisoner until his camp was liberated by the Russians in June 1945. He weighed just 90 pounds at his release. After his return, Pugh resumed his studies at Wabash, graduating in 1949.

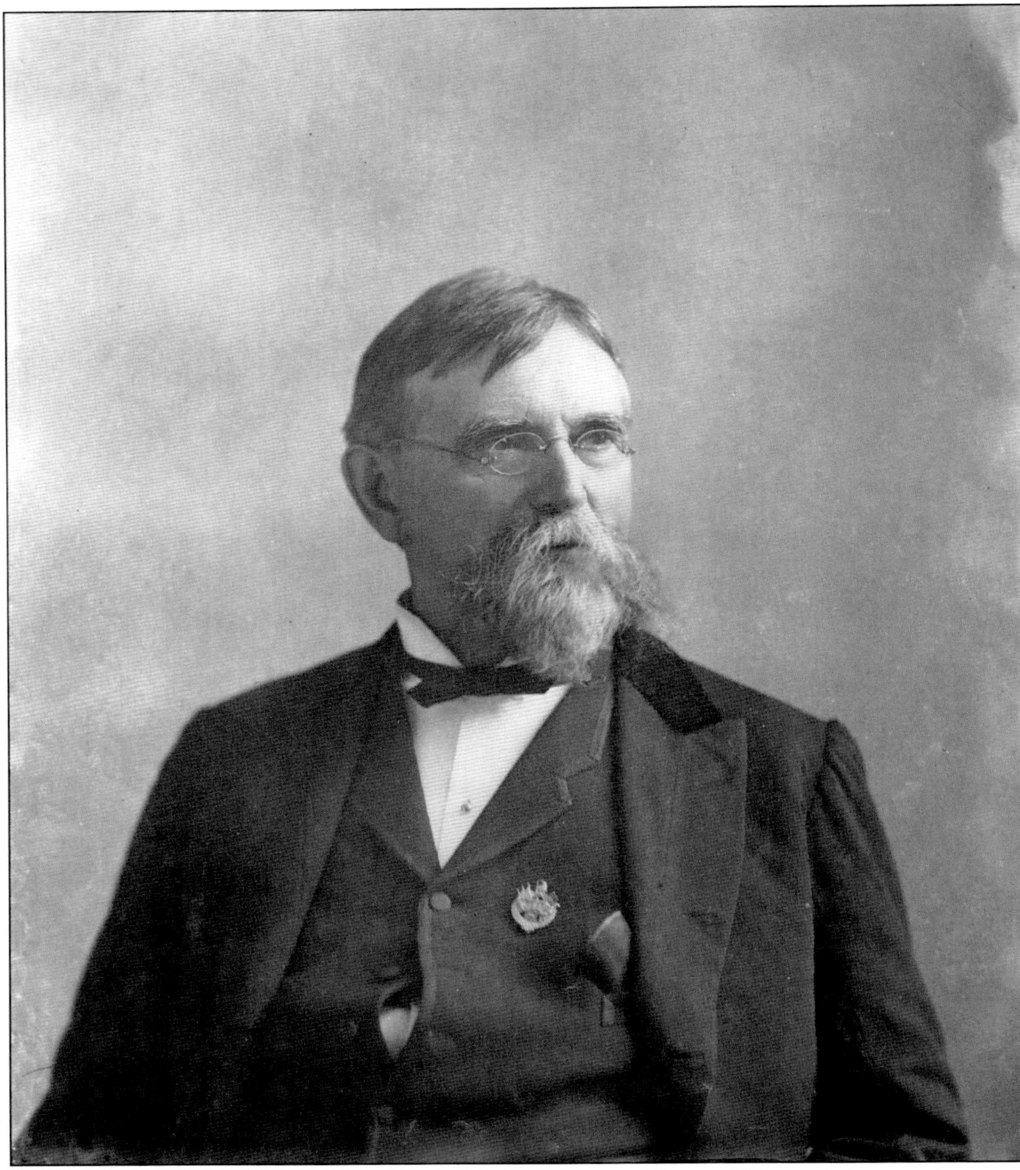

Crawfordsville's most famous soldier is undoubtedly Lew Wallace (1827–1905). Before the age of 20, Wallace served with Indiana militia units in the Mexican War. In 1861, at the outset of the American Civil War, he helped recruit troops in Indiana, which led to his appointment as colonel of the 11th Indiana Infantry. After proving his worth, Wallace was eventually promoted to major general in 1862. After the battle of Shiloh, however, Brig. Gen. Ulysses S. Grant accused Wallace of incompetence for what he perceived as unnecessary delays in moving up some reserves that could have cost the Union the battle. Wallace was deeply hurt by this accusation (which was probably false), but he served the rest of the war with distinction. Wallace can even be credited with saving Washington, D.C., from advancing Confederate forces in 1864 by delaying them long enough for Union forces to strengthen the city's defenses. Wallace commanded a mere 5,600 troops that were defeated by Confederate General Jubal A. Early's 15,000 men, but the disruption of Early's progress saved the city, as Grant himself admitted.

Along with Lew Wallace, four other men with ties to Crawfordsville became Civil War generals. Mahlon Dickerson Manson became a captain in the 10th Indiana Infantry at the outbreak of the Civil War and was promoted to brigadier general in 1862 because of his leadership on the battlefield. Manson survived being wounded twice during the conflict, and he went on after the war to become a U.S. representative, state auditor, and finally 19th lieutenant governor of Indiana.

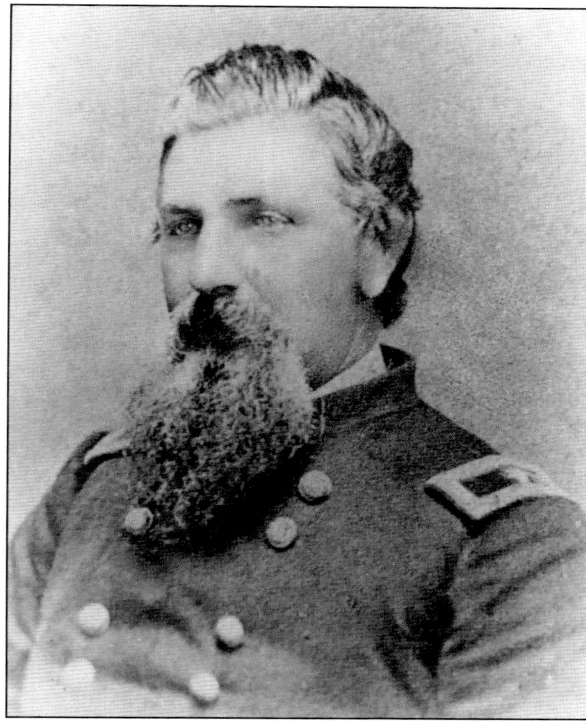

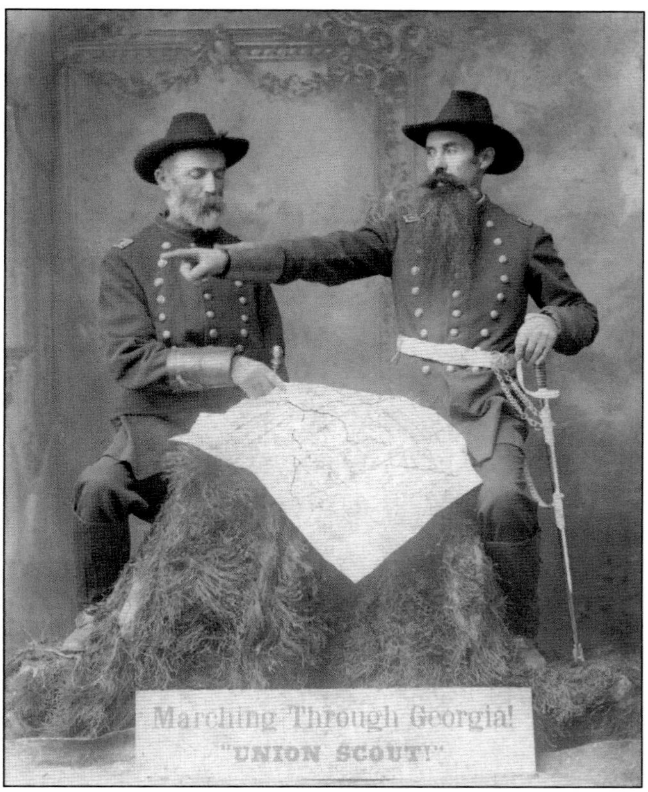

Civil War Captain Henry H. Talbot (right) and an unidentified man are pictured around a stump in a photography gallery around the time that the play *Marching through Georgia!* was staged at Crawfordsville Music Hall in February 1892. Talbot arrived in Crawfordsville a few years after the war and soon became a prominent citizen, twice serving as commander of the local Grand Army of the Republic post. Talbot passed away in 1931 at age 90.

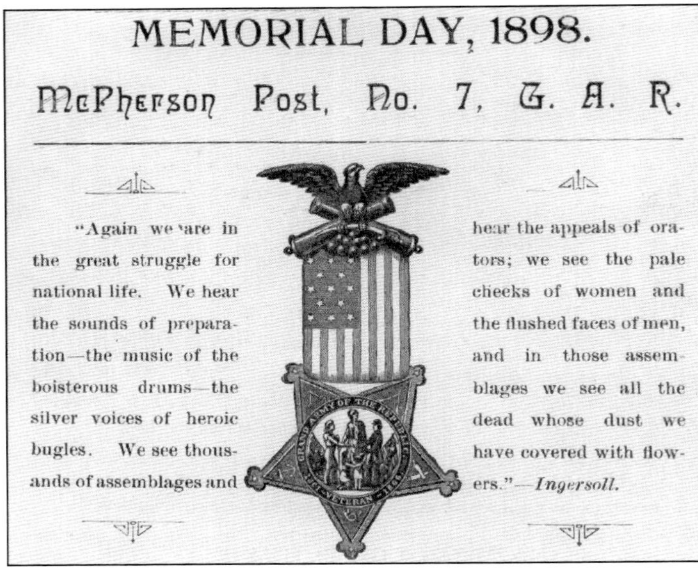

In May 1898, the Crawfordsville McPherson post of the Grand Army of the Republic prepared for its annual Memorial Day parade. The Spanish-American War had broken out a month before. The parade assembled at post headquarters (on the northwest corner of Washington and Pike Streets), where assembly was sounded at 1:30 p.m. Different columns formed (police, band, city officials), at the end of which marched the GAR members.

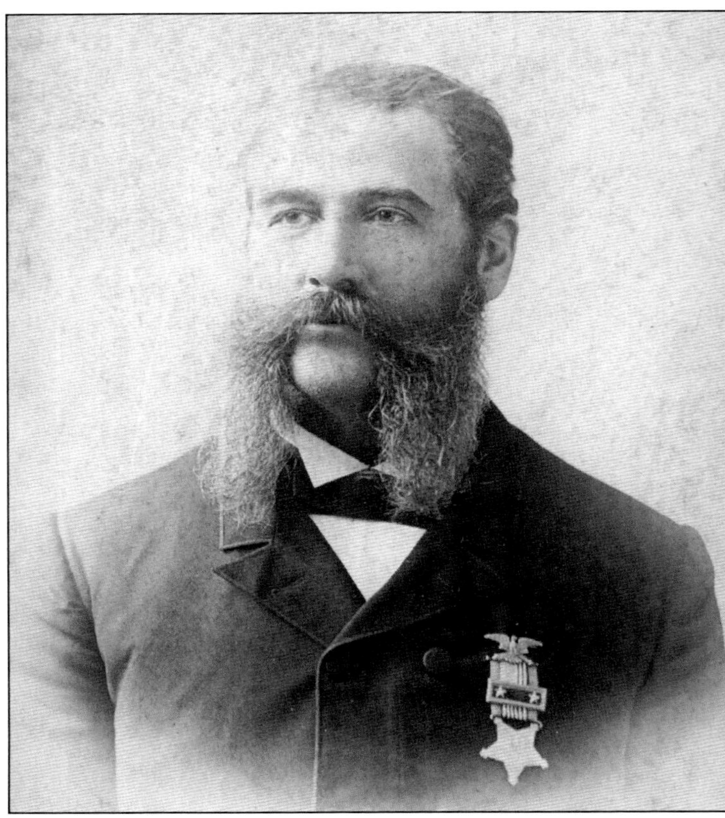

After three years as a private in the Civil War, Charles M. Travis came to Crawfordsville and studied law. He practiced with Gen. Lew Wallace before changing careers to establish a pension office, later becoming U.S. consul to Brazil during the Ulysses S. Grant administration. When the Spanish-American War broke out in 1898, Travis was quick to volunteer, becoming a major before the conflict ended. He is pictured here around 1890 with his Grand Army of the Republic medallion.

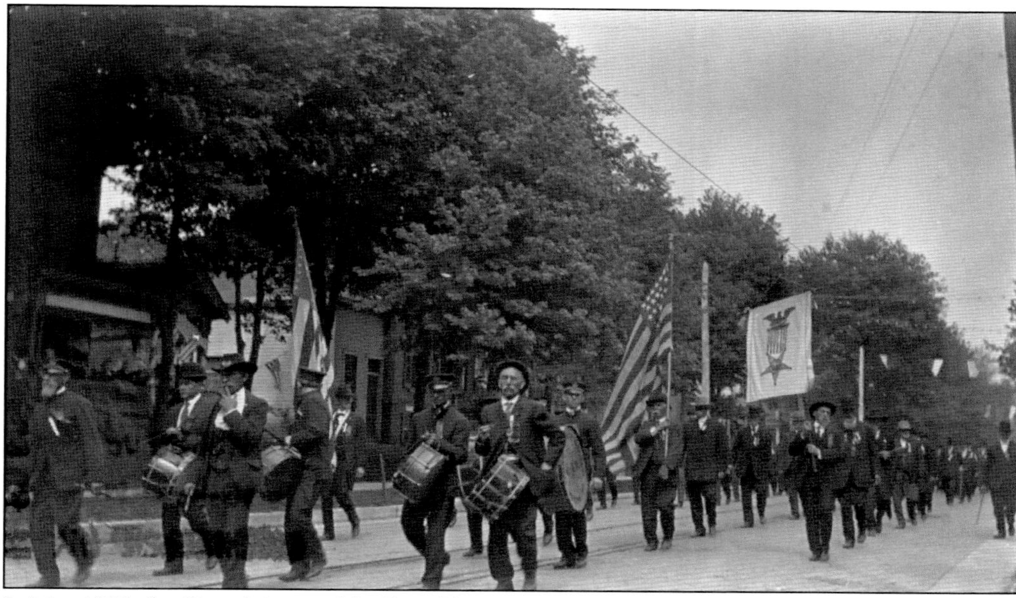

In May 1909, the Grand Army of the Republic encampment was held in Crawfordsville over several days. Activities of all sorts were planned, and veterans of several wars (the Mexican-American War, the Civil War, and the Spanish-American War) marched down Main Street (above). Charles E. Lacey took this photograph of the men passing his house at 311 West Main Street and made it into a postcard that he sent to his daughter Florence, who was attending Vassar College. The National Women's Relief Corps, an auxiliary to the GAR, was formed to perpetuate its memory. Member of the Women's Relief Corps of Crawfordsville (below), in the wagon, were ready to assist with the dinners and memorial events.

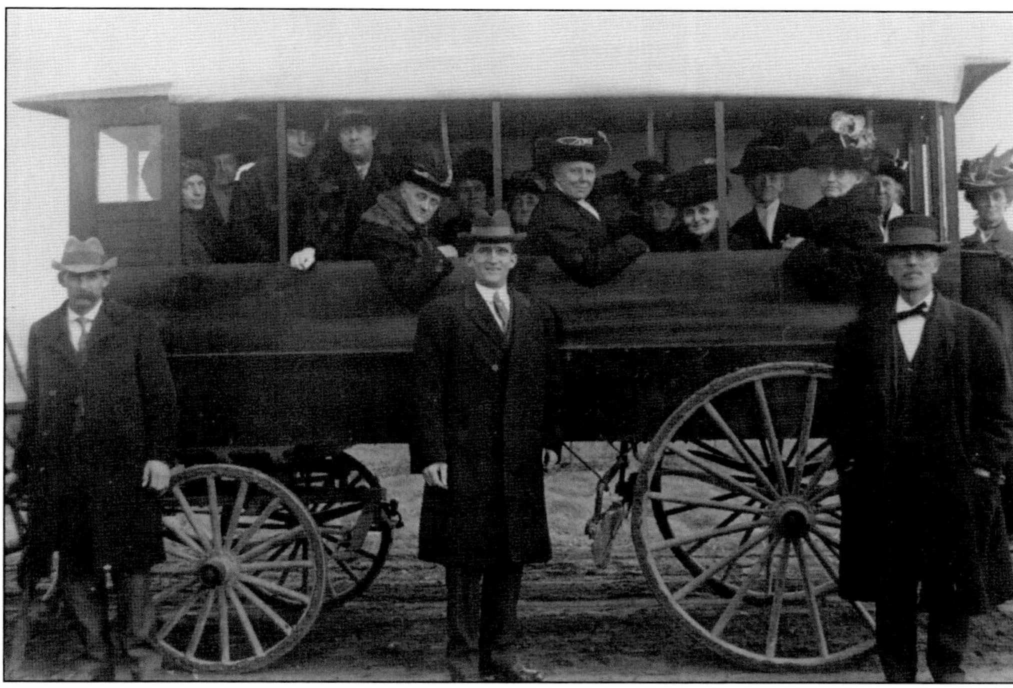

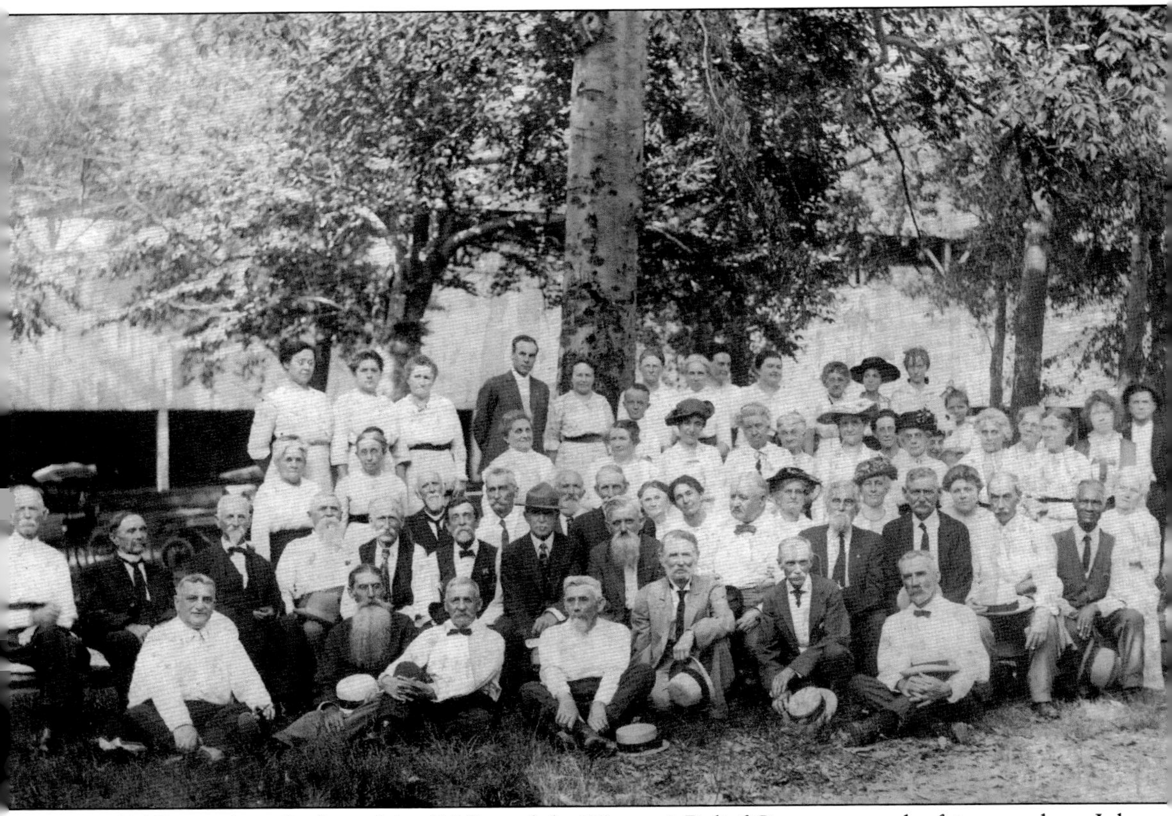

GAR members, Ladies of the GAR, and the Women's Relief Corps met at the fairgrounds on July 30, 1915, for their annual picnic. The *Crawfordsville Journal* reported, "Games were played and contests were held as though a crowd of young folks were assembled rather than a gathering of men and women who went through the troublous times of fifty years ago." Some of Crawfordsville's most influential citizens were in attendance. In the first row on the left (on the ground) sits Louis Bischof, owner of Bischof's Big Store. To the right of Bischof is Civil War veteran Capt. Henry H. Talbot (the man with the long beard). On the far right in the second row is Toliver Hawkins, who spent several years as deacon for the Second Baptist Church. When Hawkins died in 1938, the *Crawfordsville Journal* described him as "one of Crawfordsville's best known colored residents." To the left of Hawkins, with his hat on his lap, sits Dr. Edward H. Cowan. Cowan was 17 years old when he volunteered to join the Union army in 1864.

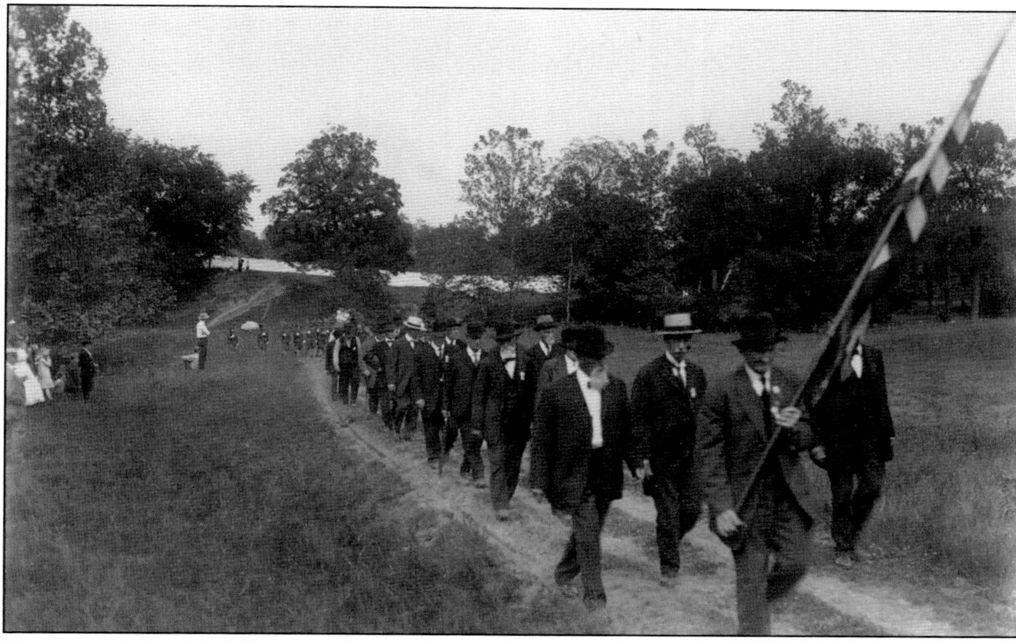

Veterans of the Civil War march proudly to their seats for the June 13, 1916, pageant held in Crawfordsville to celebrate the Indiana centennial. The Civil War ended decades earlier, but local citizens were still proud of the some 3,000 Montgomery County men who served in the conflict. Dr. Edward H. Cowan (third from right, looking at the camera) was the last surviving Civil War veteran of the county. He passed away in 1942 at age 95.

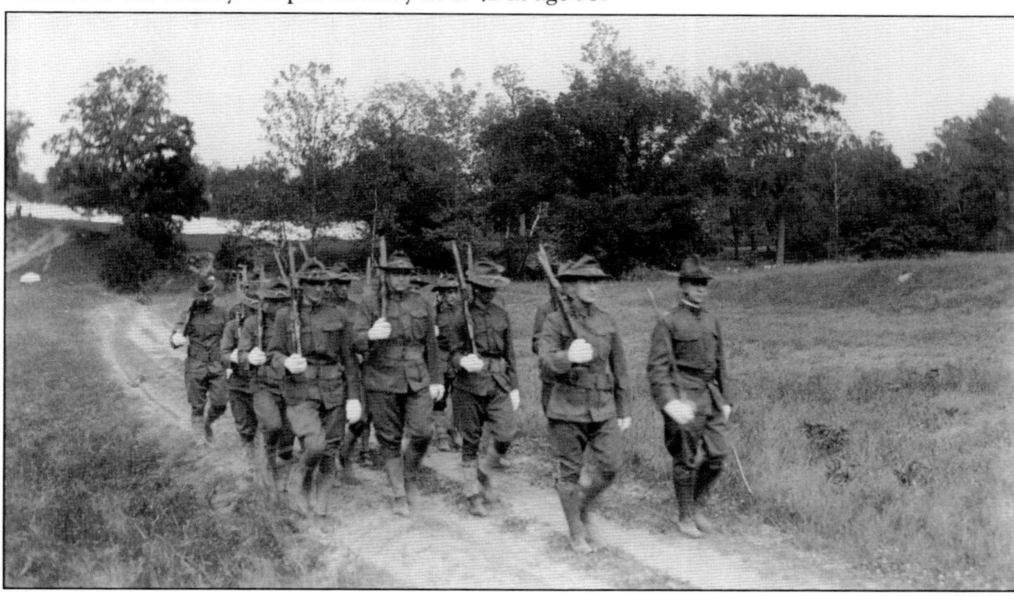

Like their counterparts of the GAR, the younger men of Company C of the 2nd Indiana National Guard march on June 13, 1916, to the grassy area where the Indiana Centennial Pageant was being held. Little did they know that in five days the guard would be mobilized to the Mexican border to aid in the continuing struggle with Pancho Villa. On June 20, 1916, the company received a rating of "very good" on its last inspection—the best in the state.

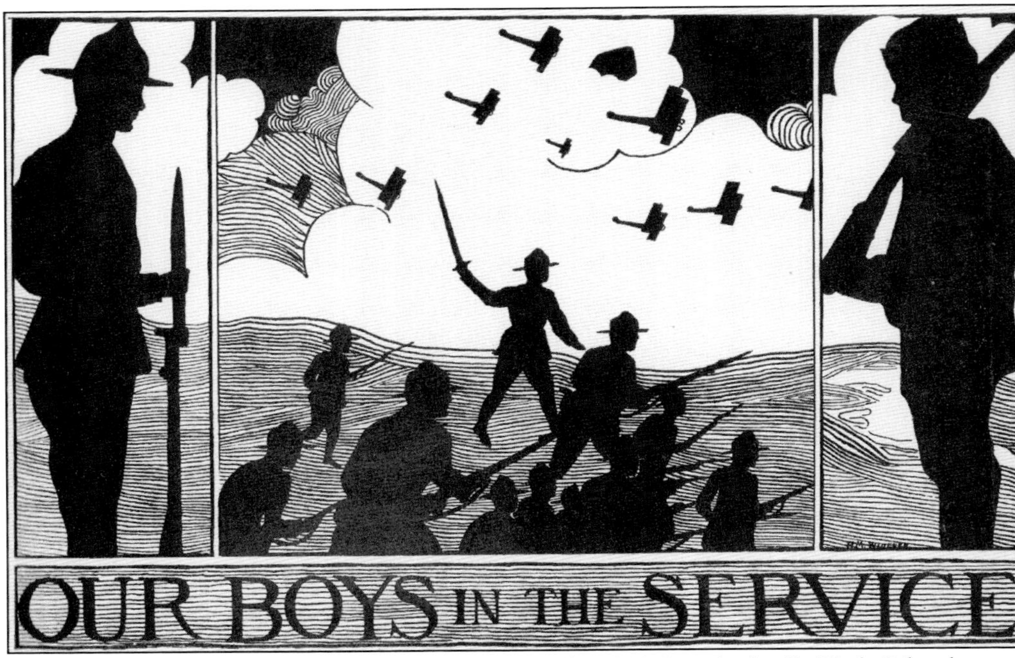

The 1918 Crawfordsville High School (CHS) *Athenian* yearbook opened with a list of the CHS men who were in the service at the time and a photograph montage of these men in uniform. The United States officially entered the war in April 1917, and within a few months U.S. soldiers were shipped to France. The publication of this yearbook honored three soldiers who died in this conflict.

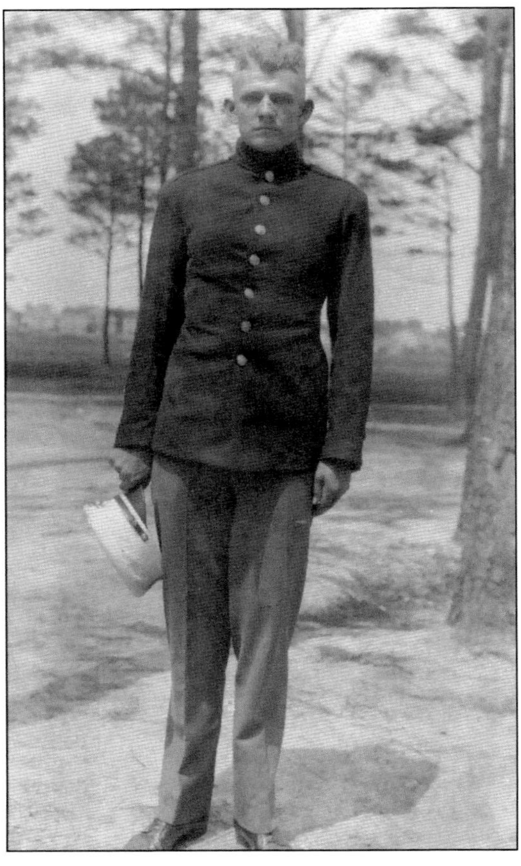

From 1918 to 1920, Frank W. Haslam served as a private with the U.S Marines on the battleship USS *Mississippi*, which was commissioned in 1917 and served until 1956. In 1926, he married Eula Mitchell in Crawfordsville and later retired after 37 years with the railroad. A 50-year member of the American Legion, he passed away in 1987. His widow donated his picture to the Carnegie Museum of Montgomery County in 2010.

Loren Barney Wray spent 30 years in the U.S. Army, serving in World War II, The Korean War, and in Vietnam before his retirement. On February 16, 1944, Wray sent this V-Mail to his parents who were living at 303 West Market Street. Wray had a fellow soldier sketch his portrait on the front of the V-Mail before it was sent.

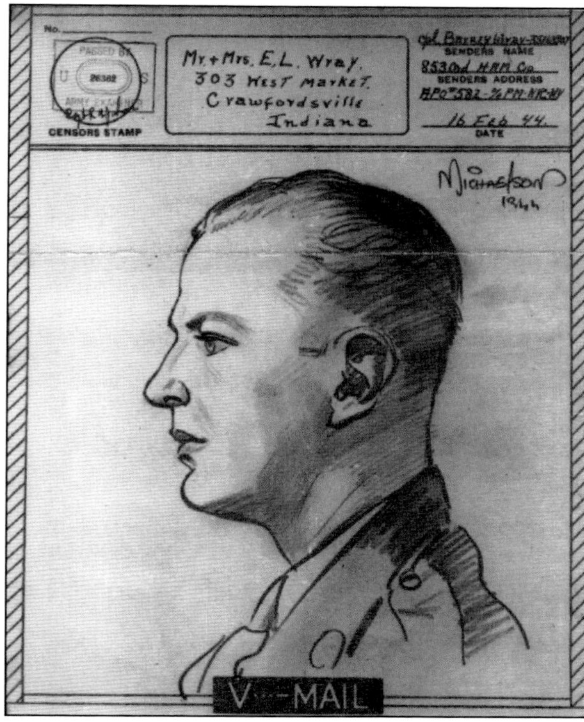

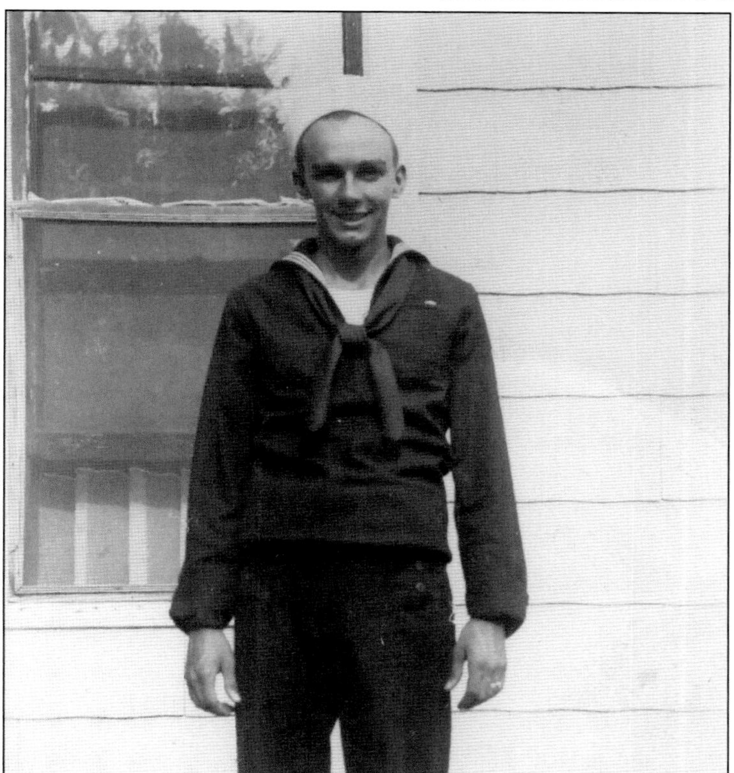

In 1943, Edward Max Fendley beams in his new uniform after returning home from basic training. Inducted at the age of 19, Fendley served aboard the aircraft carrier USS *Enterprise*, with the Central Pacific fleet, seeing action in the Gilbert and Marshall Islands and New Guinea. Fendley's older brother Donald served as a ranger in the European theater, surviving a serious wound received on D-Day.

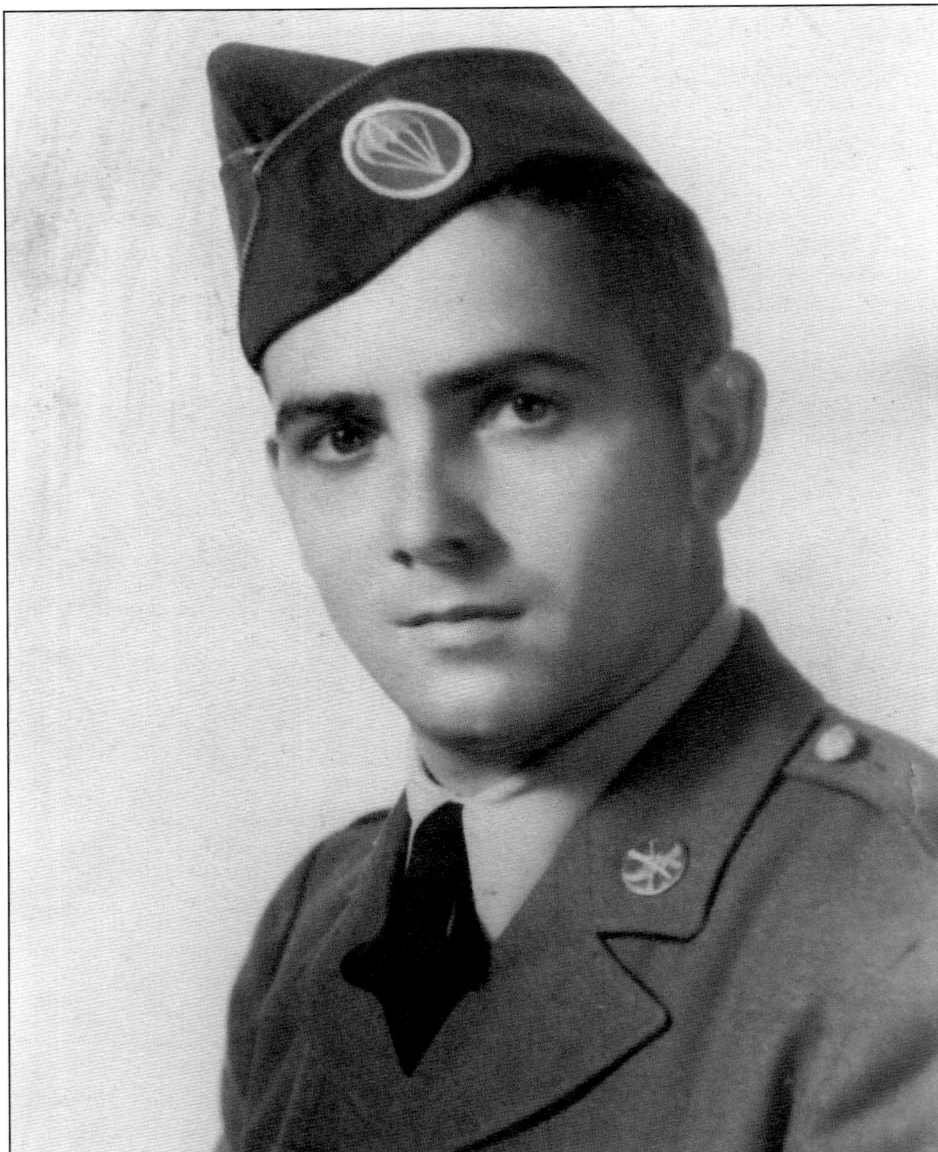

Gerald Kenneth Tilney enlisted in the U.S. Army in August 1941 and married his high school sweetheart, Jean Marie Cunningham, that December. The couple had just two weeks together before Tilney had to leave. Tilney was sent to Fort Benning, Georgia, for paratrooper training before shipping overseas in 1942. He survived several campaigns but was killed in southern France on August 25, 1944, while trying to locate enemy snipers who had pinned down his platoon. According to reports, Tilney deliberately attracted the fire of the snipers so that the platoon could move forward. For his heroic actions, he was posthumously awarded the Silver Star. In a letter dated November 10, 1944, one of Tilney's fellow soldiers remembered him as a "high lighted fellow who loved his wife and had enough will power to stay away from other women. Any time there was a church service of any kind he took time off from everything else and came after me." Gerald Kenneth Tilney was the grandson of a well-known local doctor William DeCaux Tilney (see chapter nine).

Seven

CRAWFORDSVILLE AT PLAY

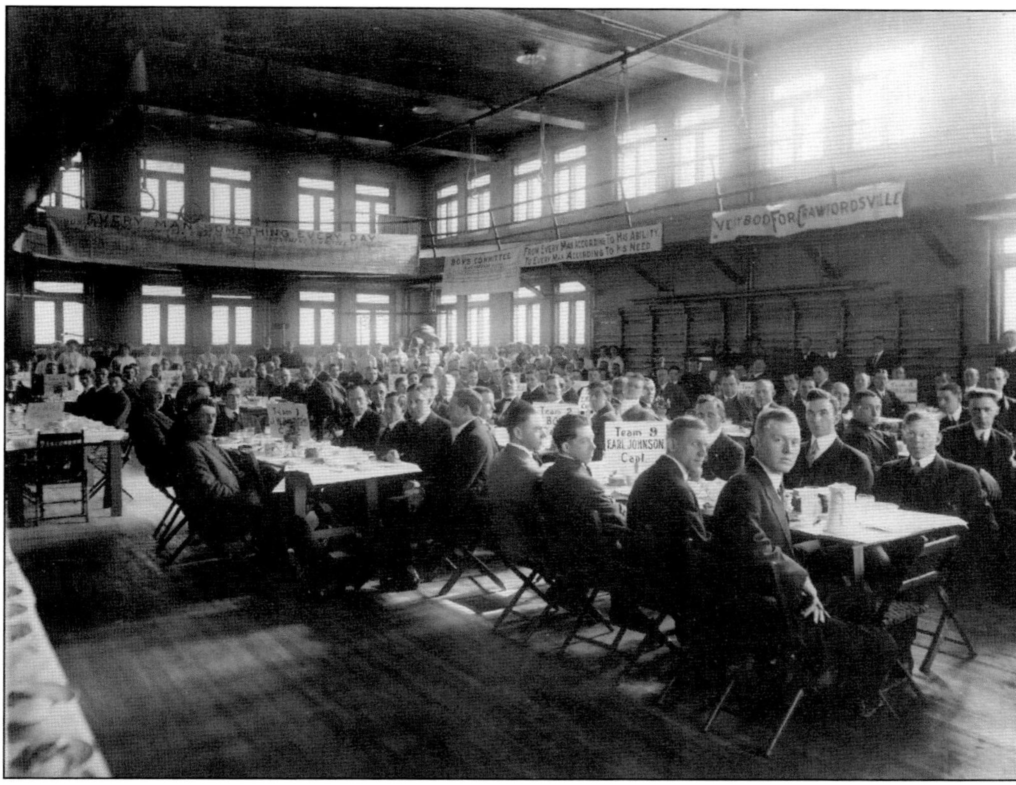

Crawfordsville's original YMCA building was constructed in 1888 on the southwest corner of Main and Washington Streets. After 20 years, the original structure was inadequate, and a campaign was begun to find a new structure. A banquet was held on January 21, 1914, comprising some 200 men divided into 20 teams. After the high school orchestra performed, toastmaster Humphrey H. Ristine explained their purpose, and campaign manager E. K. Smith instructed the teams on the raising of funds. The first campaign luncheon was held the next day (served by the ladies' auxiliary of the association), shown here, with all teams present—and with $5,535 already pledged. The *Crawfordsville Journal Review* observed that it was "the greatest spirit of enthusiasm that has ever attended a gathering of men in this city." The new YMCA did not survive the Depression, closing in 1930.

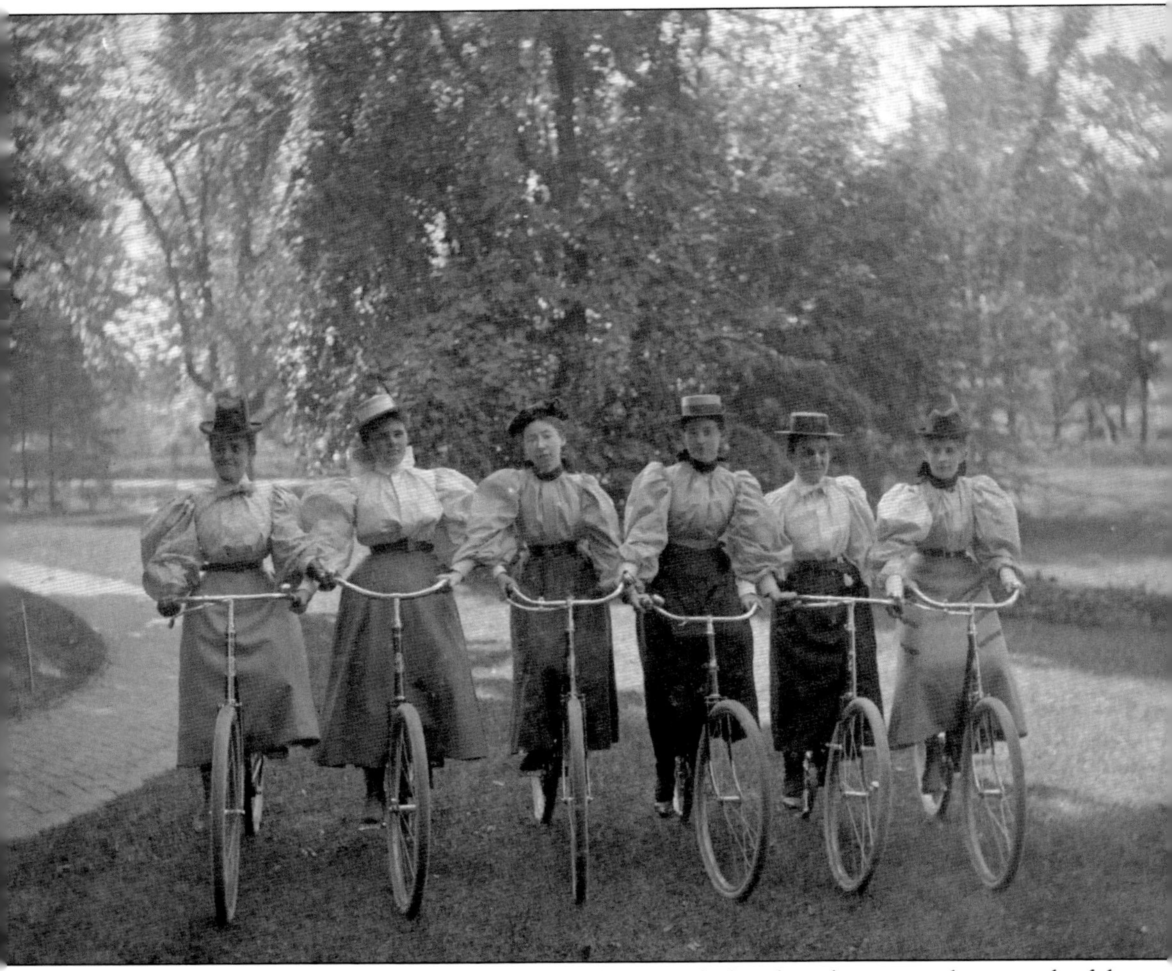

These six female cyclists, pictured here around 1905 with their bicycles, are on the grounds of the Elston Homestead, which is now part of the Lane Place Museum grounds. The cyclists include, from left to right, Maria Elston App, Margaret Noble Wallace, Mary Campbell Crane, Ethel Ronthaler McCain, Mary Elston Tullis (sister of Maria), and Rose Campbell Anderson. The women have interlocked their arms in order to remain upright and steady for the photograph. At that time, bicycle riding was a growing activity that sometimes competed with pedestrians for sidewalk space. Riding on sidewalks was prohibited by city ordinance, however, for safety reasons. The *Crawfordsville Weekly Review* of April 10, 1908, in anticipation of the summer season, reminded readers that the ordinance would be strictly enforced and that violators had been arrested in the past. The paper continued to state that "it is not an uncommon occurrence to see some person walking on the sidewalk be forced to step to one side while some bicycle fiend goes scorching by."

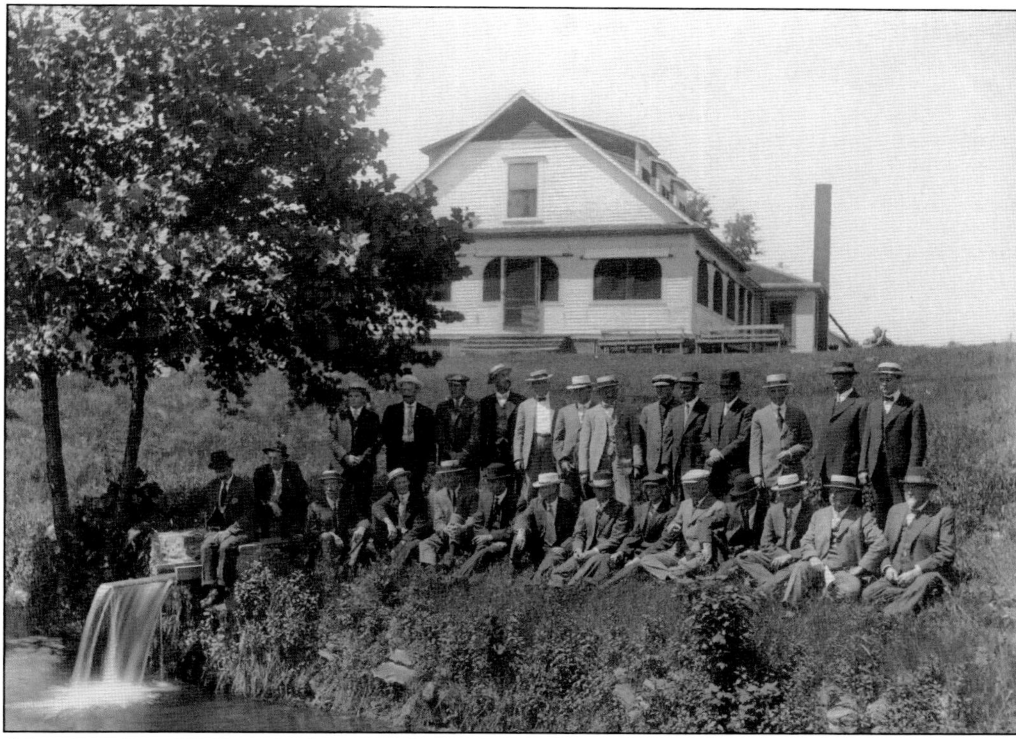

After Gen. Lew Wallace died in 1905, his widow, Susan Elston Wallace, offered to sell his estate. Crawfordsville acquired the land, which the general had dedicated much time and money developing. Men are posed here around 1906 in front of the Crawfordsville Country Club Clubhouse next to the spring that feeds the lake. The country club continues to occupy this spot today, although the original clubhouse (Wallace's summer home) burned to the ground in 2005.

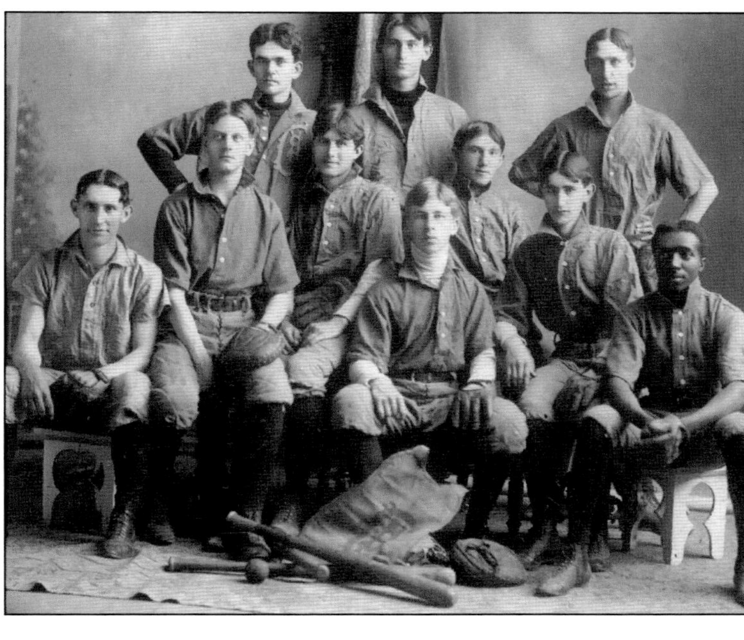

The Crawfordsville High School baseball team is pictured in 1901. Timothy Davis (front row, far right) graduated that year—one of three African Americans who graduated in a class of 20 students. The *Utopian* (High School Annual of 1902) praised the 1901 squad: "The four essentials to good base ball playing—energy, tact, perseverance and good judgment—seem to have been prevalent among the entire team."

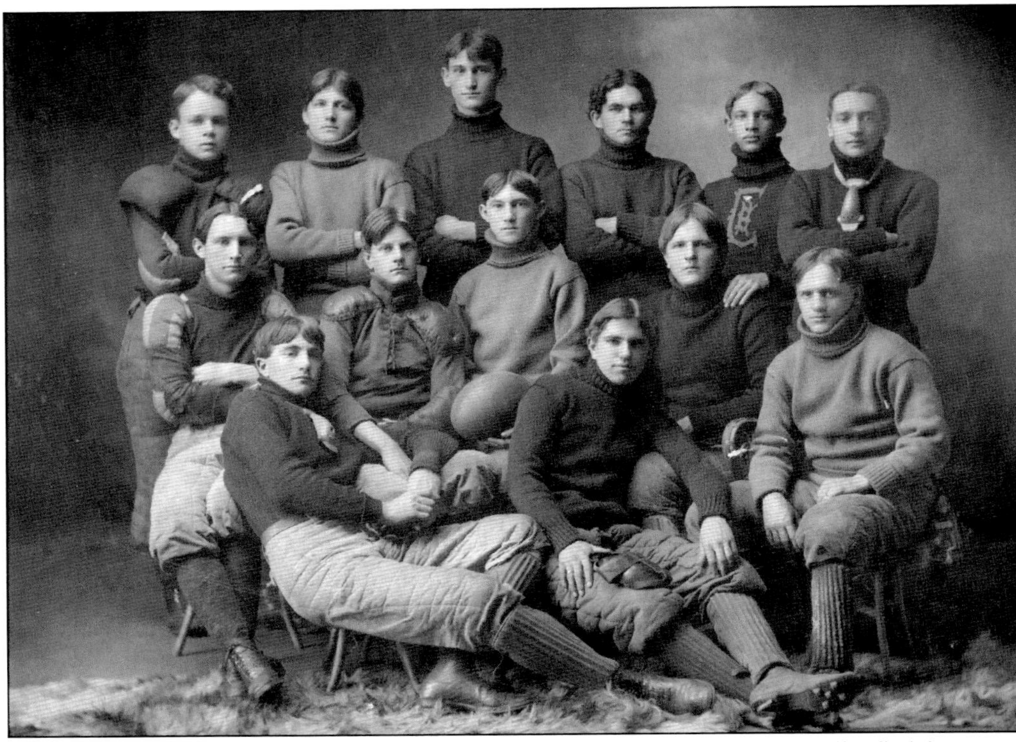

The Crawfordsville High School football team poses in 1901. Football was still a fledgling sport and often quite dangerous. From left to right are (first row) John Sidener and Ward Williams; (second row) Harry Richard, John Shepherd, Glenn Henry, Rome Williams, and Carl Alfrey; (third row) Ralph Wicks, Robert Irons, Will Sprow, Niles Haton, Frank Symmes, and Frank Glover. Irons (1903) was the manager and quarterback.

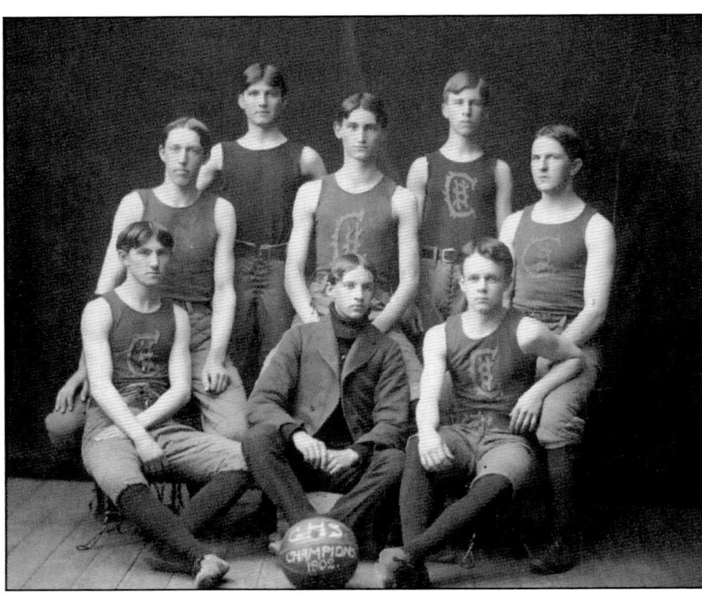

Crawfordsville High School played its first basketball game in 1900, and this "third" sport (after baseball and football) has grown in popularity ever since. The Crawfordsville High School basketball team poses here in 1901–1902. From left to right they are (first row) Glenn Henry, Frank Symmes, and Ralph Wicks; (second row) Heber Banks, Will Sprow, and Rome Williams; (third row) Robert Irons and Harter Williams. This team never lost to another high school team.

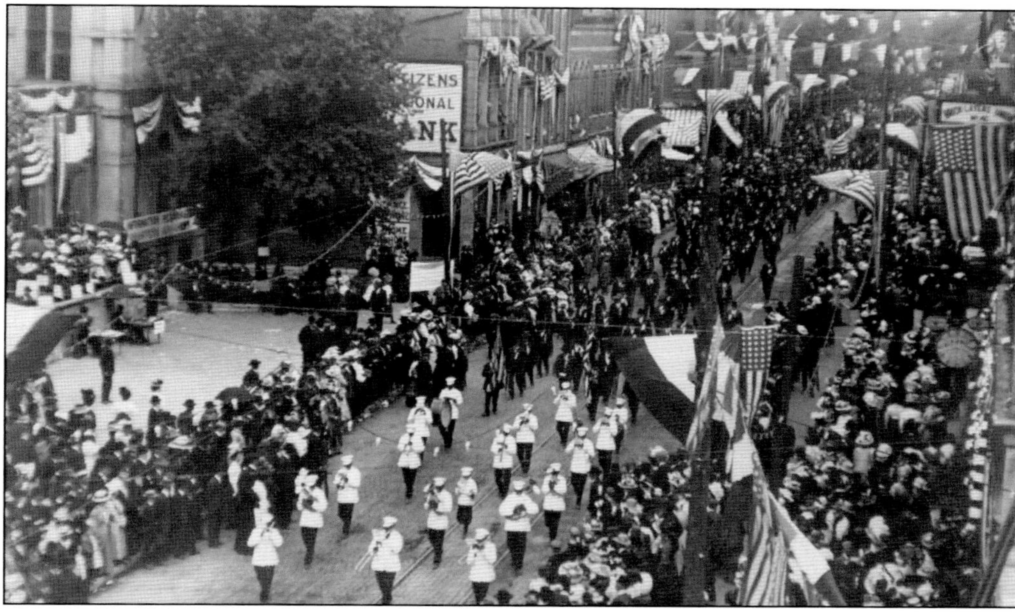

Interesting events in Crawfordsville were commemorated in postcards. This postcard shows a parade for the GAR encampment in 1909. The Citizen's National Bank appears in the background behind the courthouse, and the interurban tracks laid by the Indianapolis and Northwestern Traction Company can be seen underfoot. The band marches west on Main Street past the courthouse. This African American band often played at public functions.

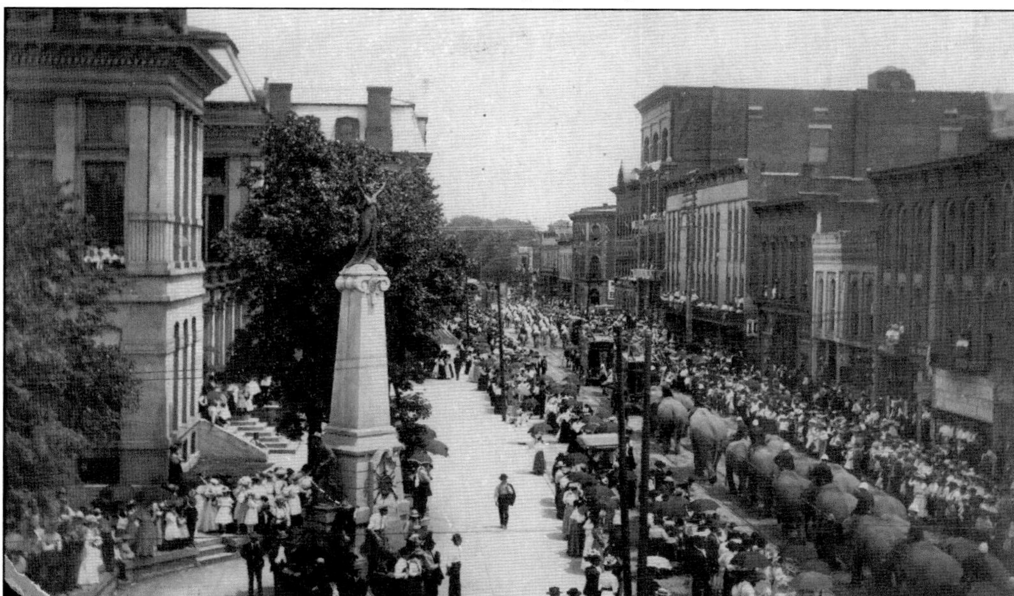

Crawfordsville was a major rail hub at the beginning of the 20th century and was often visited by traveling troupes and shows. Here the Ringling Brothers Circus parades into the city, heading east on Main Street. The Crawfordsville courthouse is to the left, along with the Soldiers and Sailors Monument that was dedicated in 1906. A large crowd thrills to the exotic elephants that are just entering East Main Street.

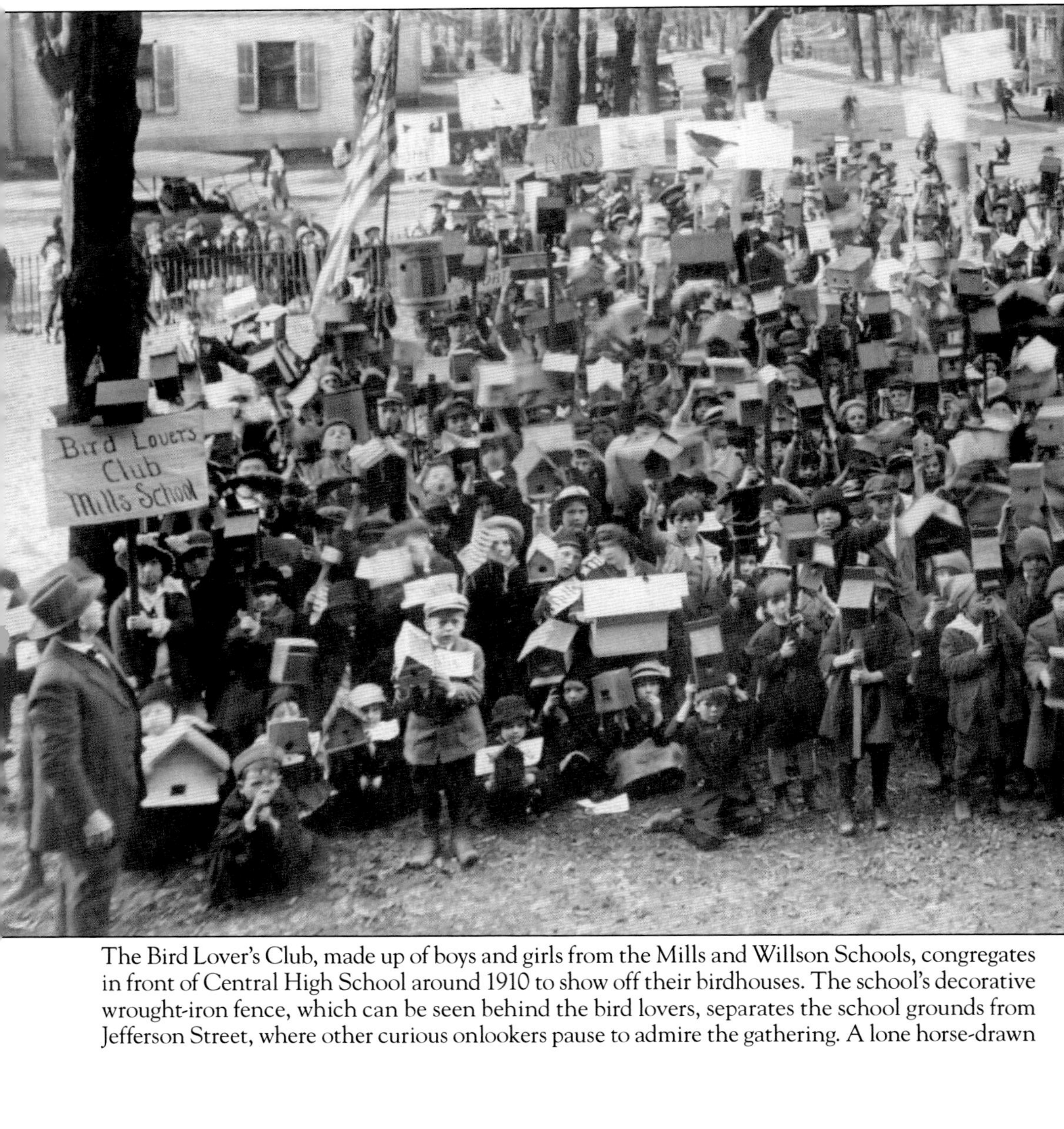

The Bird Lover's Club, made up of boys and girls from the Mills and Willson Schools, congregates in front of Central High School around 1910 to show off their birdhouses. The school's decorative wrought-iron fence, which can be seen behind the bird lovers, separates the school grounds from Jefferson Street, where other curious onlookers pause to admire the gathering. A lone horse-drawn

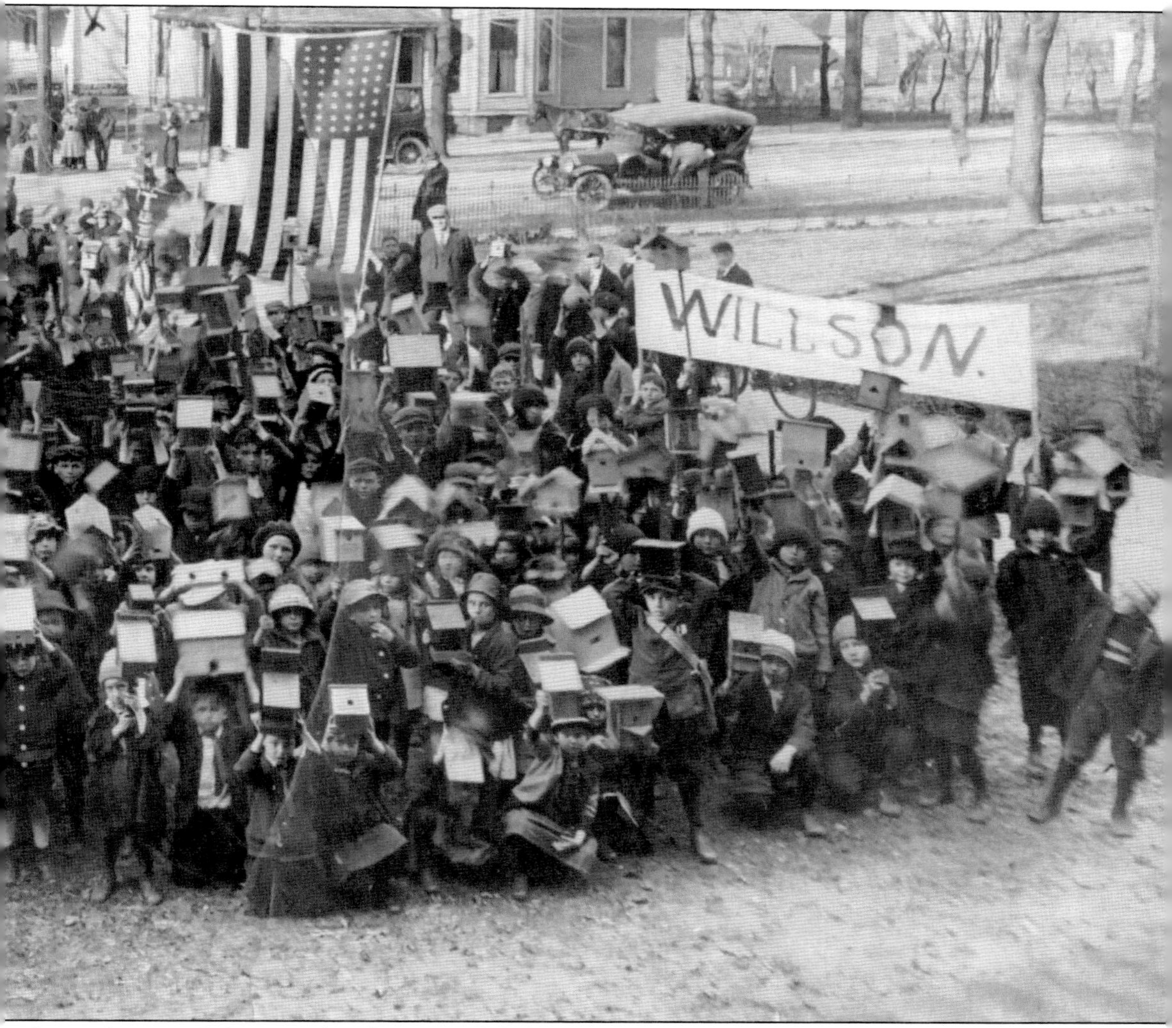

buggy (upper right) proves that the automobile has not yet taken over the streets of Crawfordsville entirely. More than 100 children are holding up their birdhouses, along with signs in support of their feathered friends ("protect the birds") and signs for the school groups (Mills students are on the left and Willson students on the right).

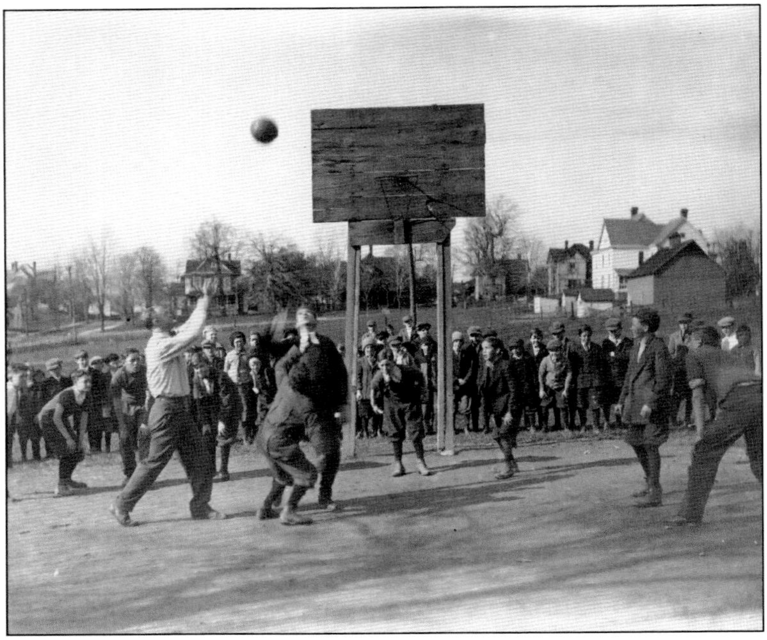

Basketball has always been a popular local sport no matter what the conditions. Here is a recess game, around 1910, whose action was captured in what appears to be mid-shot (or awkward jump ball). The game is taking place on the grounds of the Tuttle Grade School (looking west), with student players and a teacher serving as referee. Tuttle Middle School occupies this spot now, having replaced the original building in 1960.

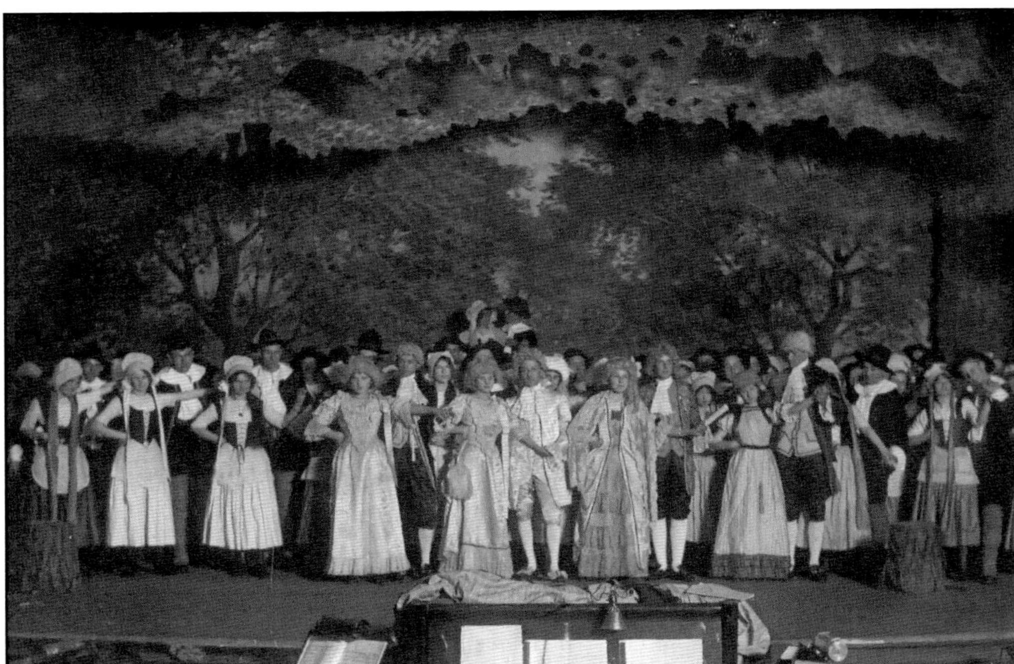

On April 2, 1912, a group of high school students presented the three-act comic operetta *Sylvia* at the Music Hall (later occupied by the Strand Theater) on 122 South Green Street. This photograph has all the actors on stage for "The Final Chorus." The performance was sold out, and the play was very successful critically and financially (it cleared more than $200, which was not a small sum for 1912).

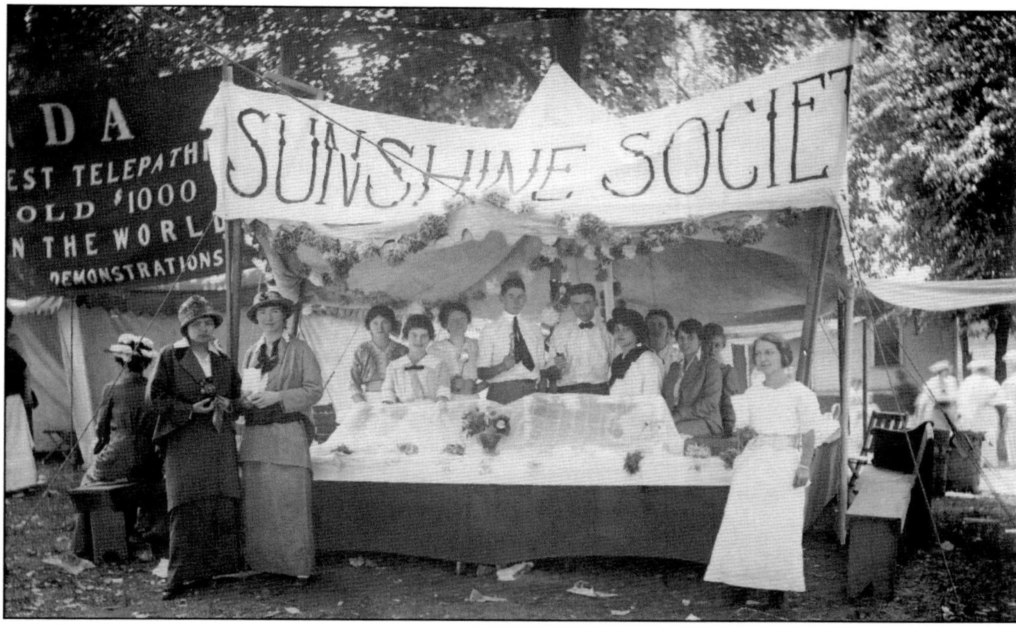

The Sunshine Society of Crawfordsville High School shows off its booth at the 1914 Montgomery County Fair. All the girls in the school comprised the 198-member society, seeking to bring "sunshine into the lives of people who most need it," according to the 1914 *Athenian* yearbook. Meetings, programs, and charity work continued year-round, benefitting the "poor and lonely" and bringing "its members to a higher and purer standard of womanhood." The Sunshine Society is still active today. The girl fifth from the right (with hat) is Maurine Dallas Watkins, the woman who wrote *Chicago*.

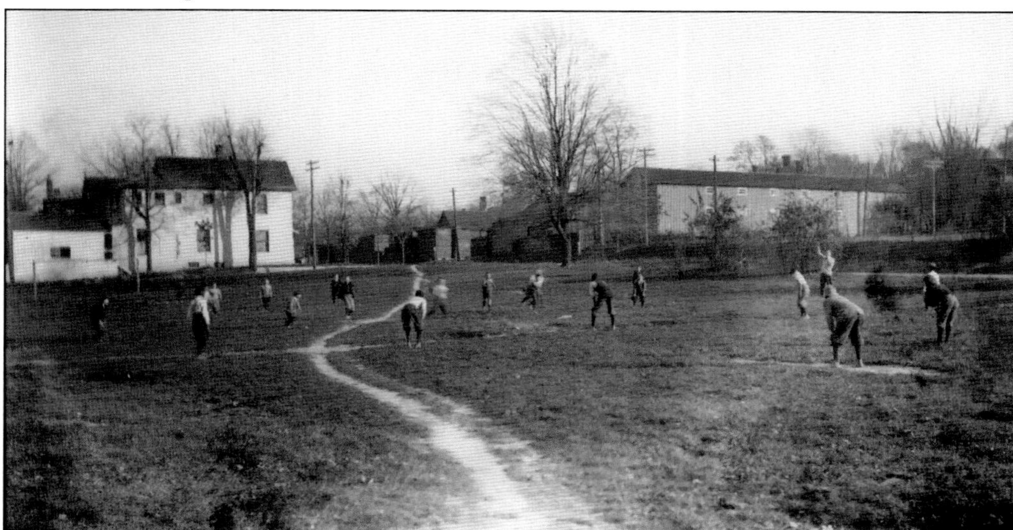

This photograph reveals a boys' game in progress around 1915. An adult acting as referee is standing with one hand raised in the air to the right side of the image. The grounds are that of Tuttle Grade School, which were located in approximately the same place as the current Tuttle Middle School fields. It appears that the African American students of Lincoln School are on a supervised visit to play with the students of Tuttle School.

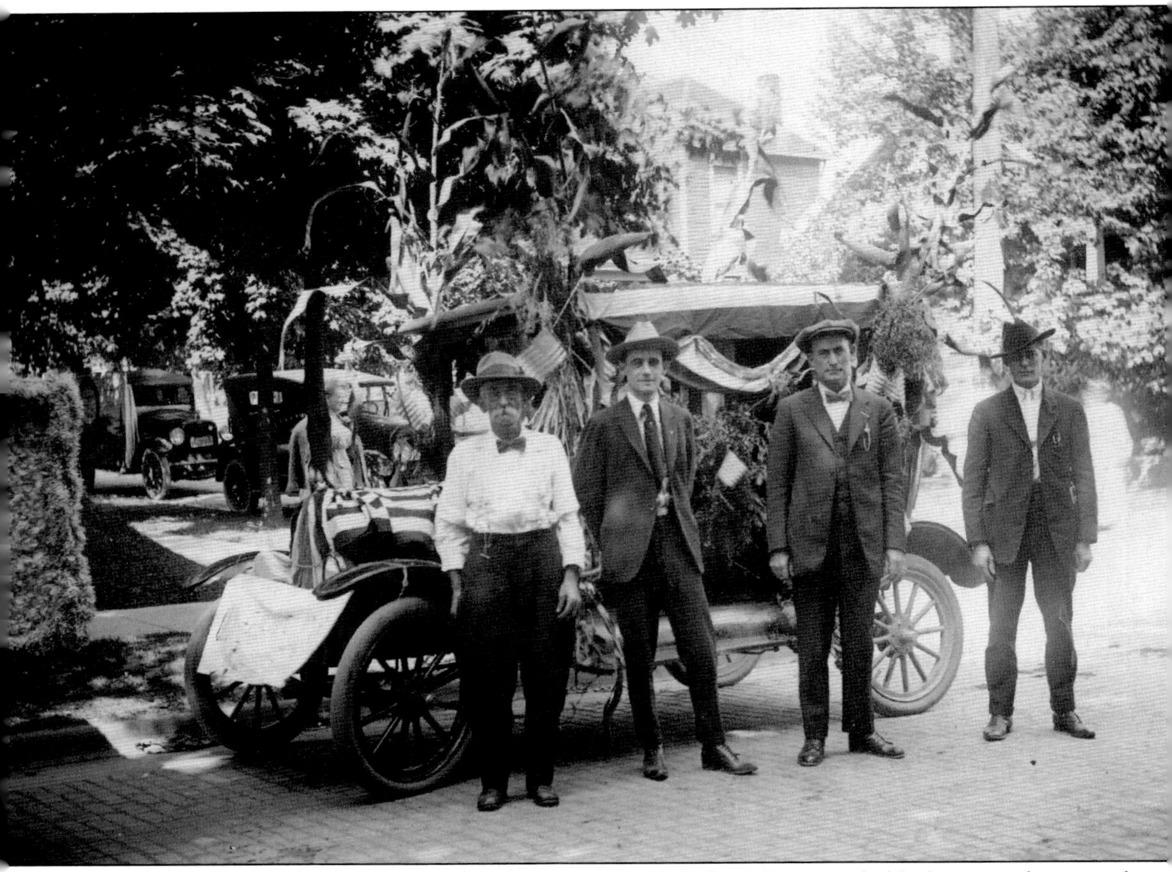

Four men show off a car decorated with corn stalks and other plants, probably for a parade, around 1915. Sam C. Snyder is on the far left, and Dud Maloney (a lawyer) is second from the left; the other two men are unidentified. In 1905, Crawfordsville had 50 miles of cement sidewalks to only 5 miles of paved streets. A. W. Bowen's *History of Montgomery County*, published in 1913, observed that automobiles "had come to stay. . . . They are now commoner here than were carriages in an early day." With cars came fast driving—to the point that the National Horse Thief Association of the county, no longer occupied by tracking down horse thieves, was involved in "bringing to justice men who run automobiles faster than speed limit and run over persons and seek to escape by going on at full speed without stopping to care for those they may have run down."

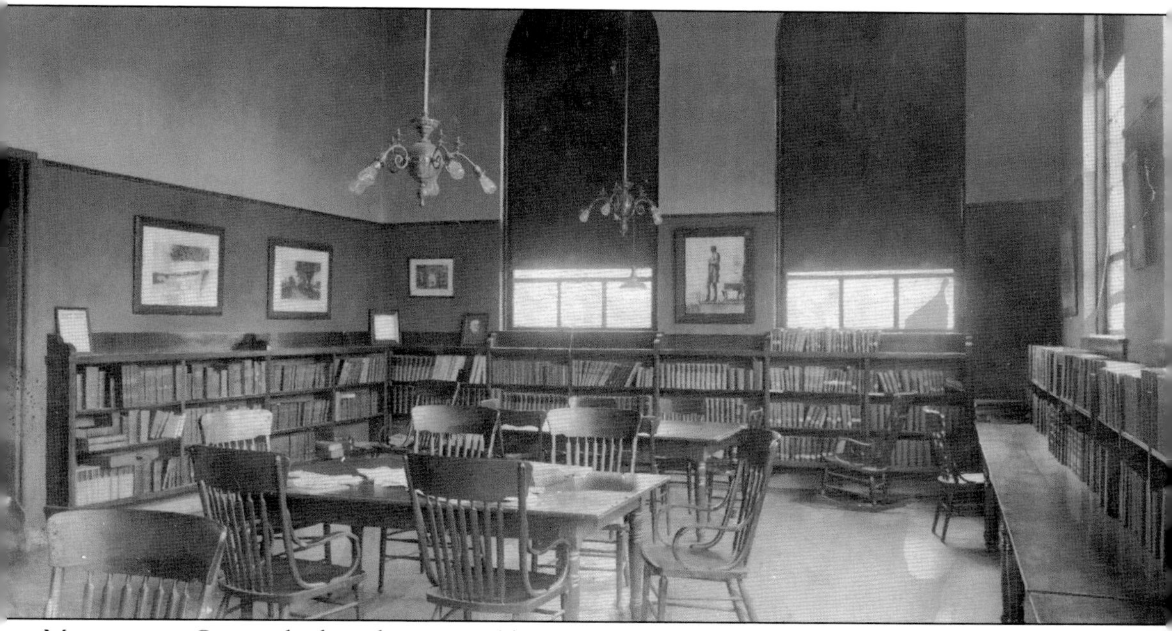

Montgomery County had a subscription library as early as 1827, but at the start of the 20th century Crawfordsville's citizens organized to petition philanthropist Andrew Carnegie for the funds necessary to construct a true public library. The Carnegie Library, built at a total cost of $26,600, was opened in July 1902 and immediately filled some of the cultural needs of the city. It was available to the public from 9:00 a.m. to 12:00 p.m. and then from 2:00 to 5:30 p.m. and 7:00 to 8:30 p.m. At the dedication ceremony on July 29, Rev. Clarence Wilson of the Center Presbyterian Church was quoted by the *Crawfordsville Daily Journal*, saying that "only those books which are positively and undoubtedly immoral should be excluded from the library and no effort should be made to suppress by exclusion any social, political or religious heresies. The people should be free to pick and choose for themselves." This c. 1915 photograph shows the north reading room, whose windows faced Washington Street and the Masonic Temple (today this room is the Sports and Popular Culture Gallery of the Carnegie Museum of Montgomery County).

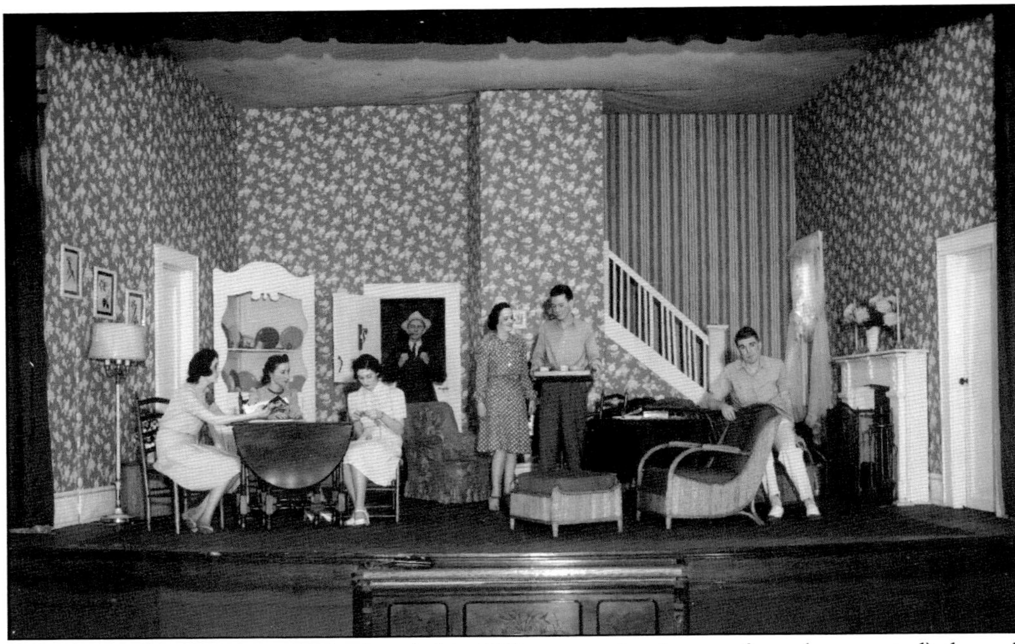

Crawfordsville's Dramatic Club, founded in 1897, was active (except for a short period) through the 1950s. Because membership was limited by the votes of the membership committee, a waiting list existed for vacancies. The list of its members for any year is full of well-known local names. In 1941, the club presented *Penny Wise*. The renowned cartoonist and future mayor (1971–1975) of Crawfordsville, Dave Gerard, can be seen to the far right on the stage.

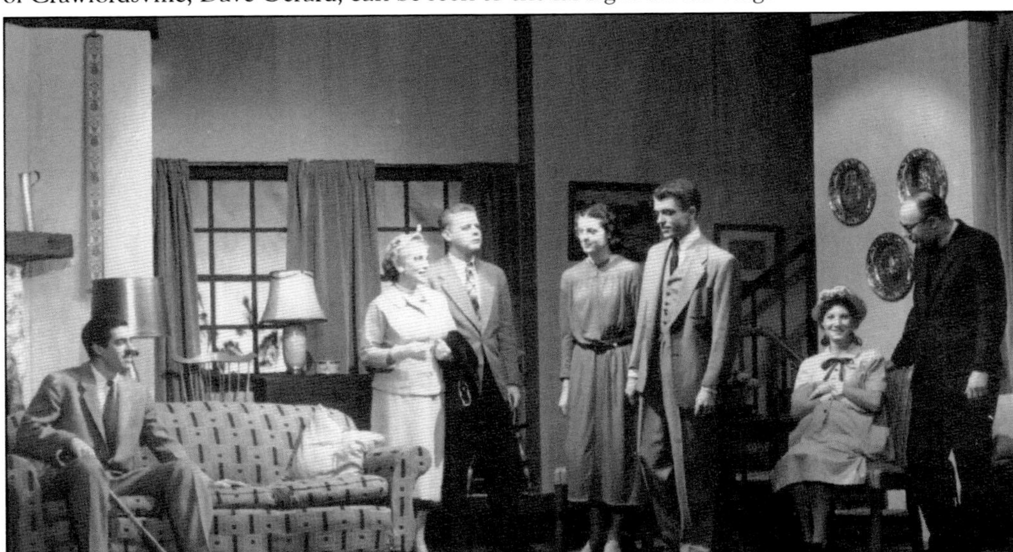

The Dramatic Club's cast of *Enchanted Cottage* by Pinero is caught here on stage during a February 17, 1957, performance. The actors are, from left to right, John S. Long, Catharine W. Evans, Paul C. McKinney, Mary Cornett, Charles Scott, Barbara Walters, and Herbert Lederer. Paul McKinney, a 1952 Wabash graduate, later became dean of students at the college from 1981 to 1993, where he also taught for 47 years.

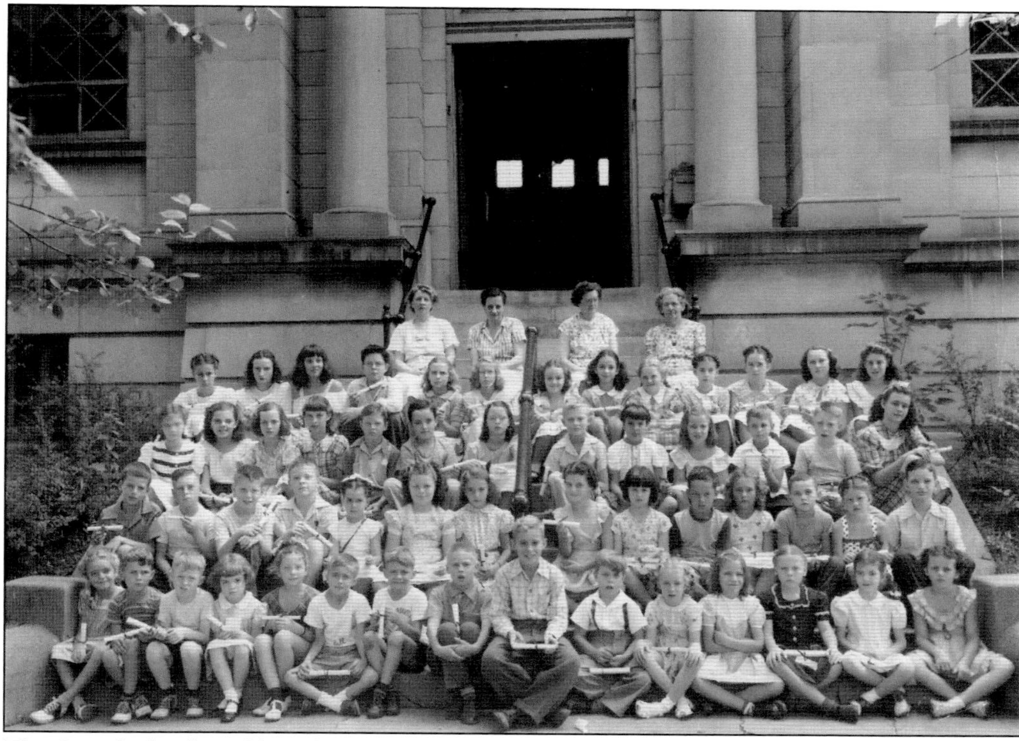

The Crawfordsville Public Library's Vacation Reading Club of 1947 ran from June 10 to August 30. Members in grades one through eight were given a list of 50 age-appropriate books and earned a red star for each book read. Ten red stars earned a place on the gold star honor roll and a diploma at the end of the summer. By the end of June, 145 children had already joined. The diploma members are pictured here on the steps of the library.

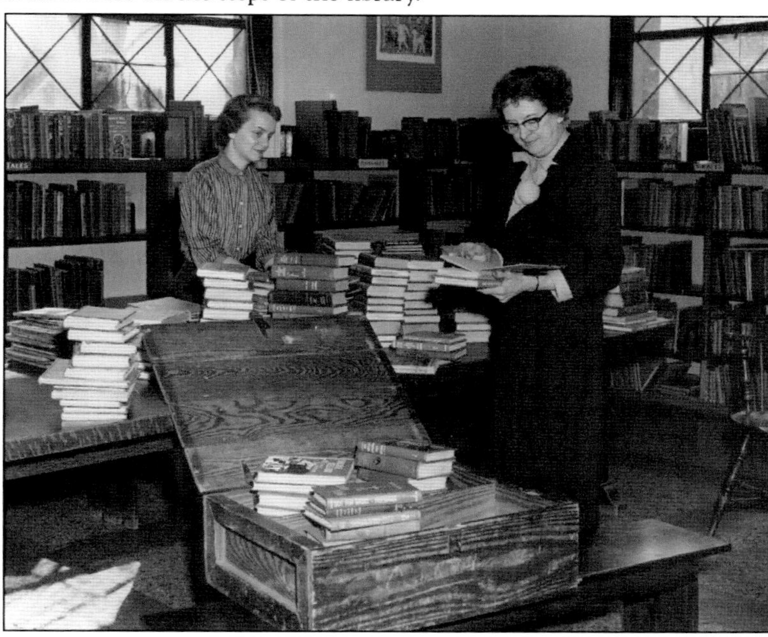

Mrs. Mary Scott (left) and Miss Elisabeth Molony of the Crawfordsville Public Library sort books in March 1955 to send to local classrooms. The library allowed teachers in Crawfordsville schools to borrow books for their classes and returned after six weeks. The previous year, teachers used more than 5,000 public library books to supplement their classroom materials.

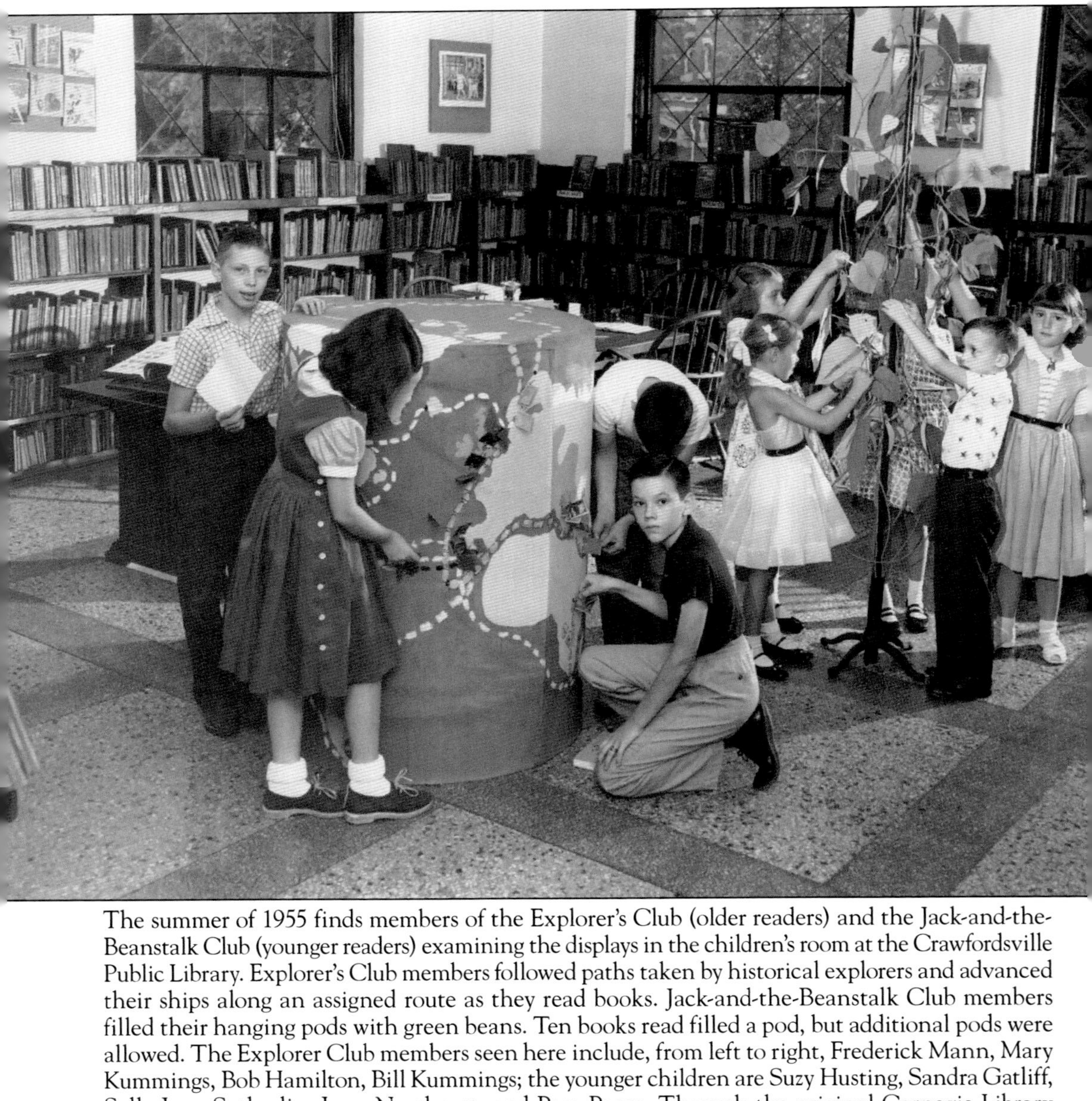

The summer of 1955 finds members of the Explorer's Club (older readers) and the Jack-and-the-Beanstalk Club (younger readers) examining the displays in the children's room at the Crawfordsville Public Library. Explorer's Club members followed paths taken by historical explorers and advanced their ships along an assigned route as they read books. Jack-and-the-Beanstalk Club members filled their hanging pods with green beans. Ten books read filled a pod, but additional pods were allowed. The Explorer Club members seen here include, from left to right, Frederick Mann, Mary Kummings, Bob Hamilton, Bill Kummings; the younger children are Suzy Husting, Sandra Gatliff, Sally Jean Sutherlin, Jerry Northcutt, and Pam Poore. Through the original Carnegie Library glass windows can be seen the Wabash Avenue Presbyterian Church on the corner of Wabash Avenue and Washington Street. The beautiful terrazzo floor of the library has been restored and is much admired now in the Carnegie Museum of Montgomery County, which has occupied the building since 2007.

Eight

Town and Gown

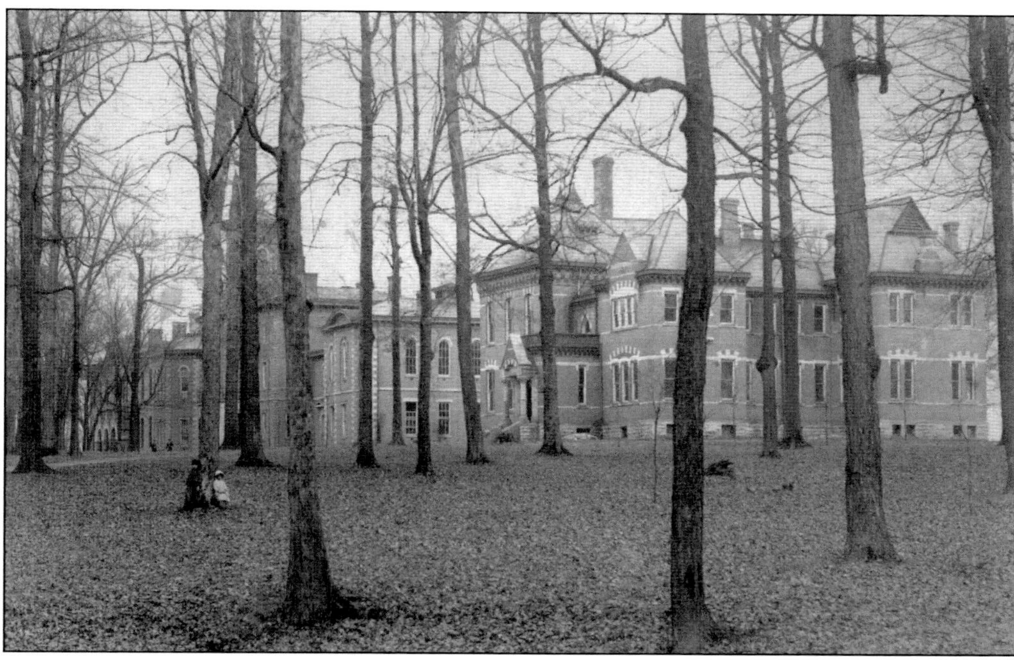

A group of Presbyterian ministers founded Wabash College on November 21, 1832. The next day a group of these men knelt in the snow to conduct a dedication service. Caleb Mills became the first faculty member in 1833, and in December of that year he opened The Wabash Teachers Seminary and Manual Labor College with 12 students. Although Mills was a Presbyterian minister, Wabash College has always been independent and nonsectarian and today is one of the few all-men's liberal-arts colleges in the country. From an original building on the corner of Blair Street and Lane Avenue, the college relocated to its present site. In this photograph, taken at the end of the 19th century, two girls pause near Peck Hall, the original science building. To the left is Center Hall, which is still in use. This area eventually became the arboretum, which contains nearly 90 species of native plants.

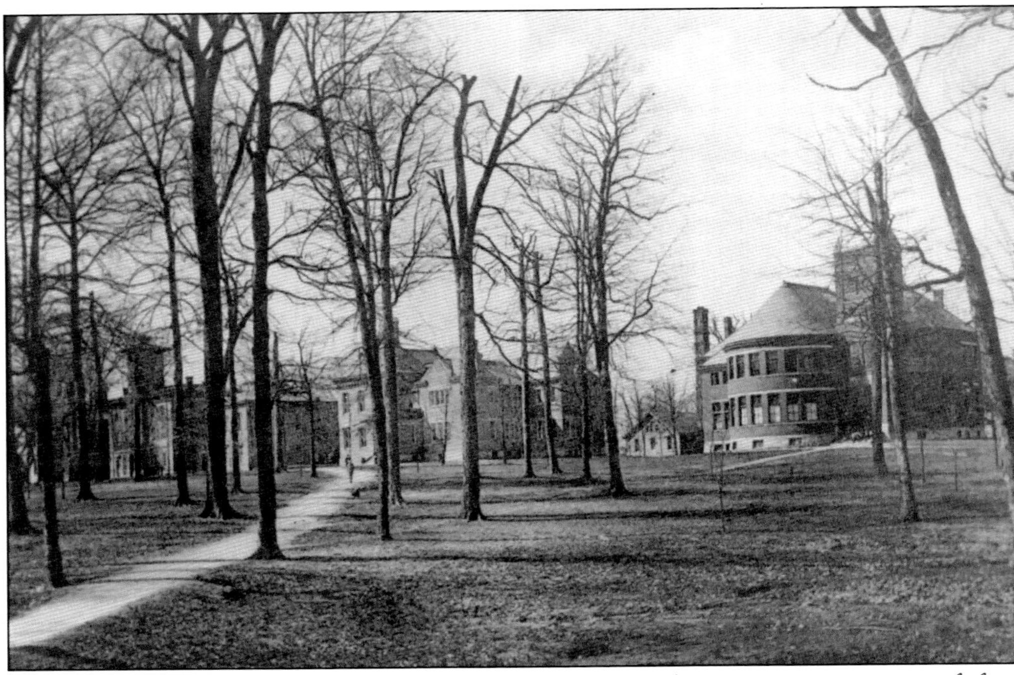

Yandes Hall (above) was completed in 1890 as the Wabash Library. It was a generous gift from Simon Yandes, an alumnus and trustee of the college. The main entrance was in the tower and is partially obscured by trees in this c. 1900 photograph, but the students lounging on its steps can clearly be seen. To the left of Yandes Hall stands Peck Hall, and to the left of Peck Hall is Center Hall. From the front of Yandes Hall (below) the view of the entrance is again blocked by foliage, but the worn path leading to its door seems well traveled. In 1959, when the Lilly Library was completed, Yandes became the home for the modern languages and art departments. In 1995, Yandes was extensively remodeled to become the Detchon Center thanks to a gift from Irwin Lee Detchon, a local resident and 1923 Wabash graduate.

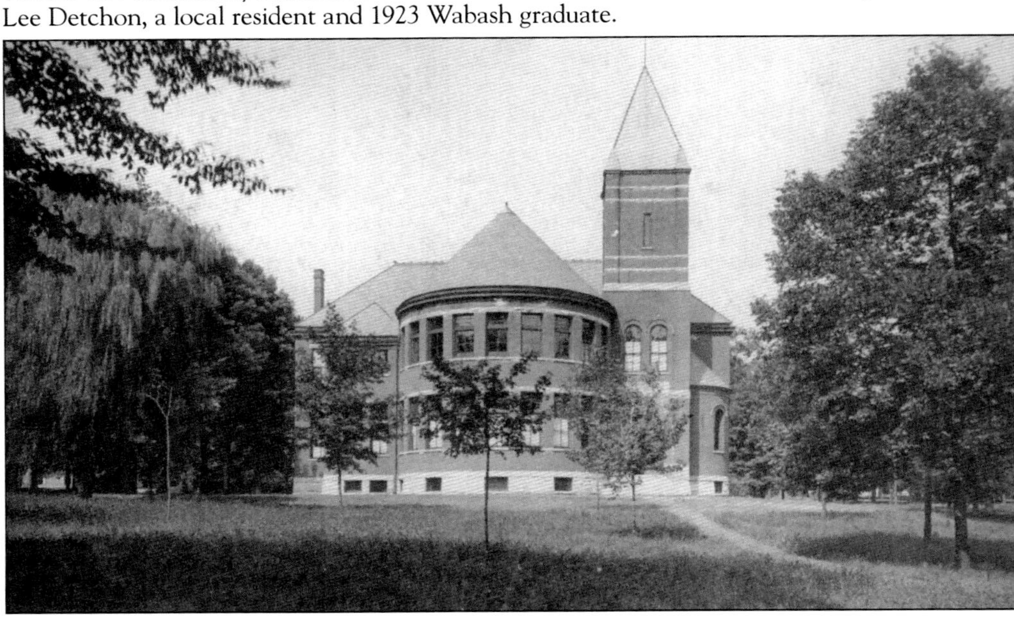

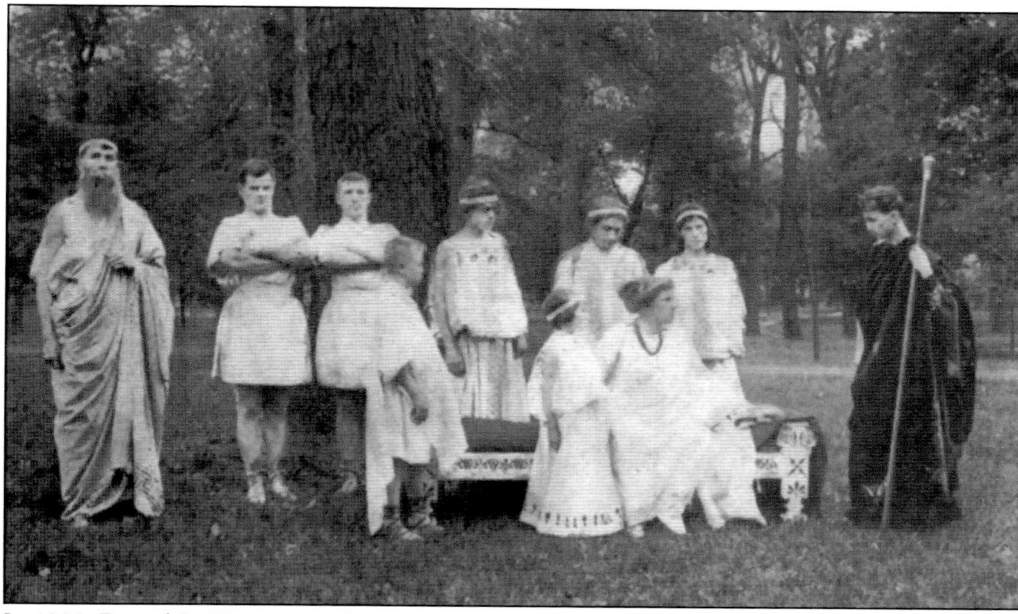

In 1908, Daniel D. Hains, a professor of Greek, was concerned about the decline of enrollment in his field. To encourage Greek studies, he decided to present an English translation of *Oedipus Rex* by Sophocles outside on the south campus using a natural amphitheater (close to where the Martindale dormitory is currently located). Encouraged by the play's success, Hains continued to put on a classical Greek drama annually through 1915. The postcard above is of a group of actors who posed to advertise the 1910 production of *Alcestis* by Euripides. The performance took place on June 14, during the commencement period, with seats selling for 75¢. Sets and costumes for the plays were extravagant, as proven below by the 1912 performance of *Electra*, written by Sophocles, at which time the price of a ticket had been raised to $1. Hains later went on to direct the very successful Montgomery County Indiana Centennial Pageant in 1916.

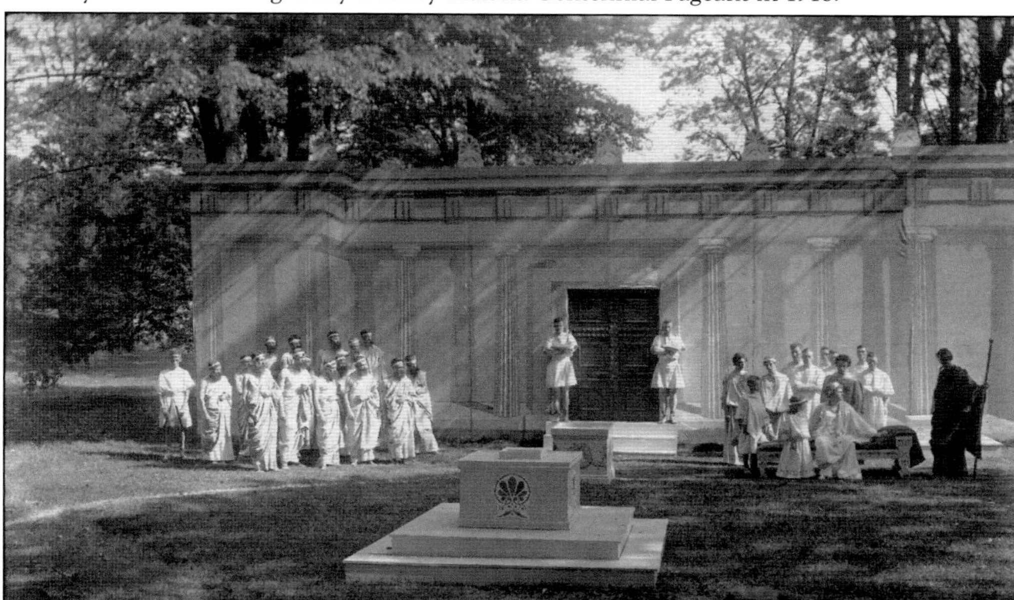

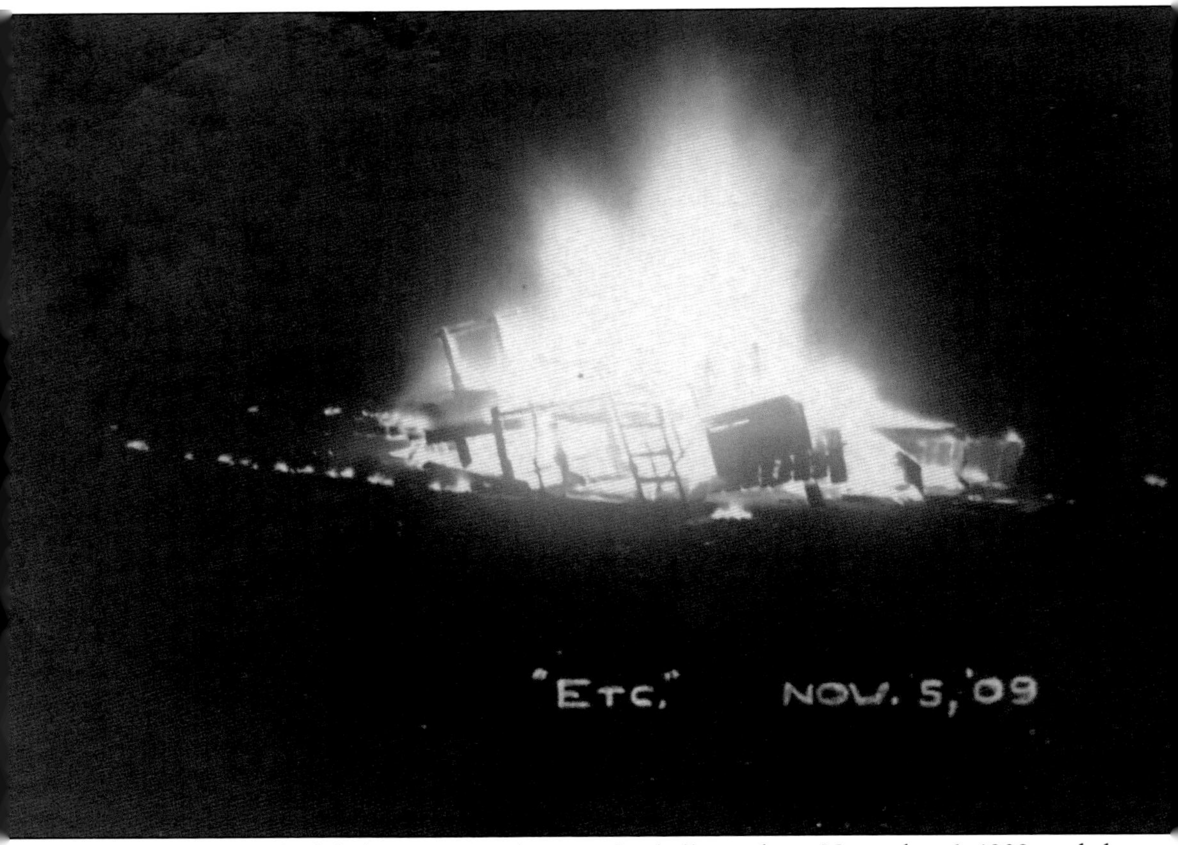

Wabash was scheduled to meet Purdue in a football match on November 6, 1909, and the Boilermakers were the favorites. A bonfire was planned for campus the night before to encourage interest in the game. The bonfire got a little out of hand, however, because students had roamed beyond the campus to scavenge fuel for the flames. The *Crawfordsville Journal* of November 6 collected the details of the damage and complaints: "Several citizens of this city, especially those living near the college campus, complained bitterly to the police this morning because of the destruction of their property by a band of college students who were working up enthusiasm for the Purdue game." Buggies, wagons, fences, lumber, and any manner of combustibles were used to feed the bonfire. The chief of police estimated the damage at $150 and promised to arrest the offenders if evidence could be secured. Perhaps the bonfire raised the spirit of the fans as well as the team, because Wabash defeated its rival 18 to 17 that Saturday afternoon. The *Crawfordsville Journal* admitted that "no Wabash college team has ever shown a better fighting spirit."

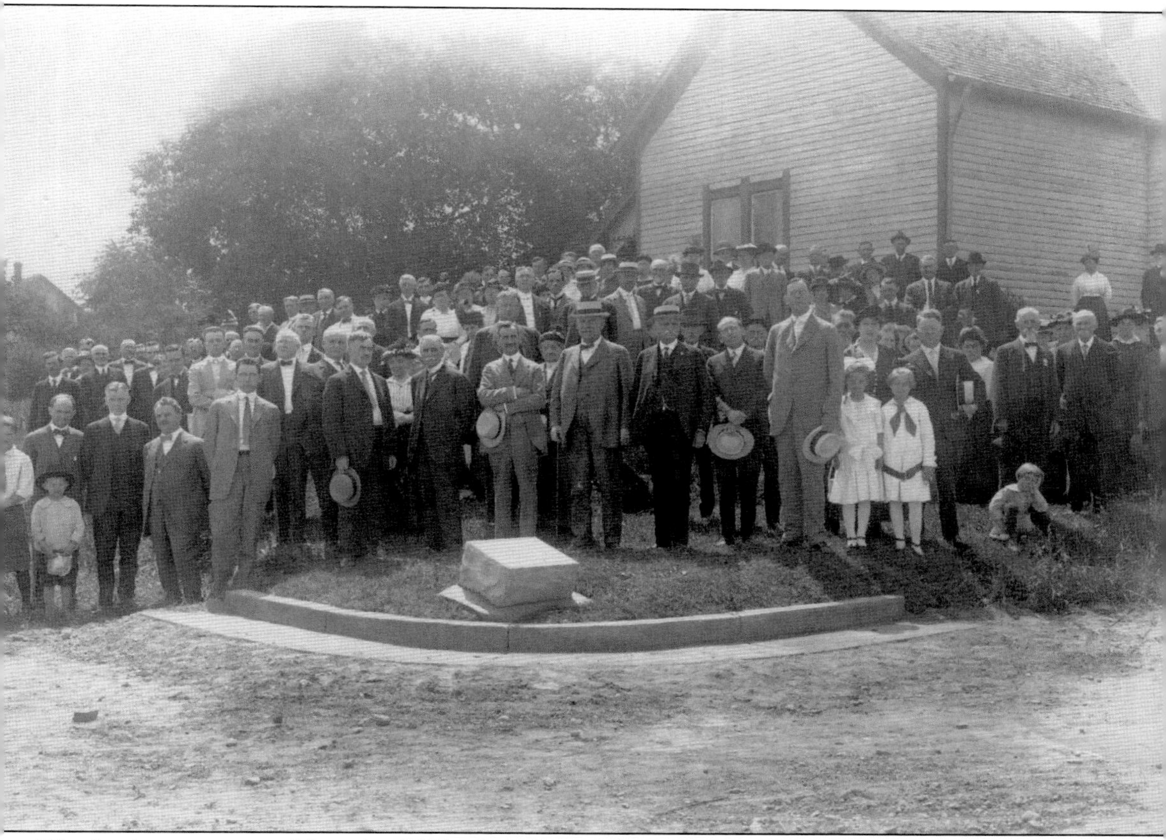

The faculty, trustees, and friends of Wabash College gather on June 12, 1916, for a public ceremony to mark the spot of Wabash's first building in Crawfordsville. One important problem needed to be solved before the event: no one remembered where that spot was. In its coverage of the ceremony, the *Crawfordsville Daily Journal* reminded its readers that "there were also found old, grey-haired men, who even had attended Wabash College and had lived in Crawfordsville most of their lives, who confessed that they had not the faintest conception as to where the first building was erected." Finally, a road contractor who had removed an old foundation years earlier convinced everyone that the historical point could be placed on the corner of Blair Street and Lane Avenue. The city constructed a cement curb at the southeast corner of the intersection, and all was ready for the ceremony. The monument itself was a tablet of Vermont granite placed atop a concrete base, which remains there today.

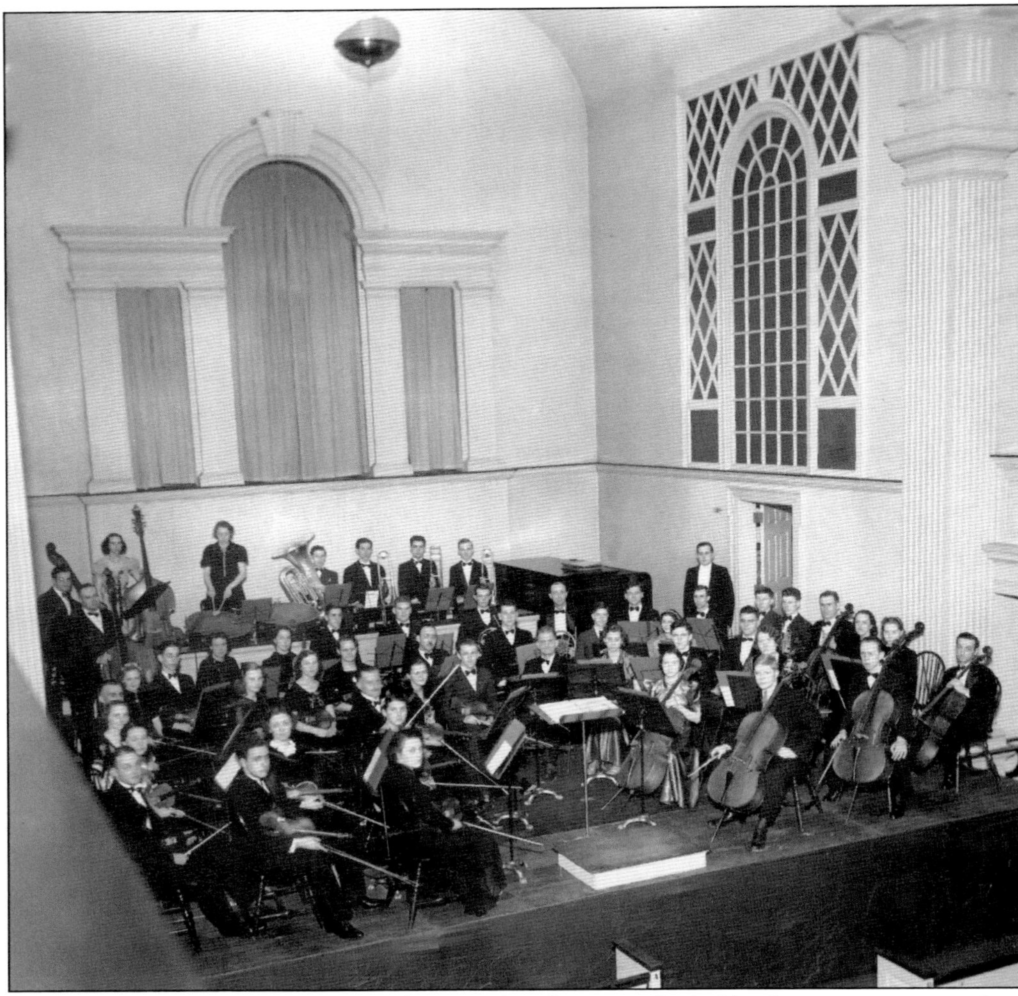

The Crawfordsville Symphony Orchestra, already active for half a dozen years, poses for a photograph around 1938 fully aware of its national publicity. Rehearsals and concerts were held in the Wabash College Chapel. (The college did not charge the orchestra, for which its students were allowed free admission to the concerts.) Regular admission for adults was 35¢, and school-age children paid 15¢. The full concert strength of the orchestra was from 50 to 60 members, and these musicians were composed of all types, including music teachers, Wabash students, and as *Time* magazine noted on May 13, 1940, "Musically knowledgeable farmers and townsfolk." To fill in for any missing instruments, four to eight professionals from the Indianapolis Symphony were hired on occasion. *Time* observed that the orchestra had its difficulties, "At weekly rehearsals the Crawfordsville musicians often play out of tune, get lost, wheeze and whiffle, come in at the wrong places, and competing basketball games lure away many a player." Yet they all improved by concert time, as *Time* noted.

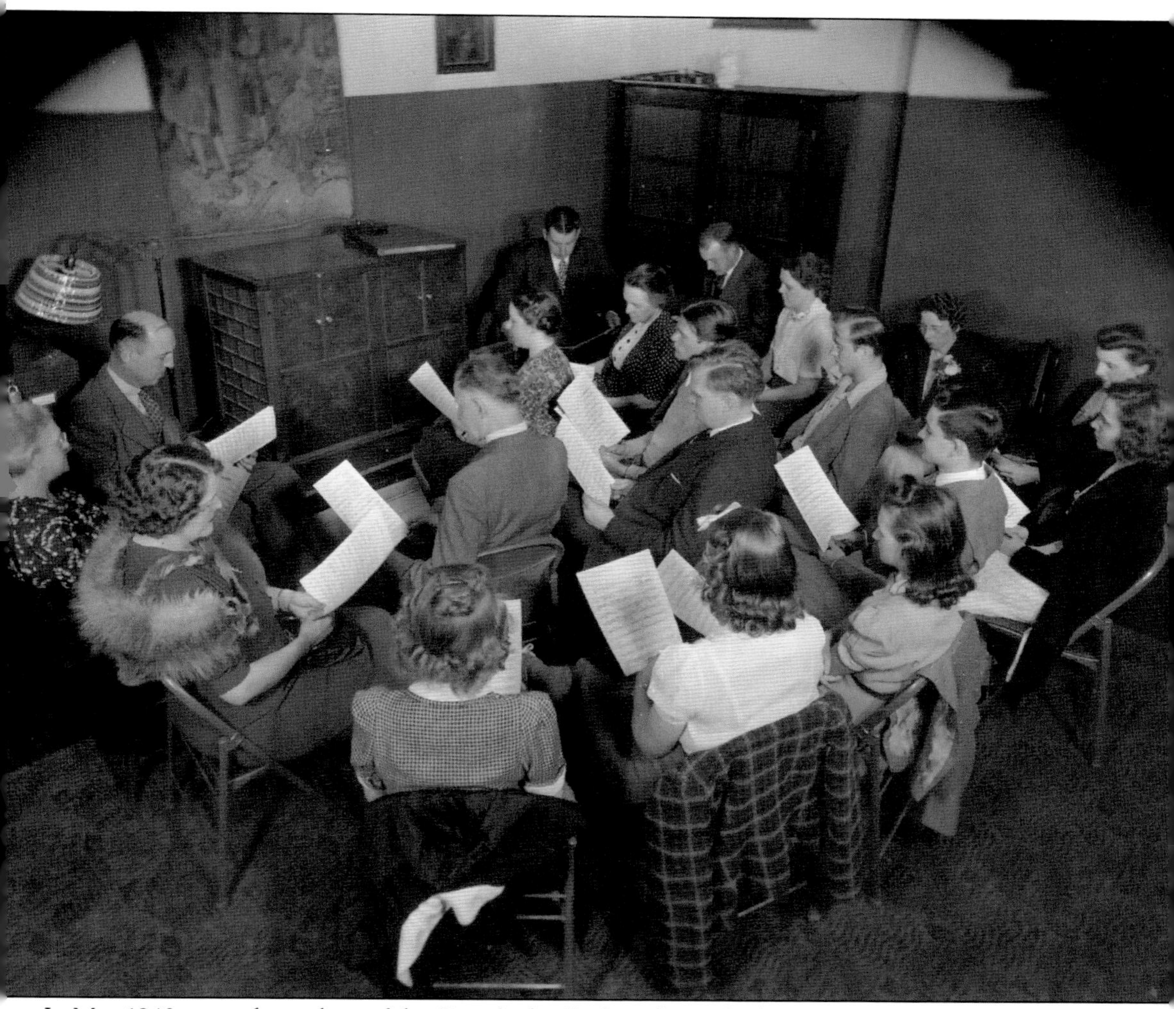

In May 1940, several members of the Crawfordsville Symphony Orchestra sit in Peck Hall on the Wabash College campus to listen to records on a Capehart phonograph. This group frequently gathered around Wabash's Capehart using the college's collection of records in order to hear how big orchestras performed the works. A Capehart phonograph was considered to be an excellent machine—technically advanced and representing the best in electronics for its time. Capehart phonographs were made by the Capehart division of Farnsworth Television and Radio Corporation of Fort Wayne, Indiana. When a representative for the advertising firm of the Farnsworth Company read the May 13, 1940, article in *Time* magazine about how the Crawfordsville Symphony Orchestra used a Capehart for inspiration, he immediately wrote the conductor to ask for a picture of such a session, stating that "this would provide further publicity for the Crawfordsville Symphony Orchestra, as well as serving our own purpose."

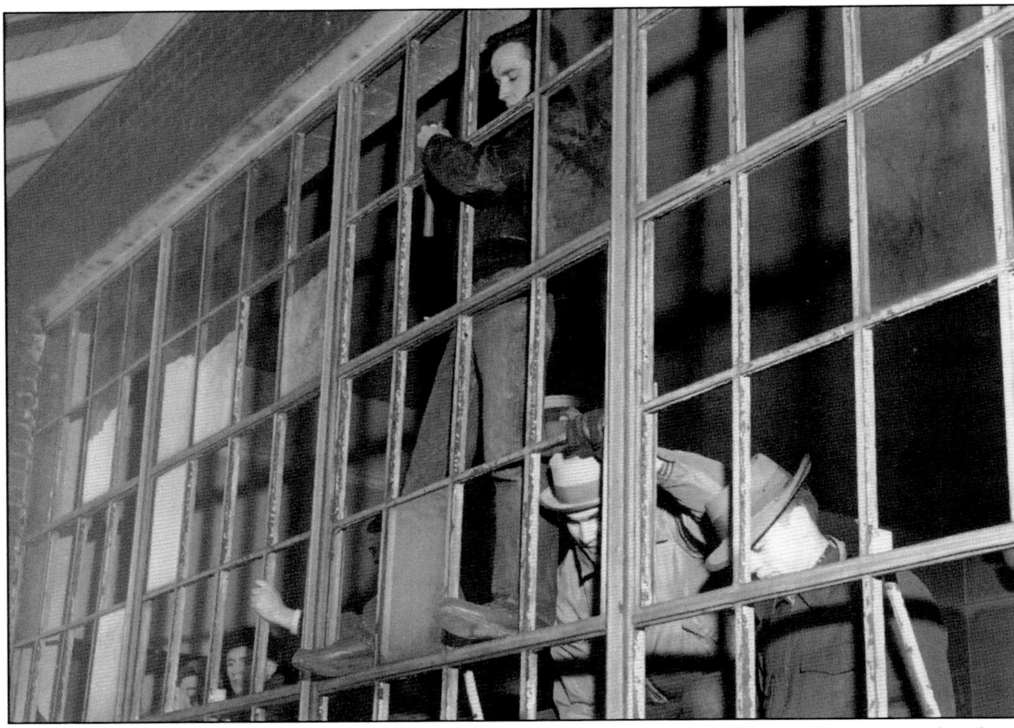

Wabash College has always tried to give back to the community, and the tradition stretches back many years. Several Wabash College students are pictured above replacing broken windows around 1953 in the original Lincoln School building, later named Horace Mann School. The building was then being refurbished into the Northside Recreation Center. This same year also finds students participating in a car wash, seen below, at the intersection of Pike and Water Streets. For many young men, the natural inclination would be to remain near campus and not venture unnecessarily into town. At the president's breakfast for seniors on June 3, 1950, Dean Byron K. Trippet admitted that Wabash students could easily be exasperated by the "social limitations of Montgomery County" simply because there were not often ample entertainment opportunities for youth their age. Wabash helps motivate students to become involved in the community, and today all Wabash freshmen participate in community service projects during their orientation week.

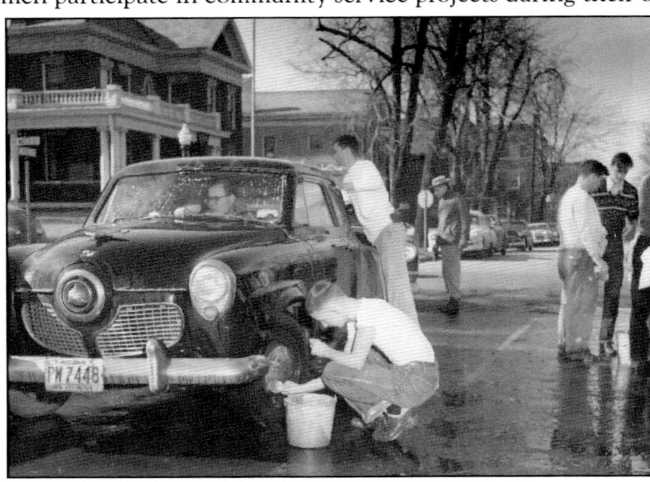

Nine

People, Famous and Forgotten

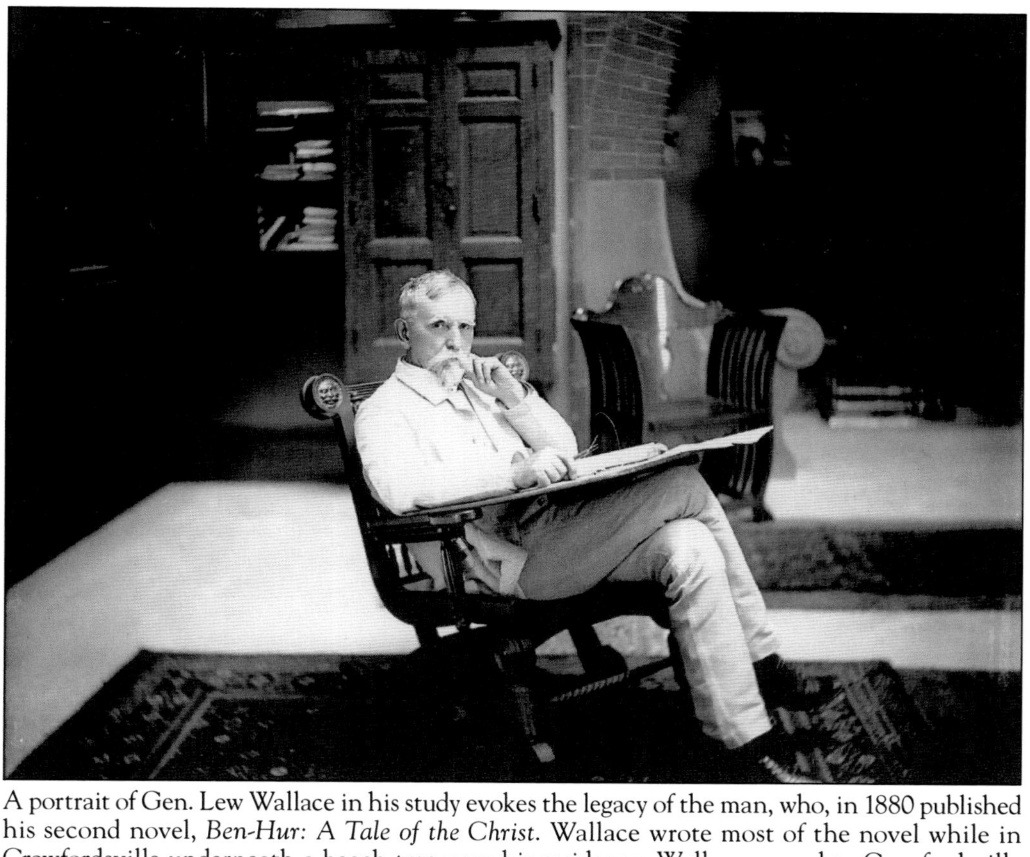

A portrait of Gen. Lew Wallace in his study evokes the legacy of the man, who, in 1880 published his second novel, *Ben-Hur: A Tale of the Christ*. Wallace wrote most of the novel while in Crawfordsville underneath a beech tree near his residence. Wallace moved to Crawfordsville in 1853 and was elected to the Indiana State Senate. During the Civil War, Wallace reached the rank of major general. Wallace was a military judge at Lincoln's assassination trial in 1865, President Hayes appointed Wallace to the position of governor of New Mexico territory in 1878, and President Garfield named him U.S. minister to Turkey in 1881. The study in which Wallace was photographed was one of his favorite projects, built between 1895 and 1898. Today the General Lew Wallace Study and Museum contains artifacts and displays pertaining to Wallace's life.

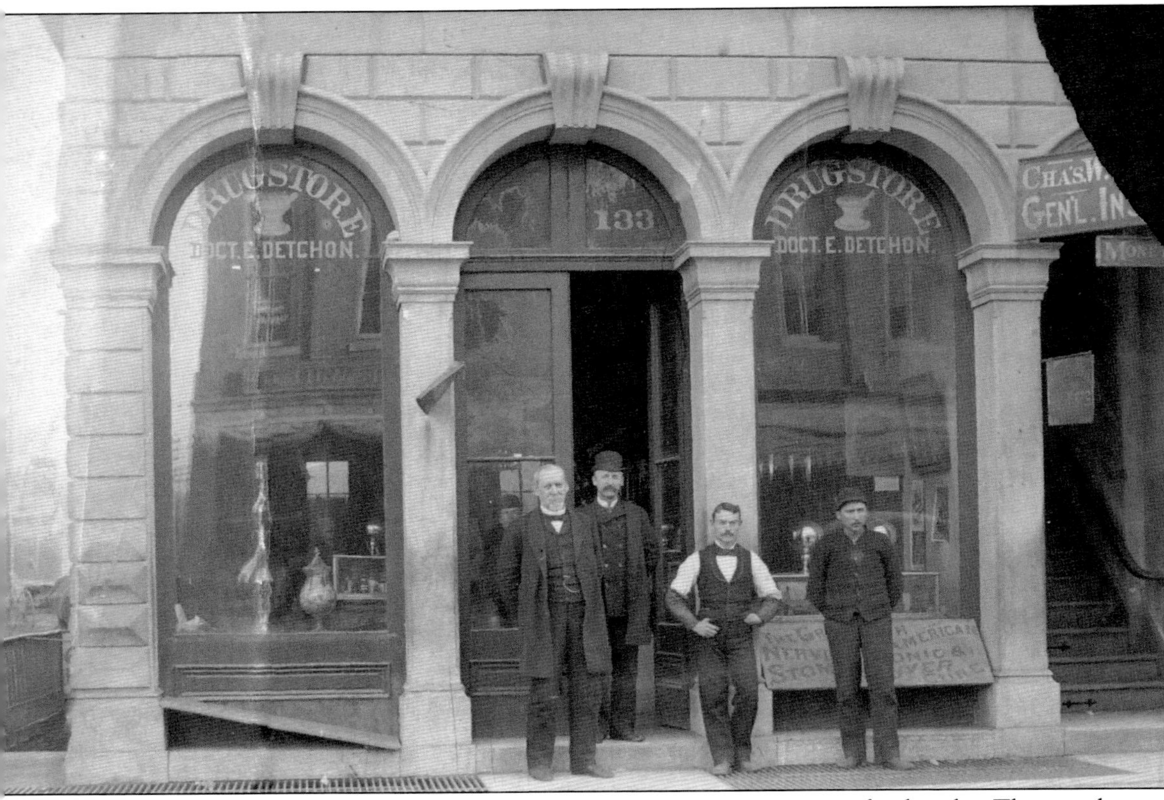

Dr. Elliot Detchon was one of Crawfordsville's most prominent citizens for decades. The popular doctor began to practice medicine in the area around 1851, and by 1871 he opened a drugstore in Crawfordsville on the southwest corner of East Main and South Green Streets. Here he stands (far left) in front of his drugstore around 1880, along with his sons Irwin (with hat, in the doorway) and Seymour (in shirtsleeves and vest). At Elliot Detchon's death in 1905, the *Crawfordsville Daily Journal* commented on his "magnetism which cemented his friendships so that those who knew him well were ardent admirers of him." Irwin was also a doctor, but he and his father became especially rich through the "proprietary medicine" business. Irwin was an 1873 graduate of Wabash College who gained fame in town for his participation in community and college enterprises. Seymour did not enter the medical field, becoming instead a well-respected broker in New York and Chicago.

Mary Holloway graduated from Penn Medical University in 1856—the first woman from Indiana to obtain a medical degree. As Dr. Mary Holloway Wilhite, she gained a reputation for her skill and education, as well as and her belief in gender equality. Hiram Beckwith's *History of Montgomery County* (1881) recorded, "Mrs. Wilhite is also an ardent supporter in woman's rights, and fully expects to see the day when woman may vote for those who make laws to govern her, and when doctors will counsel one another without distinction in regard to sex."

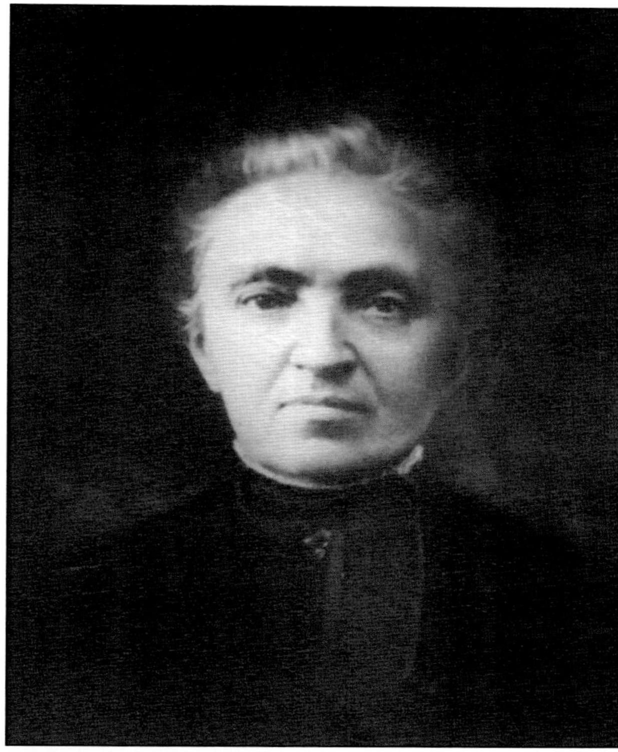

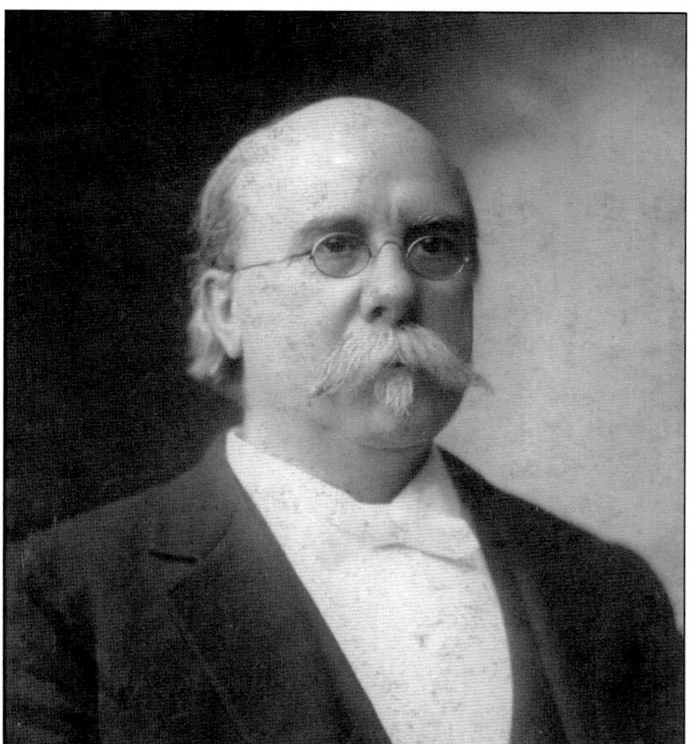

William DeCaux Tilney is pictured here around 1900 when he was 60 years old. Tilney was born in England in 1841 and served under the British government in India for three years before coming to the United States. In 1865, he relocated to Crawfordsville, where he practiced medicine and remained the rest of his life. When he passed away in 1925, the *Crawfordsville Daily Journal*'s obituary recalled that this "venerable doctor" was also known as an "interesting character." Tilney's grandson Gerald would give his life in World War II in France (see chapter six).

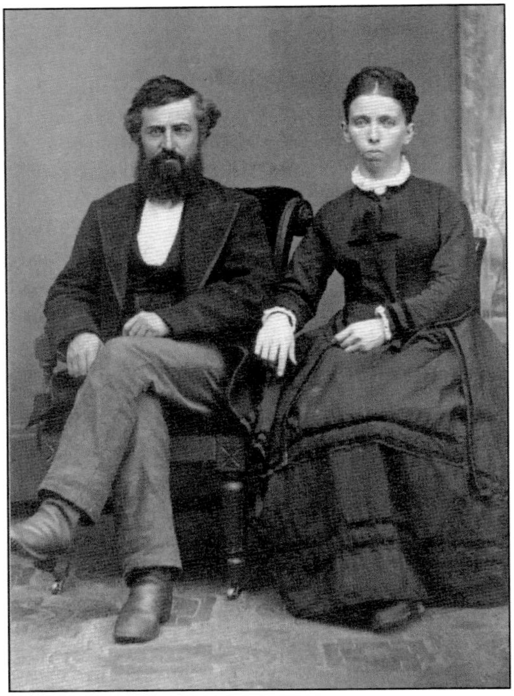

Ambrose Remley married Minerva E. Shelby in 1866, just after the Civil War, and they are pictured here a few years later. Ambrose was a veteran of the war, serving in Company E of the 72nd Indiana Volunteer Infantry. Bowen's *History of Montgomery County* remarked, "He never quailed in the face of danger and duty, no matter how arduous." Ambrose was the son of John and Sarah Remley (John was one of the area's original settlers who arrived in Crawfordsville in 1824).

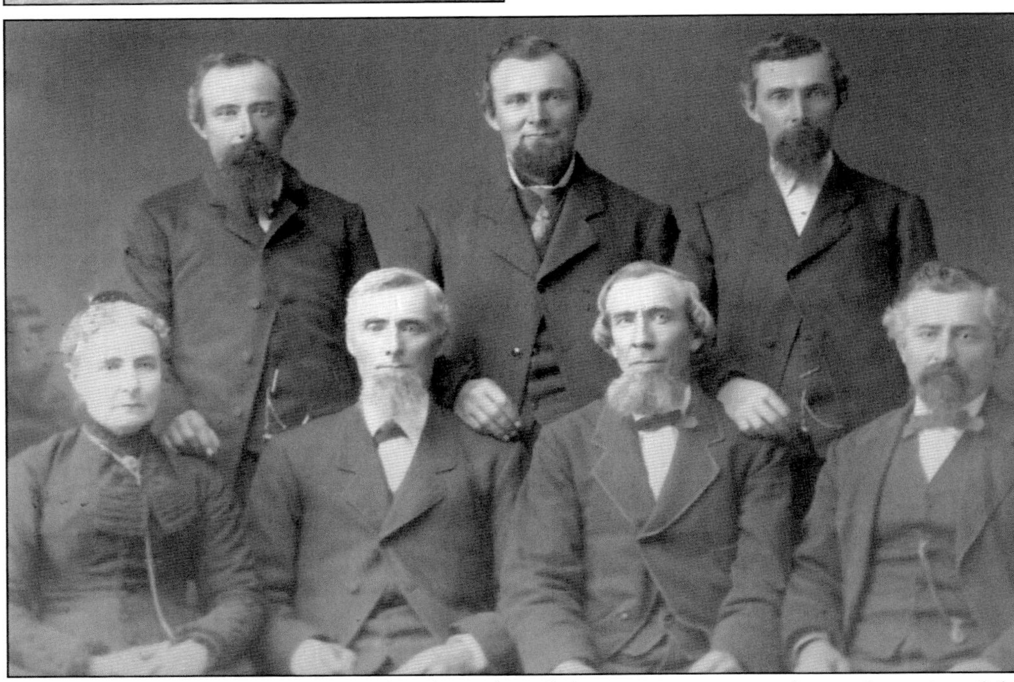

The family of John and Sarah Remley thrived, and their names appear often in histories of the area. In 1870, their offspring gathered for this portrait. From left to right are (first row) Elizabeth, James, John, and Ambrose; (second row) Daniel, William, and David. Ambrose is said to have proudly kept the gun he carried throughout the war and the walking cane his father used in making his way to Indiana.

Ambrose and Minerva Remley sit with their three children for this *c.* 1876 photograph. Sarah has been placed in front, while Fred and Harry stand beside their parents. All three children would spend most of their lives in Montgomery County and were prominent citizens at their deaths (Fred, 1953; Harry, 1957; Sarah, 1961).

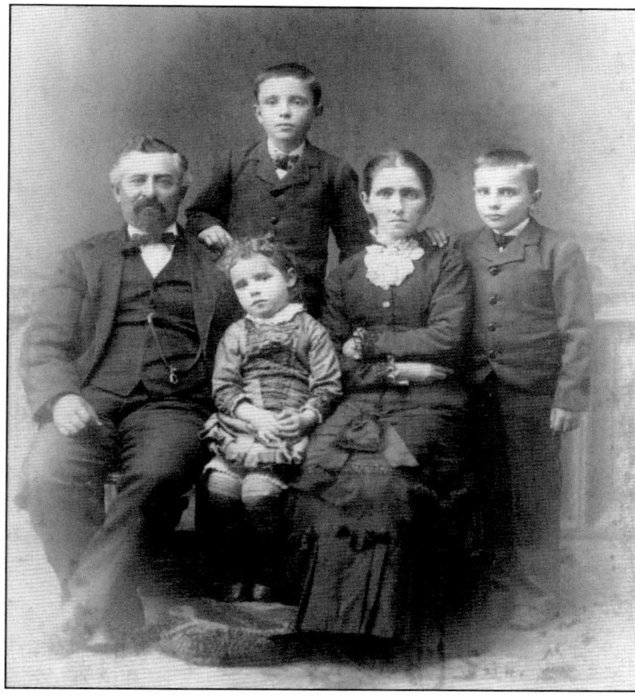

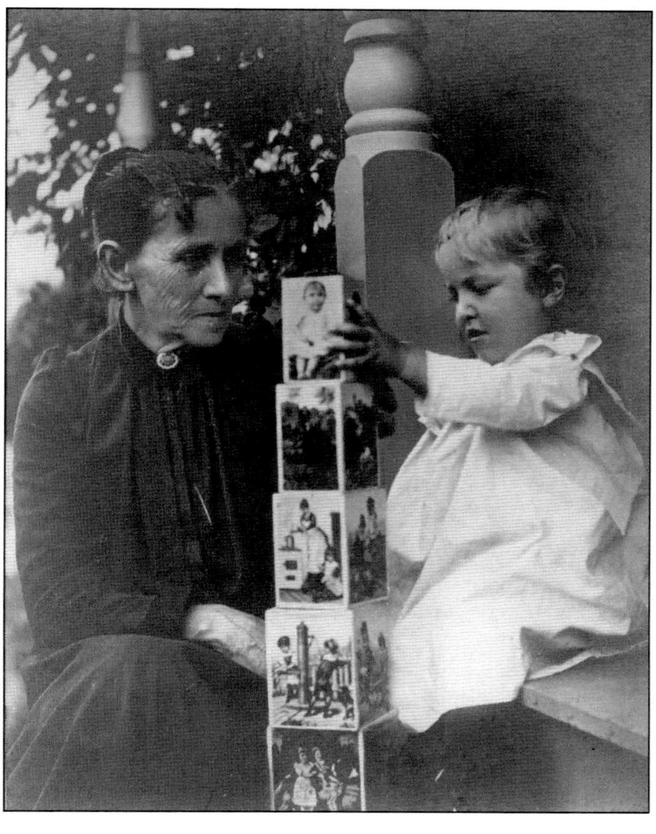

An 1899 photograph captures a moment of play between "Grandma" Minerva Remley and Walter Remley, son of Fred and Nellie Brown Remley, on Grandma's porch at 700 South Water Street. Walter graduated from Crawfordsville High School in 1915 and served in World War I with the 42nd (Rainbow) Division. His obituary remembered him for active membership in many organizations and for his relentless handshaking.

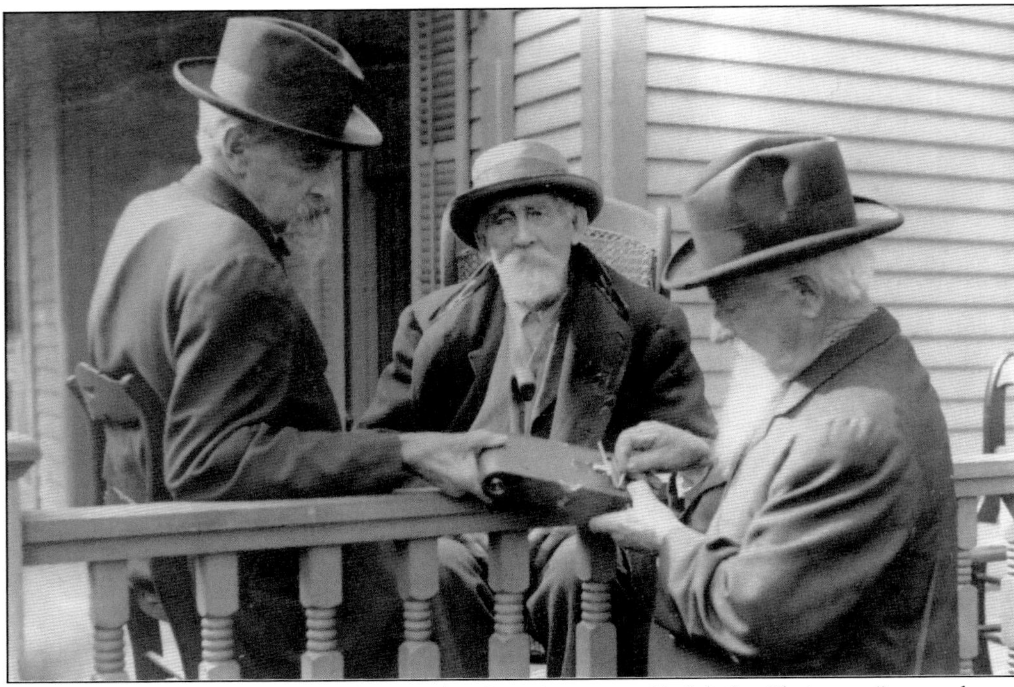

This *c.* 1910 photograph, entitled "Give the Grandparents a Kodak for Christmas," was taken at 701 South Water Street in Crawfordsville. Ambrose Remley (right) holds a Kodak camera. The photographer, Nellie Coutant, lived just a few doors away. Coutant was a talented amateur who received many prizes. She is listed in the *American Amateur Photographer* (September 1904) as having placed 23rd in the Thousand Dollar Kodak competition, which had more than 20,000 entries.

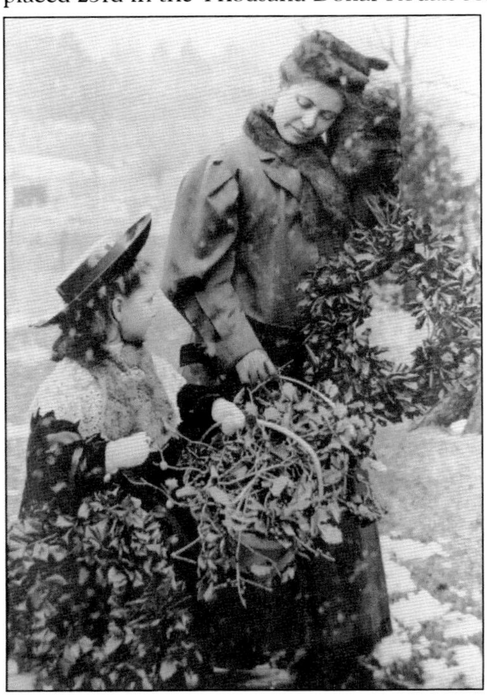

Nellie Coutant also took this photograph of two unidentified subjects sometime in the early 1900s and entitled it "Bringing Home the Christmas Greens." Coutant was entirely self-taught, but her images now reside in archives, including the New York Public Library and the Hartmann Collection at the University of California at Riverside. At her death in 1953, however, her local obituary made no mention of her photography.

Railroads crisscrossed Crawfordsville and provided a major source of local employment. William Wesley Walker was a longtime resident and 25-year employee of the Big Four Railroad. He is seen here in 1903 as a flagman on the corner of Mill and Franklin Streets. Walker resided nearby, at 818 East Franklin Street, at the time of his death in 1927. The *Crawfordsville Daily Journal* called this familiar face "one of the well known residents of this city" in his obituary.

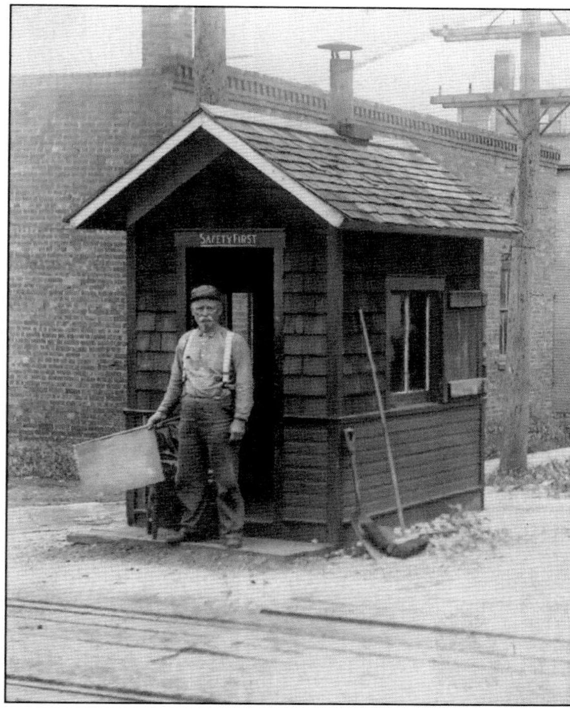

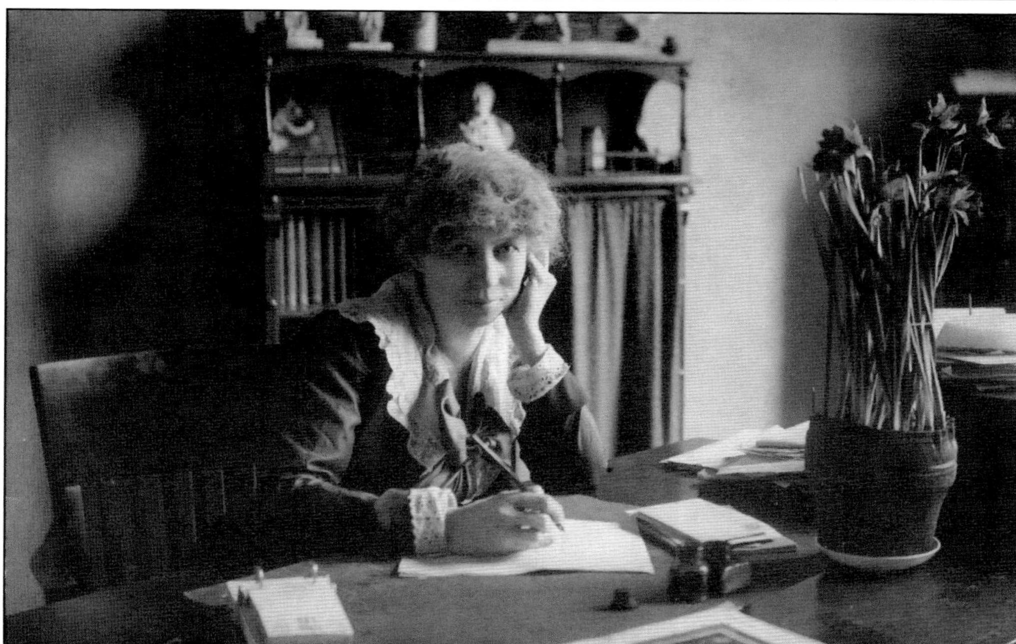

Anna Willson is seated at her desk in 1904. Willson, a nationally reputed educator and administrator, inspired generations of Crawfordsville schoolchildren. She organized clubs and societies, including the extant high school girls' Sunshine Society. In 1911, *American Primary Teacher* called the Sunshine Society "the sort of club that would delight the souls of some teachers and citizens who are lamenting the degenerating tastes of high school pupils in many cities."

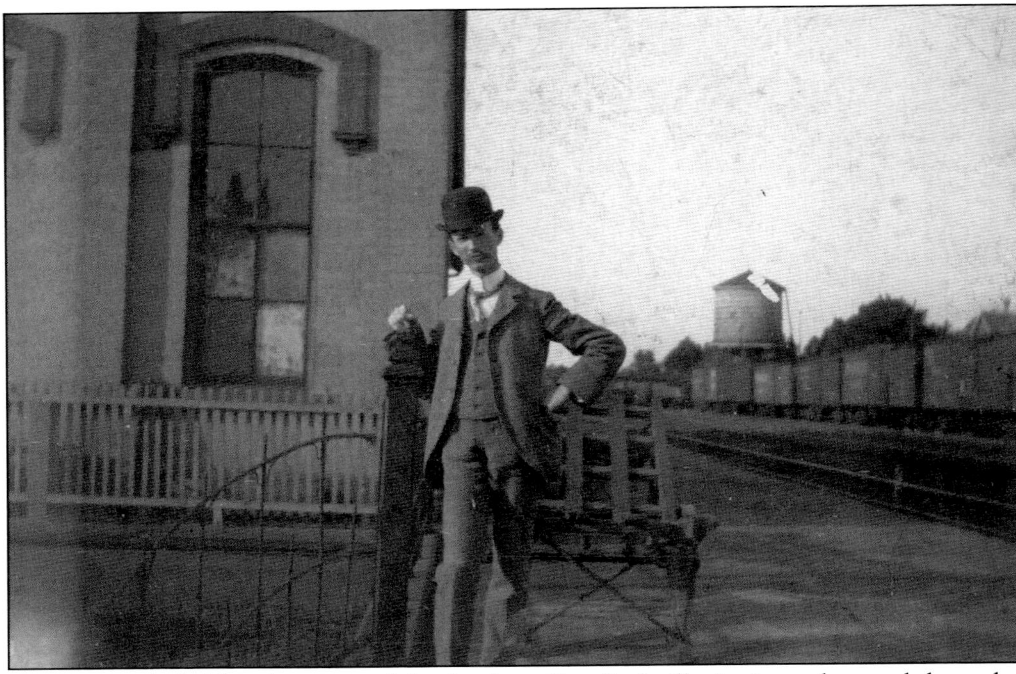

Thomas S. Clark (above), a successful tailor from Crawfordsville, is pictured around the end of the 19th century at the Big Four depot, a busy train station located at the corner of Wallace and Franklin Streets. Clark's business, located at 131 East Main Street, sold furnishing goods as well as tailored clothing. He married Mary Agatha Shoemaker of Lafayette, Indiana, in 1899. By 1902, his health had failed, and his business went bankrupt. He lived six more years in a sanitarium in Indianapolis and died in 1908. Mary Shoemaker Clark (below) is at the same station seated on a luggage cart. After her husband's death, she was left to raise two young children, James and Mary Elizabeth, and returned to live with her family in Lafayette.

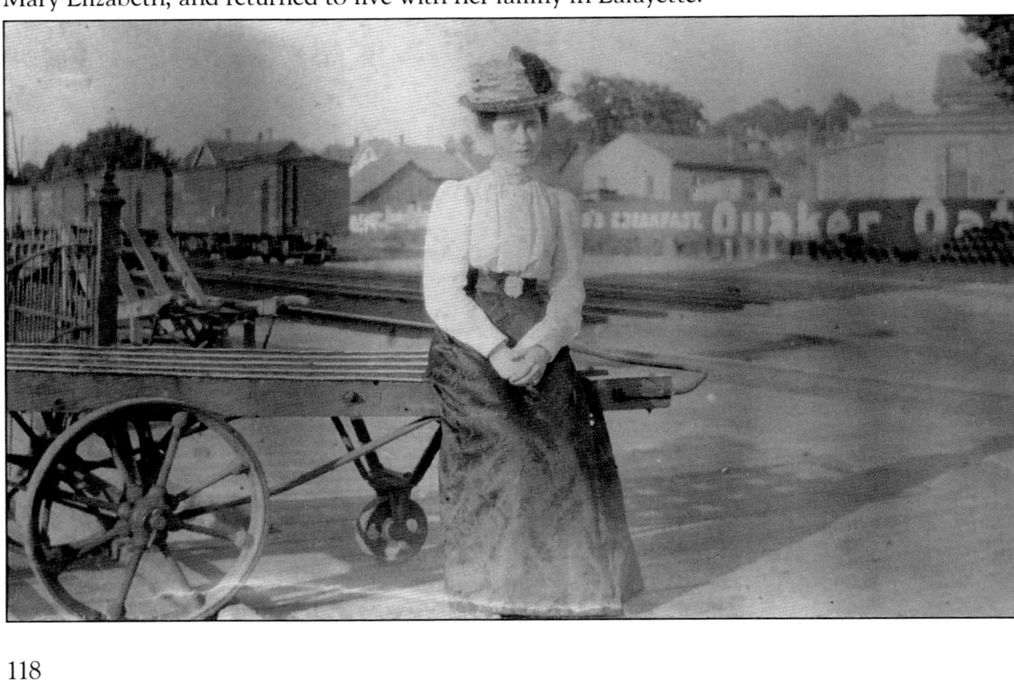

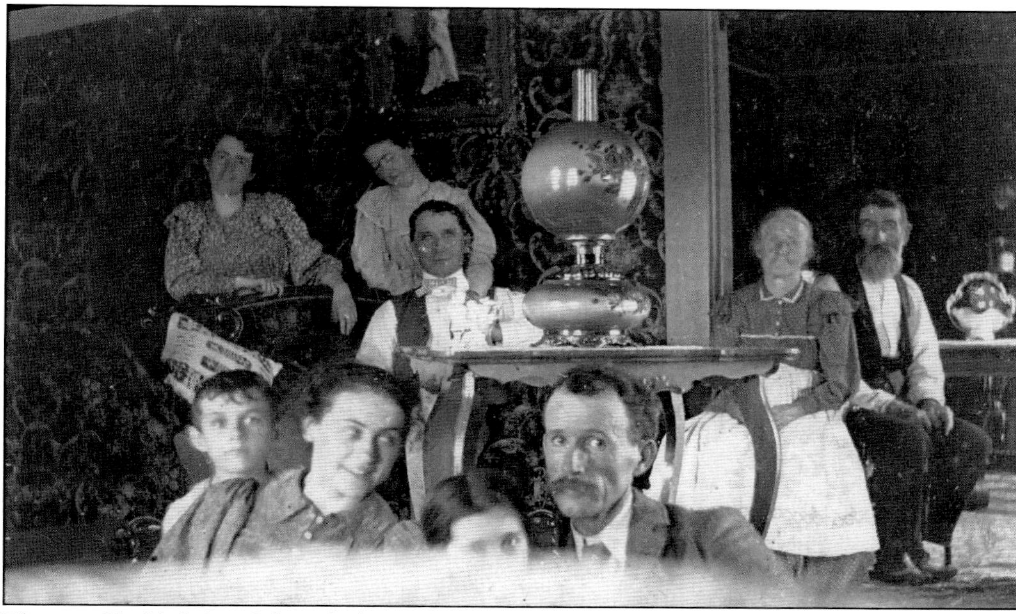

Thomas Clark's father, John Clark, was born in Dublin in 1823 but spent his last 55 years at 508 Whitlock Avenue in Crawfordsville. His family takes a moment for a photograph noted "our living room, 1899." Thomas's siblings—Lizzie, Kate, and John—are in the upper left; John Clark and his wife, Mary Slattery Clark, are to right in the photograph; Mary Shoemaker Clark and her husband, Thomas, are in the front with a niece and nephew.

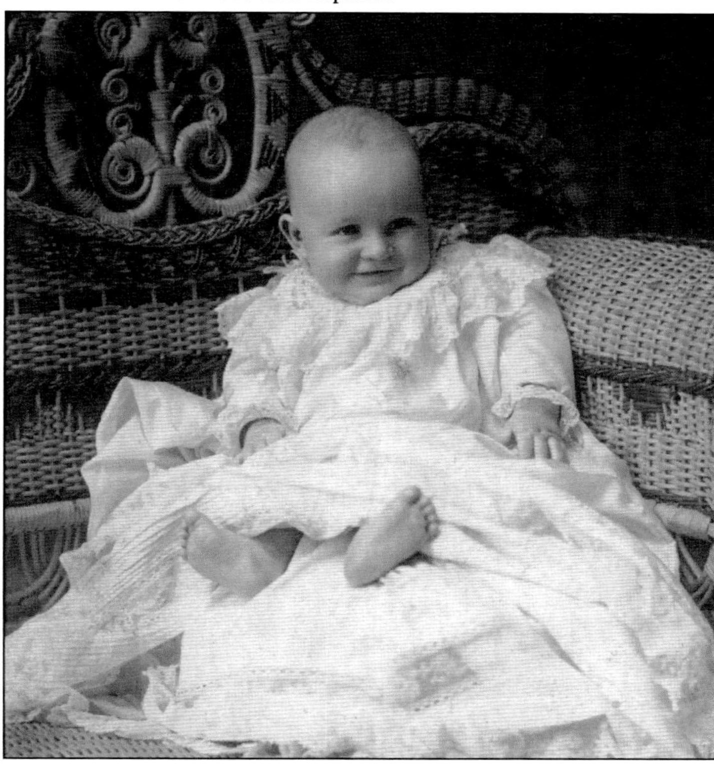

This photograph was taken in 1900 when Joseph James Clark was less than one year old. His sister Mary Elizabeth was born in 1902, three days before their father's bankruptcy notice was published in a local newspaper. Thomas Clark was falling ill at the time, and he never recovered (his obituary on July 3, 1908, said that he died from a "softening of the brain").

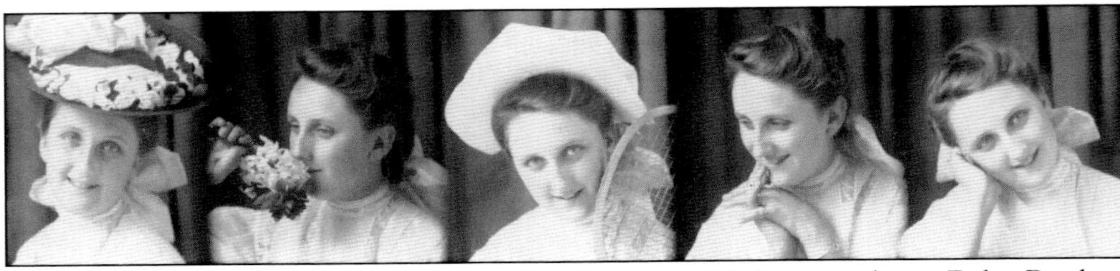

When war broke out in Europe in 1914, many Americans scrambled to return home. Esther Detchon, from a well-known Crawfordsville family, was among a group of Americans who congregated in Italy and attempted to obtain passage under the neutral Italian flag. Detchon visited the U.S. embassy in Rome on August 7, where she obtained a certificate of citizenship and requesting safe passage. The certificate also recorded her age (20), her height (5 feet, 6 inches), her eyes (blue), her nose (aquiline), as well as other distinguishing features. Within 10 days, Detchon and nearly 400 other Americans were crowded aboard the *Principe di Udine*, which sailed from Genoa to New York. The *Crawfordsville Daily Journal* was relieved to report that "one of the city's prominent young ladies" was on the passenger list and expected home soon.

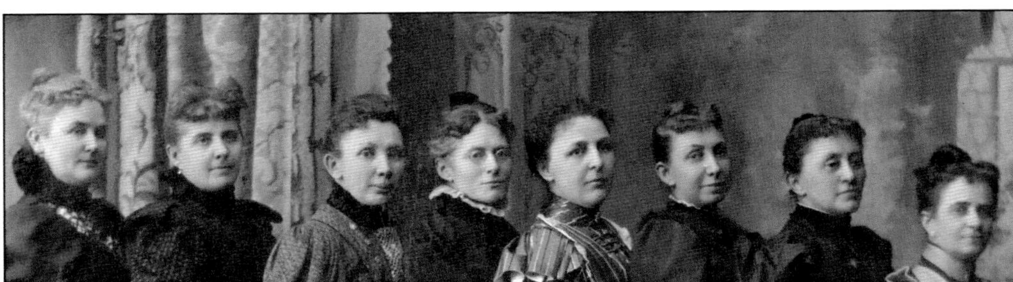

Around 1912, several school friends of Laura A. Blaine gather for a group portrait. From left to right are Jo Graham Evans, Laura Williams Crabbs, Caroline Virginia Krout, Emma Ashenhurst Sidener, May Purviance Bruner, Mary Hannah Krout, Mellie Blair, and Mattie Keeney. Of these women, the Krout sisters were noteworthy for their literary skills. The elder sister, Mary (born 1851), was a strong advocate for her sex. When still a teenager, she spoke to area groups on women's right to vote. Mary eventually became an international journalist for the *Chicago Inter-Ocean* and then the *Chicago Tribune*. Mary is also credited with helping her friend Susan Elston Wallace complete the memoirs of her famous husband after his death. Caroline (born 1852) also wrote articles for several newspapers and magazines. She took her writing skill further, however, and produced several novels with some success.

Dumont Kennedy was twice county clerk, twice prosecuting attorney, and twice mayor of Crawfordsville—but he is best remembered for his dedication to local history. Kennedy's father, also an amateur historian, erected a monument in 1881 southwest of the city to commemorate the first European settlement in the county. When the monument fell into disrepair, Kennedy spearheaded the effort to restore it. Kennedy stands in front of the monument for the rededication in 1922.

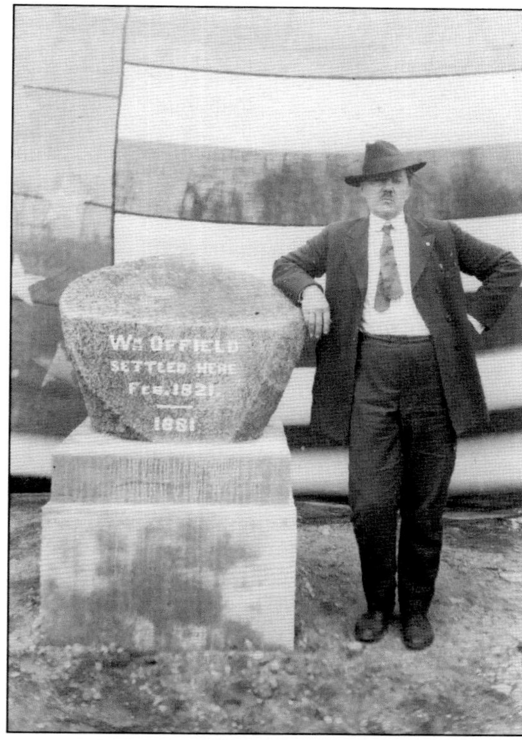

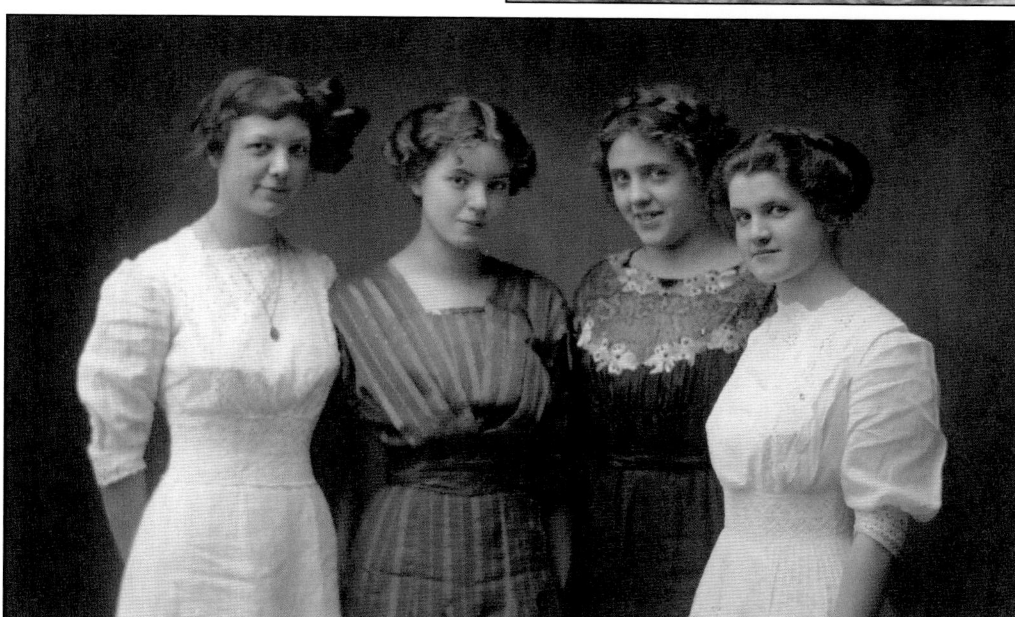

Fern Ream (third from left) poses with some of her friends around 1920. A graduate of Crawfordsville High School in 1911, Ream attended nearby DePauw University before going on to the Winona Teachers College and eventually the Music School of Cornell University. Ream taught geography and history in Crawfordsville for the junior high school (1916–1917) before becoming music supervisor for the senior high school the next year.

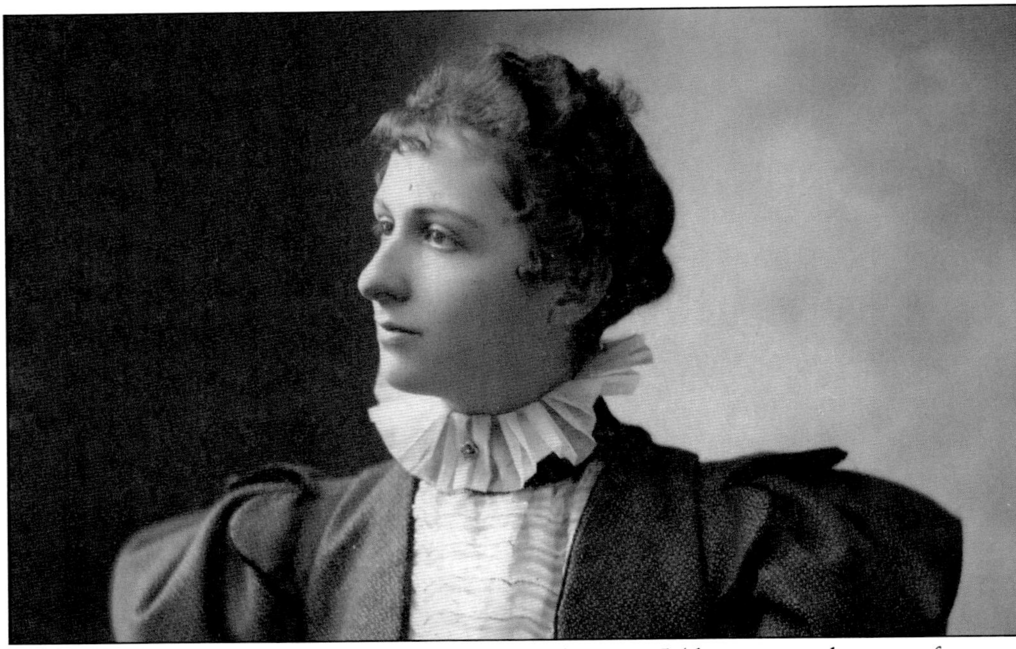

Effie Gardner, pictured here, married Tully C. Crabbs in 1895 (this portrait dates to a few years after). Tully played in the first basketball game in the state of Indiana, which was held at the Crawfordsville YMCA in 1894, the year he graduated from Wabash College. Tully ran a successful grain elevator company until it was sold 1945 and then worked more closely with the Elston Bank, where he had served as a director since 1918.

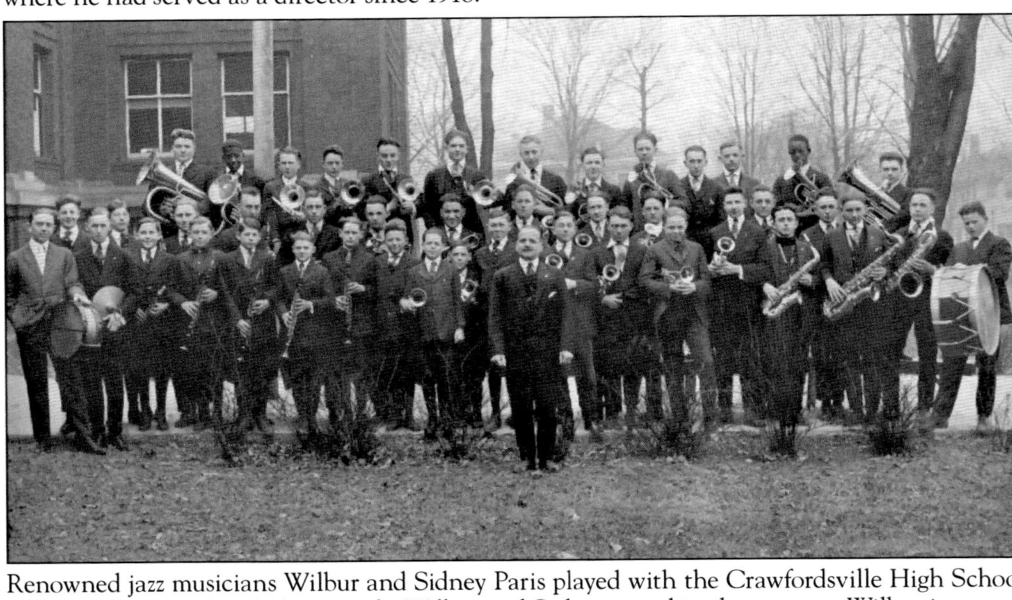

Renowned jazz musicians Wilbur and Sidney Paris played with the Crawfordsville High School band. In this 1918 band photograph, Wilbur and Sydney stand in the top row: Wilbur is second from the left and Sidney is last on the right. The two left Crawfordsville before graduating. The brothers added a "de" to their last name and started long musical careers, playing with greats Louis Armstrong, Jelly Roll Morten, and Sidney Bechet. Sidney was known for his trumpet work, while Wilbur mastered the trombone.

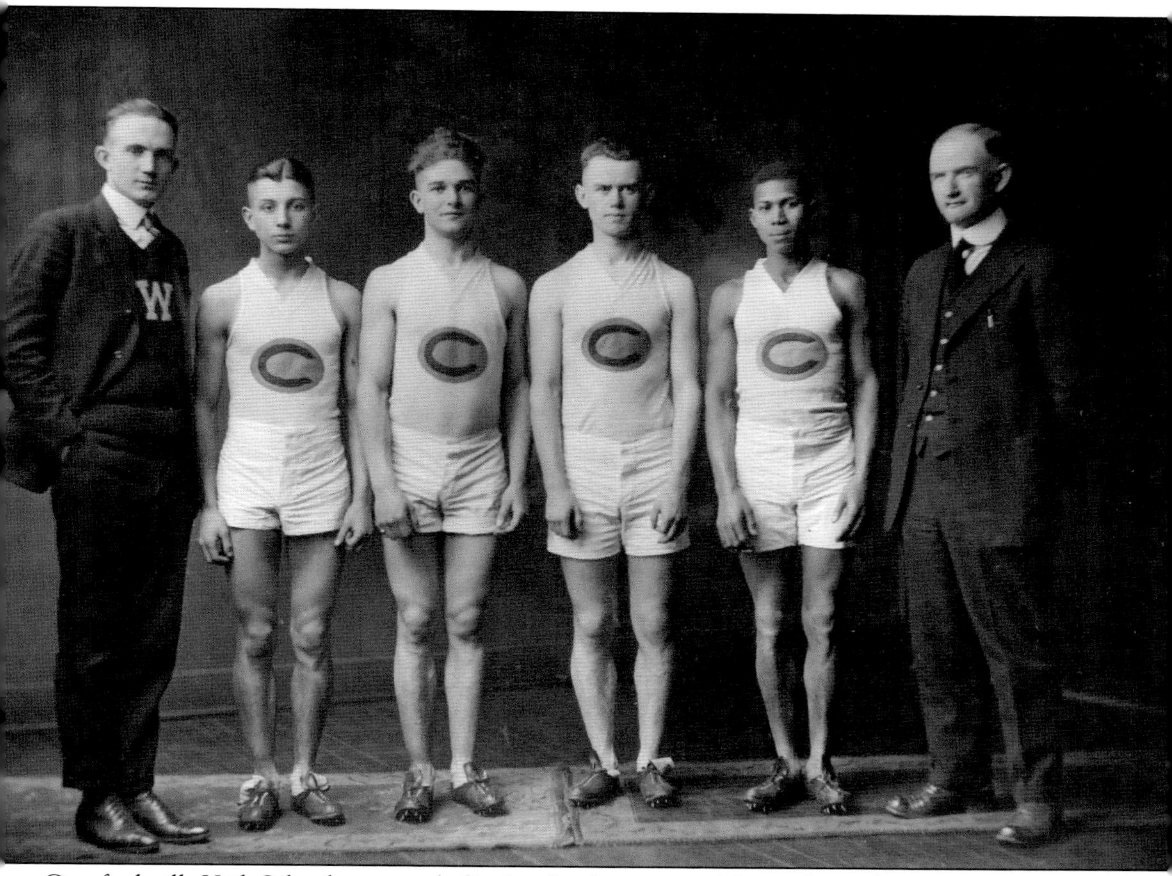

Crawfordsville High School was proud of its 1-mile relay team and featured it in the 1920 yearbook. From left to right are Parmer Sims (coach), Theodore Schweitzer, Hugh Dinwiddie, Floyd McGeath, Elbert Walker, and Frank McGeath (manager). Sims found success at CHS, especially in 1919, when the yearbook stated, "We do not know just what tactics Sims employs by way of training, but we do know that he has produced wonderful results." Frank McGeath was the father of Floyd and had a solid reputation for his work with junior high and high school athletics. The CHS track team had been invited in 1919 to the Drake Relays in Des Moines, Iowa, and was the only high school east of the Mississippi to receive this honor. CHS easily won both races in which its teams were entered. The yearbook observed, according to the *Des Moines Register*, "The only thing that kept the Hoosier athletes from smashing records was lack of competition."

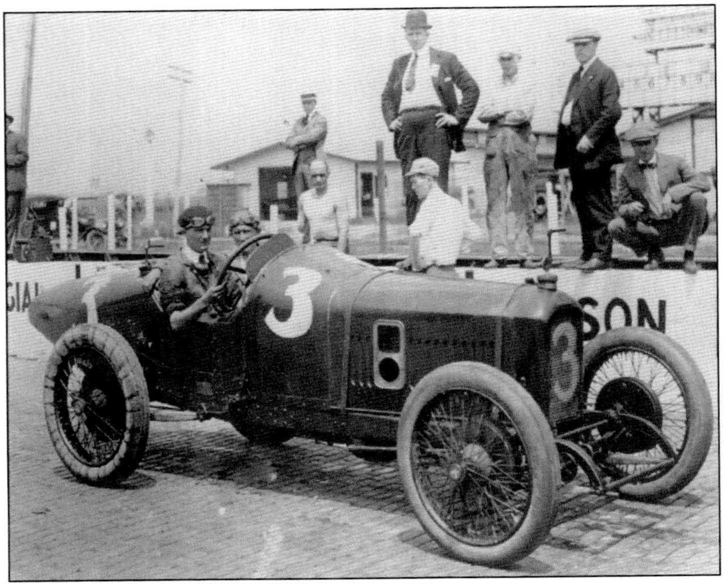

Crawfordsville-born Howard "Howdy" Wilcox, the winner of the 1919 Indianapolis 500-mile race, played an important role in the development of American auto racing. He began his short but successful racing career with a victory in 1909. Wilcox had started in all the 500-mile races at Indianapolis, according to his obituary in the *Crawfordsville Daily Journal*. He was killed in a crash during the inaugural race at the Altoona Speedway in Pennsylvania in 1923.

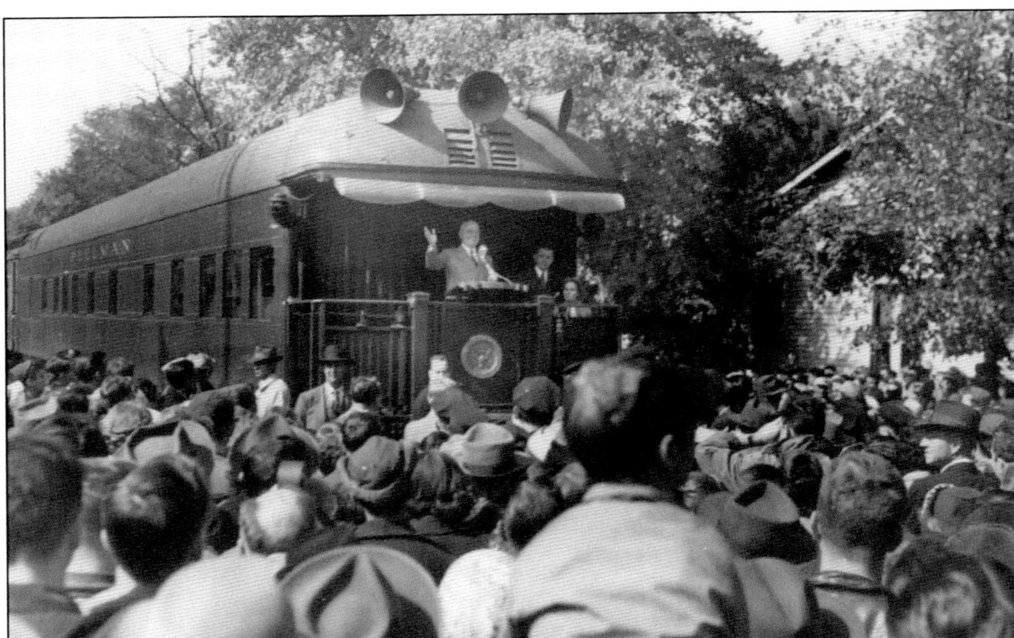

During his whistle-stop campaign for reelection in 1948 while running against Republican Thomas Dewey, Pres. Harry Truman spent 10 minutes in Crawfordsville—a Republican stronghold. On October 12, 1948, his train stopped where the tracks crossed Washington Street just north of Franklin Street. Truman is at the podium, and William "Bill" Wilson, a Wabash graduate serving as Democratic chairman for Montgomery County, stands to the right. Crawfordsville voted 3,373 to 2,230 in favor of Dewey.

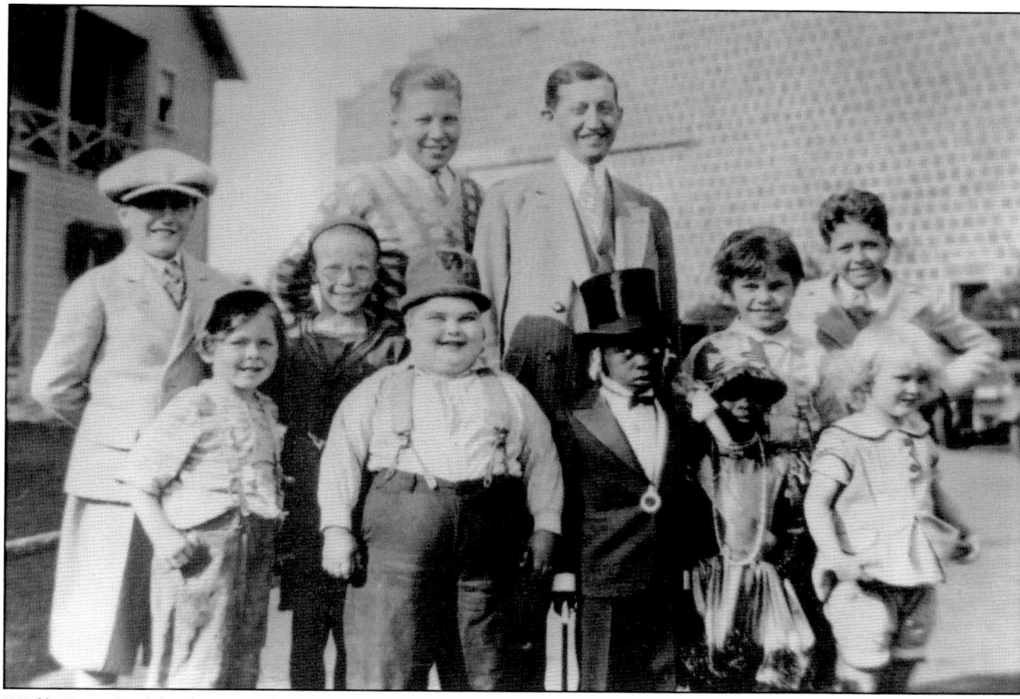

Will Hays Jr. (the boy in the suit, back right) traveled with his father, Will Hays Sr., to Hollywood in the late 1920s, where he posed with some of the *Our Gang* cast. The father gained fame for cleaning up Hollywood as the first president of the Motion Picture Producers and Distributors of America (MPPDA), serving from 1922 to 1945. The son, a 1937 Wabash College graduate, also spent time in the film industry. A longtime trustee of Wabash College, Hays Jr. served as mayor of Crawfordsville from 1964 to 1972.

Four Crawfordsville authors were honored during Library Week in March 1954. Pictured from left to right are Norwood Brigance, Will Hays Jr., John Forbes, and Richard Banta. Brigance and Forbes taught at Wabash, and Hays and Banta were graduates. Brigance was a recognized author and professor of speech and Forbes a scholar and professor of history and fine art. Hays wrote movie and television scripts, including the 1949 musical *You're My Everything*, starring Anne Baxter, and several novels. Banta was known for his work as a publisher.

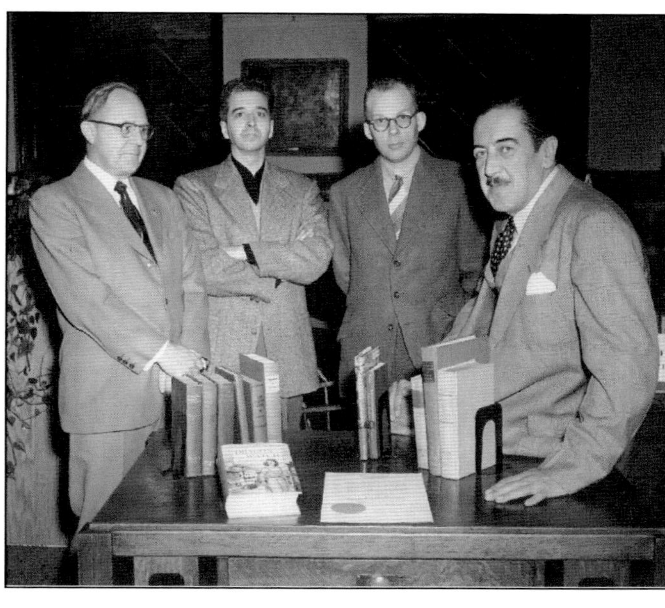

BIBLIOGRAPHY

Banta, Richard E. Crawfordsville: *One Hundred Forty-three Years in the Hoosier Athens*. Crawfordsville, IN: Crawfordsville Area Centennial Corporation, 1965.

Beckwith, H. W. *History of Montgomery County*. Chicago: H. H. Hill and N. Iddings, 1881.

Bowen, A. W. *History of Montgomery County, Indiana*. Indianapolis: A. W. Bowen, 1913.

Cantrell, Martha. *The Quilt Chronicles: A Montgomery County Heritage, 1821–1979*. Crawfordsville, IN: Montgomery County Historical Society and Crawfordsville Art League, 1979.

Cline, Pat. *Crawfordsville: A Pictorial History*. St. Louis: G. Bradley Publishing, 1991.

Crawfordsville newspapers: *Star, Daily News-Review, Journal, Journal and Review, Review, Weekly Argus, Weekly Review*

Cline, Pat, ed. *Montgomery County Legend and Lore*. Crawfordsville, IN: Montgomery County Historical Society, 1988.

Gronert, Theodore. *Sugar Creek Saga: A History and Development of Montgomery County*. Crawfordsville, IN: Wabash College, 1958.

Harvey, Robert, ed. *These Fleeting Years: Wabash College 1832–1982*. Crawfordsville, IN: Wabash College, 1982.

Hoffman, F., ed. *The Revised Montgomery County Atlas*. Crawfordsville, IN: Indiana Printing Company, 1898.

Montgomery: Your County Magazine, a monthly supplement to *Crawfordsville Journal Review*, 1976–1999.

Ogle, George A., ed. *Standard Atlas of Montgomery County, Indiana*. Chicago: Geo. A. Ogle and Company, 1917.

Riggs, Constance Kakavecos, ed. *Montgomery County Remembers*. Crawfordsville, IN: Montgomery County Historical Society and Crawfordsville Community Bicentennial Committee, 1976.

Zach, Karen Bazzani. *Crawfordsville: Athens of Indiana*. Charleston, SC: Arcadia Publishing, 2003.

INDEX

Banta, Richard, 125
Baptist church, 39
Ben-Hur building, 24, 73
Bischof, Louis (Bischof's Big Store), 13, 67, 68, 84
Brigance, Norwood, 125
Castle Hall (Commerce Hall), 19, 23, 24
Catholic church, 26
Central School, 9, 12, 28
Christian church, 9, 31
Clark family, 118, 119
Coutant, Nellie, 116
Crawford Hotel, 18
Crawfordsville Electric Light and Power, 18, 70
Crawfordsville Fire Department, 70
Crawfordsville High School, 33, 36, 37, 40, 91, 92, 96, 97, 123
Crawfordsville Public Library (Carnegie), 22, 41, 77, 99, 101, 102
Crawfordsville Symphony Orchestra, 108, 109
Crawfordsville Wire and Nail Company, 71
Culver Union Hospital, 16, 23, 75
Detchon family, 112, 120
Episcopal church, 27, 39
Fendley, Edward Max, 87
fire (1933), 21
Forbes, John, 125
Grab It Here, 76
Grand Army of the Republic, 17, 82, 83, 93
Gregg (Boss) Glove Company, 72
Haslam, Frank, 86
Hays, Will, 125
Indiana National Guard, 56, 59, 85
interurban trains, 14, 41–52
Kennedy, Dumont, 58, 121
Krout, Mary and Susan, 120
Lincoln School, 32, 38, 97, 110
Lyons, Leslie, 36
Manson, Mahlon Dickerson, 81
Masonic Temple, 14
Methodist church, 12, 27
Mills School, 28, 35, 37, 61, 94
Montgomery County Courthouse, 10, 12, 17, 22, 43, 49, 93
Otto Schlemmer Building, 20, 77
Poston Brick Company, 71
Presbyterian church, 9, 24, 29, 30
Pugh, Robert, 79
Remley family, 114–116
Ristine, Eleanor, 57, 58, 60
R. R. Donnelley and Sons Company, 78
Talbot, Henry, 81, 84
Tilney family, 88, 113
Travis, Charles, 82
Tuttle School, 32, 96, 97
Wabash College, 9, 10, 103–110
Wallace, Lew, 80, 91, 111
Wilcox, Howard, 124
Wilhite, Mary Holloway, 113
Willson, Anna, 25, 117
Willson School, 25, 34, 35, 94
Wilson Brothers Company, 74
Wray, Loren Barney, 87
YMCA, 89